Power, Agency, and Women
in the Mission of God

Power, Agency, and Women in the Mission of God

Interdisciplinary, Intercultural Conversations

Edited by
Susan L. Maros
Vince L. Bantu
Kirsteen Kim

Foreword by
Amos Yong

☙PICKWICK *Publications* • Eugene, Oregon

POWER, AGENCY, AND WOMEN IN THE MISSION OF GOD
Interdisciplinary, Intercultural Conversations

Copyright © 2024 Wipf and Stock Publishers. All rights reserved. Except for brief quotations in critical publications or reviews, no part of this book may be reproduced in any manner without prior written permission from the publisher. Write: Permissions, Wipf and Stock Publishers, 199 W. 8th Ave., Suite 3, Eugene, OR 97401.

Pickwick Publications
An Imprint of Wipf and Stock Publishers
199 W. 8th Ave., Suite 3
Eugene, OR 97401

www.wipfandstock.com

PAPERBACK ISBN: 978-1-6667-8598-2
HARDCOVER ISBN: 978-1-6667-8599-9
EBOOK ISBN: 978-1-6667-8600-2

Cataloguing-in-Publication data:

Names: Maros, Susan L., editor. | Bantu, Vince L., 1982–, editor. | Kim, Kirsteen, editor. | Yong, Amos, foreword.

Title: Power, agency, and women in the mission of God : interdisciplinary, intercultural conversations / edited by Susan L. Maros, Vince L. Bantu, and Kirsteen Kim ; foreword by Amos Yong.

Description: Eugene, OR : Pickwick Publications, 2024 | Includes bibliographical references and index.

Identifiers: ISBN 978-1-6667-8598-2 (paperback) | ISBN 978-1-6667-8599-9 (hardcover) | ISBN 978-1-6667-8600-2 (ebook)

Subjects: LCSH: Women in missionary work. | Christian women—Religious life. | Women in church work.

Classification: BV639.W7 P68 2024 (paperback) | BV639.W7 P68 (ebook)

VERSION NUMBER 05/06/24

Scripture quotations marked (NRSV-UE) are taken from the New Revised Standard Version Updated Edition. Copyright © 2021 National Council of Churches of Christ in the United States of America. Used by permission. All rights reserved worldwide.

Scripture quotations marked (NRSVA) New Revised Standard Version Bible: Anglicised Edition, copyright © 1989, 1995 the Division of Christian Education of the National Council of the Churches of Christ in the United States of America. Used by permission. All rights reserved.

Scripture quotations marked (NIV) are taken from the Holy Bible, New International Version®, NIV®. Copyright © 1973, 1978, 1984, 2011 by Biblica, Inc.™ Used by permission of Zondervan. All rights reserved worldwide. www.zondervan.com The "NIV" and "New International Version" are trademarks registered in the United States Patent and Trademark Office by Biblica, Inc.™

Scripture quotations marked (NLT) are taken from the Holy Bible, New Living Translation, copyright ©1996, 2004, 2015 by Tyndale House Foundation. Used by permission of Tyndale House Publishers, Carol Stream, Illinois 60188. All rights reserved.

To our sisters, daughters of God, faithful to the call.

Contents

List of Tables and Figures | xi
Foreword by Amos Yong | xiii
List of Contributors | xvii
Acknowledgments | xxi

1. Power, Agency, and Women in the Mission of God: An Introduction | 1
   Susan L. Maros

Conversation 1: Women in Global Christianity

2. Women in World Christianity: Social Norms and Power Imbalances | 17
   Gina A. Zurlo

3. Church Mothers: The Leadership of African Christian Women in the Pre-modern Period | 30
   Vince L. Bantu

4. In the Circle of God's Mission: Mission as Coming Home | 46
   Musa W. Dube

Conversation 2: Sexism from Multiple Frameworks

5. Challenging Sexism for God's Sake: A Psychological Perspective | 67
   M. Elizabeth Lewis Hall

6. Women Rise Up: Power, Agency, and Christianity | 82
   Grace Ji-Sun Kim

7   The Transformed and Transformative Voice
    of Hannah in 1 Samuel 1–2 | 97
        JACQUELINE N. GREY

Conversation 3: Addressing #MeToo, #ChurchToo

8   "This Won't Be Our Undoing": Sexual Violence, the
    Spirit, and the Work of the Church | 119
        DARA COLEBY DELGADO

9   #MeToo, #ChurchToo: A Pentecostal-Charismatic
    Response to Sexual Violence against Women | 139
        CHRISTIAN TSEKPOE

Conversation 4: Models of Women's Power

10 Restoring the Heart of the Nation | 157
        SHARI RUSSELL

11 What to Do with Fragile Masculine Egos | 171
        PATRICK B. REYES

12 Transforming Collectivity: Empowering Women
    Leaders through Gendered Spaces | 185
        EVELYN HIBBERT

Conversation 5: Women's Leadership

13 Agency and Mission: Rethinking the Approach
    of "Women in Mission" | 205
        KIRSTEEN KIM

14 The Expansion of Female Leadership Influence
    through Seven Developmental Domains | 222
        ANNA MORGAN

15 Pushing Through Relational Awkwardness: The
    Importance of Communication in Flourishing
    Mixed-Gender Ministry Partnerships | 239
        ROB DIXON

Subject Index | 259
Author Index | 263

List of Tables and Figures

Table 1. Christianity by continent, 2020 | 22
Table 2. Countries with the most Christians, 2020 | 22
Table 3. Countries with the highest % Christian female, 2020 | 23
Table 4. Largest denominations, 2015 | 23
Table 5. Largest non-Catholic denominations, 2015 | 24

Figure 1. Dimensions of flourishing mixed-gender ministry partnerships | 250

Foreword

Amos Yong

HAVING SUPPORTED—AS THE DEAN of Fuller Seminary's School of Mission and Theology—the multi-year planning of Fuller Seminary's Center for Missiological Research 2022 Missiology Lectures on "Power, Agency, and Women in the Mission of God: A Scholar-Practitioner Conversation," and then witnessed and participated in the conference in October of that year, I now am delighted to contribute this foreword as a faculty colleague (who has recently stepped back from the ranks of senior administration). To be clear, this book is less an apologetic for women in ministry (for instance, there is no chapter going over the well-trod ground of whether or not the Bible "allows" women to hold offices in the church) than intended to spark the imagination by exemplifying what women are already doing in mission. Even the chapters on sexism are less complaints about the limitations to that work than indicators of how missional women (and male co-laborers) have responded faithfully and innovatively against constraints. Let me share about how these accounts sparked three levels of response as I read.

For starters, we might not be surprised about what the Pew Research Center calls the "gender gap in religion,"[1] one that documents that among Christians there is a five-point differential in participation, with 52–53 percent women compared with 47–48 percent men. The percentage difference skews much larger when we look at pentecostal Christianity, my home tradition. While much of this sensibility is anecdotally communicated, another Pew Research Forum study on gender composition among pentecostal adherents in the evangelical stream put the spread at almost

---

1. Pew Research Center, "Gender Gap in Religion around the World." See also Gina Zurlo's chapter in this volume.

58 percent women and 42 percent men.² Even if we should be cautious about drawing definitive conclusions regarding the gender composition of pentecostal-charismatic movements from the small sample size of this study, these figures are not inconsistent with other research on women in pentecostal-charismatic Christianity even as the numbers would not be surprising to those who regularly attend pentecostal-charismatic churches and congregations.³ The point I am making here, partly but not only from out of the group of churches that I know best, is that women are not just a slight majority of Christians but also, in many if not most congregations and Christian communities around the world, a significant if not predominant segment of regular attendees and participants. A number of the chapters in this book address these matters directly, including addressing the missional and missiological implications.

This brings me to the next level of consideration: majority numbers mean less access to the benefits of group membership and more having to carry most of the burden of Christian labor. The life and work of congregational and ecclesial-communal sustenance is borne by women who contribute variously as ushers, deaconesses, organizers, servers, child-care providers, teachers (of the youth and children, mostly—more on these constraints in a moment), prayers, worship team members, hospitality providers, outreach agents, etc. Growing up pentecostal, I witnessed firsthand the pervasive role of ministry played by my mother, the pastor's wife, including her motivating, galvanizing, and empowering women in the congregation to do the work of the ministry, work that my mother continues to do in her retirement years (my father has recently deceased even as their church is no longer formally incorporated) by spending hours on the phone each week listening to, counseling, and praying for those who call her. In fact, if it were not for women, we may not have churches, or it is surely recognizable that Christian ministry would come to a halt! Even if leadership, preaching, and ordained, senior, and formalized pastoring have been historically reserved in many Christian traditions for men, our sisters continue their efforts, and the chapters to come show how women work individually and collectively to engage their relational, social power, to enact their God-given agency to be light and salt in the world.

And this brings us to the third level of consideration that interfaces directly with the missiological thrust of this volume: that while women often have been both denied decision-making roles in their churches and yet

---

2. See "Gender Composition among Pentecostals in the Evangelical Tradition," in Pew Research Center, "Religious Landscape Study."

3. See also Alexander and Yong, *Philip's Daughters*.

encouraged if not expected to undertake most of the ministry effort of their congregations and ecclesial communities, they were also often allowed to or, perhaps more conveniently, sent off (by male-dominated authorization boards, no less!) for work on the "mission field." Within the modern missionary paradigm, women could not be ordained to lead fully established churches (so certain New Testament texts were read as prohibiting) but newly planted mission communities that were not yet fully ecclesial allowed for women "leaders," effectively to serve as missionaries, evangelists, and "church" planters—until these "mission" communities became formalized as churches, at which point ordained men would take the pastoral leadership responsibilities. So, the North American Assemblies of God denomination, like many other churches, was willing to send out (and continues to practice the commissioning of) single women missionaries around the world. One of them, Lula Baird, was sent to Malaysia midway through the prior century, and it was under her ministry that my parents came to Christian faith and then into ministry themselves. Of course, I remain grateful for her sacrificial life, and especially how she worked within a system that gave her some freedom to pursue what she felt to be God's call on her life while also having to navigate patriarchal assumptions that constrained her efforts. The pages to come lift up similar efforts in a variety of especially contemporary spaces in which diverse experiences and perspectives are presented from a range of disciplines and backgrounds documenting what women have been and are already doing in mission leadership and related endeavors.

We all still need new models of women's agency in mission. The contributors to this volume open us up to diverse and creative possibilities of women's responses to God's missional call, including their forging of new forms of church and ministry that explode or navigate around the conventions of maleness-and-femaleness we have inherited from our forebears. If here and around the world, Christian churches continue to strain under the legacy of the colonial missionary enterprise (and its misogynistic practices), and considering that still in the West, the historic centers of Christian missionary sending, old habits of thought and practice are difficult to adjust for twenty-first century and postcolonial realities, this book's proffering of new paradigms charts constructive ways forward for missiology and women.

What you hold in your hands (or are engaging through an e-reader) is thus not only another landmark volume from Fuller's annual Missiology Lectures, but also one brimming with theological, global, and practical perspectives on the actual and yet possible contributions of women to our common missional efforts. I enthusiastically encourage fellow missioners and mission leaders to attend to the missiological tongues bearing witness across these pages.

Bibliography

Alexander, Estrelda, and Amos Yong, eds. *Philip's Daughters: Women in Pentecostal-Charismatic Leadership*. Princeton Theological Monographs Series 104. Eugene, OR: Pickwick, 2009.

Pew Research Center. "The Gender Gap in Religion around the World." *Pew Research Center*, March 22, 2016. https://www.pewresearch.org/religion/2016/03/22/women-more-likely-than-men-to-affiliate-with-a-religion/.

———. "Religious Landscape Study." https://www.pewresearch.org/religion/religious-landscape-study/religious-family/pentecostal-family-evangelical-trad/gender-composition/.

List of Contributors

Vince L. Bantu is assistant professor of Church History and Black Church Studies, Fuller Theological Seminary, and author of *A Multitude of All Peoples: Engaging Ancient Christianity's Global Identity* (2020).

Dara Coleby Delgado is assistant professor of Religious Studies and Black Studies and affiliate faculty in the Women, Gender, and Sexuality studies program at Allegheny College in Meadville, PA.

Rob Dixon is an associate regional ministry director with InterVarsity Christian Fellowship/USA and Senior Fellow for Gender Partnership with the InterVarsity Institute. He is author of *Together in Ministry: Women and Men in Flourishing Partnerships* (2021).

Musa W. Dube is the William Ragsdale Cannon distinguished professor of New Testament at the Candler School of Theology, Emory University. Dr. Dube is current continental coordinator of The Circle of Concerned African Women Theologians and past vice president of the Society of Biblical Literature (2022–23).

Jacqueline N. Grey is professor of Biblical Studies at Alphacrucis College and an ordained minister with the Australian Christian Churches (AG in Australia).

M. Elizabeth Lewis Hall is professor of Psychology at the Rosemead School of Psychology, Biola University. She is a fellow of the American Psychological Association, associate editor of Psychology of Religion and Spirituality, and past president of Division 36, Society for the Psychological Study of Religion and Spirituality of the American Psychological Association.

Evelyn Hibbert is the founder and Colloquium Chair of the Angelina Noble Centre, a research center for women involved in cross-cultural ministry. She is also the Regional Vice President of the Global Region of the Evangelical Missiological Society.

Grace Ji-Sun Kim is professor of Theology at Earlham School of Religion. She is the author, co-author, or editor of twenty books, including: *Invisible* (2021), *Hope in Disarray* (2020), and *Intersectional Theology* (2018). She is an ordained minister in the Presbyterian Church (USA).

Kirsteen Kim is Paul E. Pierson professor in World Christianity and associate dean for the Center for Missiological Research, Fuller Theological Seminary and author of numerous articles and books, co-editor of the book series *Theology and Mission in World Christianity* (Brill) and lead editor of *The Oxford Handbook of Mission Studies* (2022).

Susan L. Maros is affiliate associate professor of Christian Leadership at Fuller Theological Seminary and author of *Calling in Context: Social Location and Vocational Formation* (2022).

Anna Morgan is a co-pastor of Word of Life Church, Washington, DC, and vice president of academics at Ascent College.

Patrick B. Reyes is seminary dean at Auburn Theological Seminary and author of *The Purpose Gap* (2021) and *Nobody Cries When We Die* (2018).

Shari Russell is Anishinaabe from Saskatchewan and residing in Hamilton, ON. She is ordained with The Salvation Army serving as the Territorial Indigenous Ministries Consultant and has been seconded to NAIITS: An Indigenous Learning Community as the associate director.

Christian Tsekpoe is an ordained minister of the Church of Pentecost, and Director of Postgraduate Studies and Research as well as the Head of Mission Department at the Pentecost University, Accra, Ghana. He is author of *Intergenerational Missiology: An African Pentecostal Perspective* (2022).

Gina A. Zurlo is the co-director of the Center for the Study of Global Christianity at Gordon-Conwell Theological Seminary and is the co-author of the *World Christian Encyclopedia*, 3rd edition, and co-editor of the *World Christian Database*. Dr. Zurlo's latest books are *Global Christianity: A Guide to the World's Largest Religion from Afghanistan to Zimbabwe* (2022) and *Women in World Christianity: Building and Sustaining a Global Movement* (2023).

Acknowledgments

THIS TEXT IS A collective effort not only of the individual authors who have contributed their time and wisdom but, additionally, of people in the background who have made this work possible. The Center for Missiological Research at Fuller Theological Seminary sponsored the 2022 Missiology Lectures that were the germinating spark for this book. The editors express appreciation in particular to Yoknyam Dabale, Chantelle Gibbs, and Erik Aasland for their support in the organization of the lectures, and Hanjun Kwon for his excellent assistance in the preparation of this manuscript.

—1—

Power, Agency, and Women in the Mission of God

An Introduction

Susan L. Maros

> "Mission in the third millennium will need to include women, deliberately, radically and conscientiously; otherwise, it will be incomplete and not in service of Jesus' life and ministry."[1]

FOR MORE THAN TWENTY-FIVE years as an educator, I have been engaged with the formation of in-service Christian leaders—pastors, mission leaders, leaders of non-profits and NGOs as well as Christians who are leading in business, government, and other non-faith-based contexts. A common thread among these individuals is a concern for being light and salt in the world (Matt 5:13–16). They want to be grounded in Scripture, attentive to the leading of the Spirit, and an effective and generative missional presence in their communities and organizations. They are concerned with issues of power they see enacted in their contexts and how to address these issues in a biblically and theologically grounded manner. One of their purposes

---

1. Longkumer, "Not without Women," 306.

in pursuing higher education is to expand their knowledge and build their skills for the work to which God has called them.

Many of my courses have a significant population of students from countries all over the world. In once recent course for example, I had students from Zimbabwe, Nigeria, Korea, Japan, Norway, Canada, and the United States. I routinely schedule synchronous video sessions in the early hours of my day to account for students located in Africa, Central Asia, and East Asia. When we talk about the nature of power and agency, we're talking from diverse cultural contexts with diverse assumptions about the role of women in the mission of God.

Considering the following vignettes drawn from experience.

- During a class break, a young man turned to a fellow classmate, a woman in her 50s with years of experience as a senior leader in several major corporations, and commented, "We all know that everyone is more comfortable with men in leadership."

- A young woman interning in a large church noted that her male colleagues were being tapped for additional responsibilities while she and another woman intern were not. When she asked her pastoral supervisor about what she noticed, the pastor explained, "You're going to get married." The pastor assumed the women were in ministry only temporarily until they were married and that they would, at that time, discontinue ministry work.

- A woman and man co-leading a mission team entered a church together to meet with the pastor about an event later in the week. The pastor walked past the woman, without acknowledging her presence, greeted the man, invited him into the pastor's office for a conversation while the female co-leader was left standing.

- A gifted preacher graduated with her MDiv and could not find a call in her denomination despite having won a prestigious award for her preaching and having served as a popular guest preacher for several years.

- A woman from West Africa expressed frustration in the midst of a conversation about women in ministry. "Why are you forcing your Western, White feminism on me?" she said to her US-American classmates. "It doesn't work in my context. What you see as affirmation of my capacity as a woman is actually a form of imperialism."

- A staff member in an evangelical campus ministry noted with pride that his ministry published statement affirming women in leadership.

When asked the gender diversity in senior leadership and on the board, he sheepishly noted they were all men. Upon asking a senior leader in the ministry about this dynamic, he was told "We can't find qualified women to fill senior roles."

The stories women and men share about gender-based challenges in mission and ministry are many and varied. In every context, cultural norms and expectations play a part in what roles women are expected to fill and in what ways they are expected to exert power. In faith-based contexts, these cultural norms include faith-based assumptions and values. What that community understands *God* intends for women is a central aspect of how women are viewed, how their gifts are utilized within their contexts, and to what degree they are seen as having agency to act.

My role as an educator in engaging these stories is to help the collective work of hearing, reflecting upon, and processing experience. Missiology as a discipline has formed me to welcome diverse voices and to recognize that cultural distinctives are always a part of the conversation, whether they are recognized or not. A long history of scholarly discussion around contextualization and enculturation suggests the work of missions is ever evolving in our capacity to engage across cultural and linguistic differences. Furthermore, as eminent Peruvian missiologist and theologian, Samuel Escobar, has noted, "Christian mission in the twenty-first century has become the responsibility of a global church."[2] Mission is now from everywhere, to everyone. I must help equip my students for a globalized, intercultural conversation whether they cross cultural, geographical, and linguistic boundaries or remain in their hometown to engage people across the street.

This intercultural dynamic is the context for the conversation about the role of women in the mission of God. The discussion about the role of women in the United States, particularly in the evangelical community, has, for the last thirty or forty years, focused on the question of whether or not women can exert legitimate power in leadership, particularly whether a woman can hold the office of elder or pastor, and situates the discussion in the interpretation of a set of biblical passages.[3] As recently as June 2023, the Southern Baptist Convention reaffirmed their stance denying women ordination to pastoral roles and acting to disaffiliate congregations that had done so, including Rick Warren and Saddleback Church.[4] Meanwhile, the wider conversation within the United States has included contentious

---

2. Escobar, *New Global Mission*, 12.

3. See, for example, Clouse and Clouse, *Women in Ministry*; Grenz and Kjesbo, *Women in the Church*.

4. Shellnutt, "Southern Baptists Reject Rick Warren's Saddleback Appeal."

engagement around issues such as human trafficking, abortion, and sexual assault. As vital as these concerns are, they do not necessarily attend to intercultural concerns on these topics as well as additional issues that are distinctive to other regions of the world. A Black woman in the United States, for example, has concerns that are not identical to a Black woman in Ghana. A Korean-American woman and a Korean woman may share some cultural heritage yet have distinctive experiences based on their national and geographical locations. A conversation about the ways in which women engage power must include attention to women in various parts of the world even as it attends to the particularities of a distinctive mission, church, or organizational context.

Women have always been a part of the missional work of the church as has been ably demonstrated by the seminal work of Dana Robert and Ruth Tucker as well as more recent work by authors such as Leanne Dzubinski and Anneke Stasson.[5] Women continue to be a vital part of God's work in the world. The ways in which women are limited in their organizational authority hinders the expansion of God's work yet that work is never fully thwarted. "Some of my best men are women," William Booth is famously said to have remarked about the workers in his revivalist ministry that became the Salvation Army. Some of God's best and most effective missionaries, apostles, prophets, evangelists, pastors, and teachers continue to be women, whether or not their organizations, families, and cultures affirm women in positions of organizational leadership.

While this text is honest about the limitations that women experience and the cost of those limitations personally, organizationally, and missionally, the focus of this work is not on naming the problems. God is at work and God's daughters have been and continue to be a vital part of that work. We seek to articulate the ways in which women utilize their personal and collective agency to address powers—spiritual, organizational, and cultural.

The status of women in the world and in the church represents a fundamental missiological issue of our day. In this introduction, I consider the difficulty of defining power and agency then consider the benefits of engaging these concepts in an intercultural and interdisciplinary conversation. I conclude by outlining the five conversations that are the heart of this book.

---

5. See, for example, Dzubinski and Stasson, *Women in the Mission of the Church*; Robert, *Gospel Bearers*; Robert, *American Women in Mission*; Tucker, *Extraordinary Women of Christian History*. Note also many texts of historical reference cited throughout this book.

Essential Concepts

This volume is focused on an intercultural and interdisciplinary discussion of power, agency, and mission. The authors of the chapters do not share a single definition or perspective on power. Each brings their own academic discipline, ministry experience, and contextual, cultural perspective to their work. Let us briefly consider how we might define power and agency, and look at the importance of having an intercultural and interdisciplinary discussion.

Defining Power and Agency

"Power" is a term used often and yet it is a slippery concept with limited clarity of definition. One reason why conversations about power are so challenging is that participants in those conversations come with differing sets of assumptions. Scholars in different disciplines end up talking past one another because they each use the term power with different ideas about the nature of the concept and the domain it occupies. Likewise, practitioners and scholars can end up talking past one another because of differing layers of abstraction and application in addition to differing ideas of what domains are being engaged.

As I have argued elsewhere, much of the discussion in organizational dynamics literature focuses on the power of the individual leader to effect action in a specific group of people.[6] Indeed, leadership theorist Peter Northouse's definition of power emphasizes the role of the individual to effect change. He writes, "People have power when they have the ability to affect others' beliefs, attitudes, and courses of action."[7] While there is some attention to followership in the literature—for example, Barbara Kellerman's groundbreaking book *Followership*[8]—the focus of much of the discussion within leadership literature is on the agency of the individual leader. The concept of agency is a corollary to power in that agency is the capacity to take action. Insofar as an individual or group is able to engage their environment and to make choices about their context, they are enacting their agency. Who has agency, why, and how, along with how they exercise their agency is another topic that is seen differently depending on context and academic discipline.

---

6. Maros, "Introduction," 2–3.

7. Northouse, *Leadership*, 9.

8. For a review of this literature, see Uhl-Bien et al., "Followership Theory"; Bastardoz and Vugt, "Nature of Followership."

Another arena of focus of discussion about power relates to the power of organizations. An organization is a "formalized group of people who are working together for a common goal."[9] An international missions organization, a church, and a non-profit all fit under this definition along with for-profit institutions. Leadership scholars may consider how power is distributed within organizations considering concerns related to the distribution of authority to make decisions about how tasks will be completed. Often, this discussion is interested in how the individual leader engages the organization to effect change and, thus, the interaction between individual and organizational power is the locus of the work. Much of the leadership literature is written from and for a US-American context and thus embodies the individualist cultural framework so dominant in this cultural environment. This leaves concerns about individual and organizational power in collectivist contexts unaddressed.[10]

Other discussions about power center on the influence and impact of social structures. This form of power is embedded in cultural norms and practices. Missiological anthropologists look at social structures as they consider kinship terms or questions of worldview. Sociologists consider such things as the impact of a social group on an individual's identity formation. To some scholars and practitioners, the existence of social power is central and obvious from their experience and the experience of their community. To others, particularly those who do not work in fields that require then to cross geographical, cultural, and linguistic boundaries, the existence of social power as meaningful to present experience may be highly contested. For example, much of the current discussion within the United States around diversity is floundering on the rocks of differing perspectives on the impact of social structures. For some scholars, the significance and impact of race is clear and vital while, for others, an emphasis on social power is seen as a violation of key values such as meritocracy and self-sufficiency.[11] Many of the authors in this book demonstrate attention to their social locations. Their perspectives on the role and experience of women reflects the authors' experience in an inequitable society that fails to acknowledge its inequity. If the ultimate aim of God's mission in the world is to see all women and men thriving in relationship to God, one another, and creation, then acknowledging the ongoing presence of social inequity is essential.

9. Maros, "Introduction," 3.

10. For a discussion of individualism and collectivism as cultural constructs and their impact on leadership in international organizations, see Hofstede et al., *Cultures and Organizations*, 89–134.

11. There is a wide body of literature engaged with these concerns. For one introduction, see Emerson and Smith, *Divided by Faith*.

Mission historians note the criticism of Western mission movement as paternalistic and imperialistic.[12] The history of interaction between mission and power is challenging to identify and address.[13] While scholars are helpful in identifying theoretical frameworks useful to explicating experience, practitioners have a vital role to play in naming specific instances of dynamics in practice. The usefulness of a scholar-practitioner conversation is to allow for both the abstractions of theory and the particularities of practice to mutually inform one another. Likewise, an intercultural conversation enriches our collective understanding and practice.

Significance of Intercultural Engagement

The term "intercultural leadership" refers to leadership work that moves between cultures in an interdependent manner rather than simply crossing cultural lines. Intercultural leadership is particularly significant for any mission conversation in this globalized world.[14] A whole body of literature has developed over the last several decades looking at intercultural leadership competencies.[15] This is relevant to the present discussion because the conversation of women's participation in the mission of God needs to include voices from multiple perspectives and needs to foster intercultural competencies, capacities that focus on the ability to engage interdependently between cultures, not simply communicate across cultures.

The movement from focus on cross-cultural ministry to focus on intercultural ministry reflects a shift in awareness that we do not simply live in communities in which diverse people reside but that we must learn to engage one another interdependently. Concerning the mission of God, I adapt what Anthony Gittens writes concerning religious orders in his Catholic context, agreeing with him that assimilation is no longer a legitimate aim but that, given the changes in the world, "the future of international [missions] communities must increasingly and intentionally become intercultural. Without the tectonic shift from 'international' to 'intercultural' there will simply be no viable future [for missions]."[16]

Cross-cultural ministry focuses on the individual or groups doing the boundary crossing. Much of the conversation assumes, without naming it,

---

12. Robert, *Christian Mission*, 93–96.

13. For one discussion about the nature of the relationship between the concept of power and missions, see Longkumer et al., *Mission and Power*.

14. McConnell, *Cultural Insights for Christian Leaders*, 25–26.

15. See, for example, House, *Culture, Leadership, and Organizations*.

16. Gittens, "Challenge of Intercultural Living," 13.

that the people doing the boundary crossing are the people with the resources—financial, social, and theological. Suggestions of cultivating servant-oriented attitudes may be included yet these, too, are rooted in assumptions about the agency and the power of the individuals doing the boundary crossing. We do not consider refugees, for example, as cross-cultural ministers even though they do a great deal of crossing of geographical, social, cultural, and linguistic boundaries.[17] Nor do we consider that these individuals are often persons of Christian faith. Power dynamics in the social construction of identity keep the focus on cross-cultural ministry as being from the powerful to the powerless with the powerful setting the agenda.

An intercultural approach sees the value in diverse opinions and perspectives. The business literature suggests that organizations with diverse boards and diverse decisions-makers tend to be more resilient and agile.[18] The idea is that a diversity of perspectives will lead to stronger decisions. The different groups present in a given context need one another and need to engage in an interdependent manner. One benefit of an intercultural conversation is the possibility of considering concepts of power and agency from a collectivist perspective in addition to the individualist perspective that is so dominant in literature published in the United States. How might groups of individuals who might otherwise be seen as lacking power join their collective capacity to engage their systems and structures with their collective agency? Discussion across difference of culture and context enhances one's understanding of one's own home culture. We enrich one another's understanding of the nature and character of God and of God's work in the world when we lift our eyes up from the next steps on our individual paths and consider the tapestry of God's work around the world and in locations both similar to and different from our own.

Beyond the benefits of resilience and agility, being intercultural is coherent with biblical visions of the church. God's mission in the world has always been for all the peoples. The selection and creation of Israel as a nation was for the purpose of being a kingdom of priests (Exod 19:16) ministering the presence of God to the world. Jesus' cleansing of the temple (Matt 21:12–13) was a lashing out to the religious authorities who had taken over the court of the Gentiles, that place where the nations were to be welcomed to worship, and made it a place of commerce. The image of the Church standing in eternity is one in which all the peoples of the world are present in their distinctive identities (Rev 7:9).

17. Hanciles. *Migration and the Making of Global Christianity*.

18. See Slater et al., "Business Case for Commitment to Diversity." For a comment on some necessary additional dynamics, see Jayne and Dipboye, "Leveraging Diversity to Improve Business Performance."

Interdisciplinary, Intercultural Conversations

This book began its life as a set of lectures and panel discussions in the annual Missiology Lectures at Fuller Theological Seminary, centering a conversation between scholars and practitioners from a variety of cultural and disciplinary contexts. Our aim was to name the resources women bring to addressing organizational, cultural, and sociological structures of power as an expression of participation in the mission of God. These resources include individual and collective agency to engage, overcome, and dismantle barriers to the full-orbed expression of God's *shalom* in our various communities.

The participants were not all missiologists but a missiological assumption undergirded the conversation and this text. Our starting point is the *missio Dei*: God's active engagement in the world into which we are invited to participate. To quote Jürgen Moltmann, "It is not the church that has a mission of salvation to fulfil in the world; it is the mission of the Son and the Spirit through the Father that includes the church."[19] God is fundamentally a missionary God, actively engaging humanity, actively working in creation. And, "Since God is a missionary God," writes David Bosch, "God's people are a missionary people."[20] To participate in the *missio Dei* is to participate in God's love toward people. The intention of our work in this book is to participate in equipping the church to respond to God's invitation to women to participate in God's work in the world.

The aim in forming the conversations—both in the Missiology Lectures and in this volume—is to foster an intercultural and interdisciplinary conversation. Participants were selected to cover a variety of missiological disciplines. No one book can be fully and completely a conversation that welcomes people from all over the world and facilitates a truly intercultural dialog yet this text is an attempt in this direction. The authors come from a variety of countries, identities, theological environments, and social settings. They are academics and practitioners joining together in a scholar-practitioner conversation. The individual authors of chapters speak from their distinctive academic disciplines and, often, from their particular social settings. While no individual represents the entirety of their group, having voices from a diversity of groups fosters steps towards an intercultural dialog. We are in the process of working out what it might look like to have a foretaste of heaven in which these conversations can happen without fear or anger. What we have here is more of a snapshot in time of a particular conversation than it is the give-and-take of live dialog. This, too, is the nature of

---

19. Moltmann, *Church in the Power of the Spirit*, 64.
20. Bosch, *Transforming Mission*, 280.

books. Yet we hope that the discussions contained in these pages might be thought-provoking and assist the reader in recognizing intercultural conversations in their own context or being motivated to seek out intercultural conversations in their discipline or area of practice.

This conversation began with an assumption that God has created and called women to exercise agency, recognizing that this question is still contested in many of the communities in which women are engaged in missional endeavors. Addressing the agency of women in the mission of God requires attention to the social, cultural, and theological challenges uniquely experienced by women in their distinctive contexts. These challenges include, but are not limited to, organizational practices limiting the mentoring and development of women in leadership roles, the impact of movements like #MeToo and #ChurchToo, and the intersectional challenges experienced by Black, Indigenous, and women of color.

The chapters of this book are offered in the form of five conversations. Each of these conversations focuses on a central idea related to our overarching theme. Each author in the conversation brings content from their particular academic discipline and specific cultural context. Where possible, we have included authors from a variety of nations as well as a range of academic disciplines. We include scholars and practitioners, seeking engage both theory and practice. These conversations are an exploration of power and agency, looking at a variety of means and strategies women have engaged individually and collectively to participate faithfully in the mission of God.

Conversation 1: Women in Global Christianity

The church has always been international and intercultural, even while "church history" as traditionally taught in the United States has focused on the thread of the narrative that moves through one particular cultural branch of the church: Jerusalem to Rome, Europe to the United States. Gina Zurlo's chapter considers the roles women play in church and culture around the world. Vince Bantu focuses on the history of women's pre-colonial witness and mission in Africa while Musa Dube offers a case study for the ways in which women have been collaborating in scholarship and practice, enacting their agency to impact their communities looking at the case study of the Circle of Concerned African Women Theologians. This first conversation sets a broad perspective on the nature of power and how women participate in their societies and faith communities as an expression of the *missio Dei* throughout history and across the world.

Conversation 2: Sexism in Multiple Frameworks

When we talk about limitations on women's agency and power, sexism is one of a number of common barriers. Our second discussion features chapters by a psychologist (Elizabeth Hall), a theologian (Grace Ji-Sun Kim), and a biblical studies scholar (Jaqueline Grey). Each is dealing with the impact of sexism on women's lived experience from the perspective of their differing academic and cultural contexts. Hall presents a compelling argument for the cost of benevolent sexism on the capacity and competencies of women. Kim considers the ways in which the reading and application of biblical texts have been demeaning and detrimental to women, suggesting an alternative theological approach to the recognition of women's power, particularly the capacity of women of color to contribute to the mission of God. Grey explores the story of Hannah and considers the ways in which power and agency are engaged in this narrative, particularly focusing on the ways in which sexism is evident in Hannah's engagement with the people in her family and with Eli.

Conversation 3: Addressing #MeToo, #ChurchToo

Dara Delgado and Christian Tsekpoe address one pressing concern when discussing the experience of women in the church and in society: the problem of the response (or lack of response) of the church to the physical and sexual abuse of women. This dialog brings together two cultural perspectives: one from the United States and one from Ghana. This intercultural conversation highlights the ways in which power and agency—of women who have been abused and of those who wish to support them—takes different forms depending on the cultural context. Each speaks prophetically to their context and, in so doing, offers an enrichment to the global conversation.

Conversation 4: Models of Women's Power

Shari Russell, Patrick Reyes, and Evelyn Hibbert each offer distinctive perspectives on the power and agency of women in particular social and organizational contexts. Each brings their disciplinary distinctives to the themes and concerns they highlight as well as drawing from their traditions and cultures. Each of these authors responds to dominant White, male, Western views from the perspective of Black, Indigenous, and People of Color (BIPOC) communities as each author is a scholar who is actively engaged in seeking to dismantle barriers standing in the way of BIPOC women scholars experiencing welcome into academia dominated by White men.

Conversation 5: Women's Leadership

In the final conversation, three authors offer different perspectives on the dynamics of women's leadership formation. Kirsteen Kim considers Korean women as case study of the contribution of women even while access to institutional power and gendered norms limit the formal role women play. She considers how the US-based discussion of gender limits our capacity to recognize and acknowledge the value of women in traditional roles. Anna Morgan and Rob Dixon are two practitioner-scholars deeply embedded in their organizational and ministerial contexts. Each is engaged in the development of women (and men) for leadership in the church and the world, primarily working in US-American contexts. These two authors offer some concrete and practical constructive thoughts on the development of women in leadership and the communication practices needed for women and men to work well together.

Conclusion

Scholarly inquiry into the participation of women in God's mission addresses widely differing sets of concerns and perspectives depending on the scholar or practitioner's discipline and their community's social, cultural, and geographical location. Likewise, how we think about, study, and write about power is dependent on both the particular arena in which we are working and upon the social and cultural locations that we inhabit and from which we do our work. Often, individuals and communities from these differing disciplines and cultural/social locations will talk past one another as each starts from a different set of assumptions and is concerned with different aspects of power. A fully orbed investigation into the ways in which women enact personal and collective agency requires attention to a variety of aspects of power—personal, communal, organizational, social systems, and spiritual power—as well as the distinctives of the contexts in which women are working and ministering.

This book conducts such an investigation through a global scholar-practitioner conversation. In so-doing, it fulfills the need for an accessible academic book that addresses the gender issues that women face as Christian disciples, whether in formal leadership role or engaging leadership in informal means, and considers these issues in the context of world

Christianity. In an era when mission is "from everywhere, to everywhere," when local churches strive to be missional, and when Christians are engaged in intercultural ministry, a different kind of discussion is needed. An interdisciplinary and intercultural conversation about women will enrich the church's ongoing effort to be faithful to God's call to women (and men) to participate in God's work in the world.

Bibliography

Bastardoz, Nicolas, and Mark van Vugt. "The Nature of Followership: Evolutionary Analysis and Review." *Leadership Quarterly* 30 (2019) 81–95.

Bosch, David J. *Transforming Mission: Paradigm Shifts in Theology of Mission*. 20th anniversary ed. Maryknoll, NY: Orbis, 2011.

Clouse, Bonnidell, and Robert G. Clouse, eds. *Women in Ministry: Four Views*. Downers Grove, IL: InterVarsity, 1989.

Dzubinski, Leanne M., and Anneke H. Stasson. *Women in the Mission of the Church: Their Opportunities and Obstacles throughout Christian History*. Grand Rapids: Baker Academic, 2021.

Emerson, Michael O., and Christian Smith. *Divided by Faith: Evangelical Religion and the Problem of Race in America*. Oxford: Oxford University Press, 2000.

Escobar, Samuel. *The New Global Mission: The Gospel from Everywhere to Everyone*. Downers Grove, IL: InterVarsity, 2003.

Gittens, Antony J. "The Challenge of Intercultural Living: Anthropological and Theological Implications." In *Intercultural Living: Explorations in Missiology*, edited by Lazar T. Stanislaus and Martin Ueffing, 13–21. Maryknoll, NY: Orbis, 2018.

Grenz, Stanley J., and Denise Muir Kjesbo. *Women in the Church: A Biblical Theology of Women in Ministry*. Downers Grove, IL: InterVarsity, 1995.

Hanciles, Jehu. *Migration and the Making of Global Christianity*. Grand Rapids: Eerdmans, 2021.

Hofstede, Geert, et al. *Cultures and Organizations: Software of the Mind*. 3rd ed. New York: McGraw-Hill, 2010.

House, Robert J., ed. *Culture, Leadership, and Organizations: The Globe Study of 62 Societies*. Thousand Oaks, CA: Sage, 2004.

Jayne, Michele E. A., and Robert L. Dipboye. "Leveraging Diversity to Improve Business Performance: Research Findings and Recommendations for Organizations." *Human Resource Management* 43 (2004) 409–24.

Kellerman, Barbara. *Followership: How Followers Are Creating Change and Changing Leaders*. Boston: Harvard Business School Press, 2008.

Longkumer, Atola. "Not without Women: Mission in the Third Millennium." *International Review of Mission* 100 (2011) 297–309. doi:10.1111/j.1758-6631.2011.00074.x.

Longkumer, Atola, et al., eds. *Mission and Power: History, Relevance, and Perils*. Regnum Edinburgh Centenary Series 33. Oxford: Regnum International, 2016.

Maros, Susan L. "Introduction: Engaging Power." *Journal of Religious Leadership* 19 (2019) 1–17.

McConnell, C. Douglas. *Cultural Insights for Christian Leaders: New Directions for Organizations Serving God's Mission*. Grand Rapids: Baker Academic, 2018.

Mickelsen, Alvera. *Women, Authority, and the Bible*. Downers Grove, IL: InterVarsity, 1986.

Moltmann, Jürgen. *The Church in the Power of the Spirit: A Contribution to Messianic Ecclesiology*. Translated by Margaret Kohl. New York: Harper & Row, 1977.

Northouse, Peter G. *Leadership: Theory and Practice*. 6th ed. Los Angeles: Sage, 2013.

Robert, Dana L. *American Women in Mission: A Social History of Their Thought and Practice: The Modern Mission Era, 1792–1992*. Macon, GA: Mercer University Press, 1997.

———. *Christian Mission: How Christianity Became a World Religion*. Blackwell Brief Histories of Religion Series. Malden, MA: Wiley-Blackwell, 2009.

———. *Gospel Bearers, Gender Barriers: Missionary Women in the Twentieth Century*. Maryknoll, NY: Orbis, 2002.

Shellnutt, Kate. "Southern Baptists Reject Rick Warren's Saddleback Appeal." *Christianity Today*, June 14, 2023. https://www.christianitytoday.com/news/2023/june/saddleback-sbc-women-pastors-appeal-rick-warren-southern-ba.html.

Slater, Stanley F., et al. "The Business Case for Commitment to Diversity." *Business Horizons* 51 (2008) 201–9.

Tucker, Ruth. *Extraordinary Women of Christian History: What We Can Learn from Their Struggles and Triumphs*. Grand Rapids: Baker, 2016.

Uhl-Bien, Mary, et al. "Followership Theory: A Review and Research Agenda." *Leadership Quarterly* 25 (2014) 83–104.

Conversation 1

Women in Global Christianity

— 2 —

Women in World Christianity
Social Norms and Power Imbalances[1]

Gina A. Zurlo

CHRISTIANITY HAS ALWAYS BEEN majority female[2]—after all, history shows that women were the last at the cross and the first at the tomb. In fact, demographers, social scientists, historians, and other scholars have stated for decades that women are more religious than men. The Pew Research Center's Gender Gap in Religion around the World study claimed that, indeed, Christian women reported higher rates of church attendance, prayer, and religious self-identification than Christian men. Many sociological studies have also indicated this gender imbalance in religious identity, belief, and practice.[3] Estimating the nineteenth-century missionary movement from the United States as two-thirds female, historian Dana Robert even described World Christianity as a "women's movement."[4] She asked, "What would the study of Christianity in Africa, Asia, and Latin America look like if scholars put women into the center of their research?"[5] The findings presented in this chapter are a result of the Louisville Institute funded Women

1. This chapter is adapted from Zurlo, *Women in World Christianity*.
2. Braude, "Women's History," 87–107.
3. Trzebiatowska and Bruce, *Why Are Women More Religious?*
4. Robert, *American Women in Mission*, 203; Robert, "World Christianity," 180–88.
5. Robert, "World Christianity," 180.

in World Christianity Project, which was the first global comprehensive research project to assign a percent Christian female to every Christian denomination in every country of the world. Those data are now available, for the first time, in the *World Christian Database*. However, as this chapter illustrates, social norms and power imbalances make it extremely difficult to find accurate data related to women in World Christianity. A lack of data and knowledge naturally leads to a lack of acknowledgement of women's contributions, and a lack of power, influence, and authority to enact change.

Social Norms and Power Imbalances

The 2019 Human Development Report of the United Nations was titled, *Beyond Income, Beyond Averages, Beyond Today: Inequalities in Human Development in the 21st Century*. Chapter 4 was dedicated to gender inequalities in the world, with several striking findings:

- Gender inequality is one of the most persistent inequalities across all countries.
- The world is not on track to achieve gender equality by 2030.
- If current trends continue, it will take 202 years for women to achieve complete economic equality with men.
- Gender equality in health, education, and economics has been slowing in recent years.
- Although substantial progress has been made in the last 25 years, there is no place in the world where women have complete equality with men.

These statements are not to erase the tremendous achievements women have made in recent years. Women today are the most qualified they have ever been in history. Fewer are dying in childbirth, and more are obtaining secondary education. If this is the case, though, why is the gender gap so persistent? The report highlights two underlying realities: social norms and power imbalances. Social norms dictate "men's roles" and "women's roles" in society, as well as set rules of behavior and attitudes that meld communities together. However, biases are widespread throughout social norms. The Multidimensional Gender Social Norms Count Index reported that 86% of women and 90% of men worldwide held gender social norm biases.[6] Power imbalances occur when these biased social norms expect men and women

---

6. UNDP, *Human Development Report 2019*, 154, 156.

to perform certain duties, but women are excluded from decision making that limits their opportunities and choices.

Social norms are extremely difficult to change. In many cases, people lack the information or knowledge to act or think differently. It is also an issue of what is at stake, particularly for those with more power: "A social norm will be stickiest when individuals have the most to gain from complying with it and the most to lose from challenging it."[7] In many places around the world, social norms are shifting away from traditional gendered expectations in both the public and private spheres. This is natural with increased women's education, political participation, and control over their own bodies and reproductive rights. These shifts typically critique prevailing beliefs and attitudes about how men and women should act in society. Indeed, it is beliefs about what people *do* and what people think *other* people should do that dictate what happens in the social sphere. At the same time, these beliefs and practices typically serve as active barriers that sustain gender inequalities now and likely in the future.

In the first few centuries of Christianity, women gained new opportunities for leadership and public activity in joining nascent churches, and their contributions helped grow Christianity from a fledgling movement into a world religion.[8] However, Christianity, Christians, churches, and Christian theology have also served as active barriers to women's opportunities, and this is difficult to change. While women make up the majority of church members worldwide, they are often prohibited from holding official leadership positions, are excluded from decision-making bodies, and their ministries are considered secondary to the main task of the Sunday morning worship service, where men are on public display. Church life, like everything else in the world, is gendered. Men and women experience life differently, and they experience Christianity differently.

Feminism

In the Western world, first-wave feminism of the late nineteenth and early twentieth centuries largely addressed legal obstacles to women's rights related to voting and property; that is, it was a movement about political power. Second-wave feminism emerged in the early 1960s with a much broader scope to address issues such as sexuality, reproductive rights, domesticity, domestic violence, marital rape, and divorce law. It also demanded change in patriarchal structures and cultural practices that deemed women less

7. UNDP, *Human Development Report 2019*, 158.
8. For example, see Stark, *Rise of Christianity*.

than men. Concentrated in Europe and North America, both first- and second-wave feminism were largely the initiatives of White, middle-class women, working under the assumption that women everywhere faced similar oppression to them. That is, they assumed all women suffered the same because of patriarchy and sexism. However, this approach ignored the intersectionality of oppression related to race, class, ethnicity, religion, colonialism, and politics. Women around the world soon challenged this narrow outlook and argued that their oppression was fundamentally different than that of White Western women; women suffer multiple and intersecting oppressions, not some "common condition" shared by all women worldwide.[9] The distinction between second-wave feminism and majority world feminist perspectives gave rise to so-called "third world" feminism (a term now largely out of vogue), transnational feminism (a popular term), and global feminism (or, feminisms); some use these terms interchangeably. Globally, women are not a monolith, their oppression is not the same everywhere,[10] and women's activism is not uniform around the world.

The 1970s and 1980s marked a turning point for women, but it should not be understood that White Western feminism was imported to Africa, Asia, Latin America, and the Pacific Islands. Much like Black women in the West responding to the color blindness of second-wave feminism, women in the Global South have claimed their agency to identify their own sources of oppression and advocate for their own rights separate from White Western women. For example, White female missionaries naively assumed that women's roles abroad should be re-shaped according to Western gendered norms, and as a result indigenous women often *lost* agency and power with the arrival of Christianity, not gained it. Thus, use of the term "feminism" in the Global South is not a reference to White Western second-wave feminism, but instead to how women in these places have created their own movements toward equality.

Data

Despite historians' assertions that Christianity has always been a majority female faith, uncovering the role of women behind its status as a world religion is only a recent phenomenon. World Christianity consists of 2.5 billion Christians, at least 52% of whom are women, that speak a wide variety of languages, come from different cultural backgrounds, and express their faith in a multitude of ways. However, placing women at the center

9. Herr, "Third World Feminisms."
10. Mohanty, "Feminist Encounters," 30–44.

of historical, social scientific, and theological investigation demands new frameworks. Existing approaches that attempt a gender-neutral take on the history and status of World Christianity paint with a broad brush that erases women's unique experiences and contributions to the development and sustainment of the Christian faith. Spotlighting the experiences of women does not exclude those of men. As gender and religion scholar Bernadette Brooten describes, "To listen to women is not to refuse to hear men; it is to let those who have been mute speak."[11] Focusing on women means moving their experiences and stories from the periphery to the center, from the margins of study to the core.

Endless examples illustrate women's deep involvement in global Christianity, both from regional and ecclesiological perspectives. Women are more likely to show up for church activities throughout the week, both at Sunday morning services and weeknight Bible studies. Catholic pilgrimage sites around the world are mostly visited by women. In Brazil, women are the majority of practitioners of popular Catholicism and many of its rituals are almost exclusively led by women. Membership in the Church of Christ in Congo, an ecumenical Protestant umbrella organization with at least sixty-four member denominations, is majority female. All congregations in Eswatini are majority female. Catholic sisters outnumber brothers on every continent and in most countries. There are more female missionaries than male from the United States. The examples are endless.

World Christianity

Christianity has been the world's largest religion over the last 120 years, representing 35% of the world's population in 1900 and 32% in 2020.[12] By 2050, it is anticipated Christianity could increase to 34%, but that largely depends on birth rates and potential conversions to Christianity in India and China, the world's two most populous countries. In this analysis, "Christian" refers to anyone who self-identifies as such or is in some way affiliated to a Christian congregation or denomination; this is measuring Christianity by membership, not beliefs or practices. Global Christianity experienced a dramatic change in the twentieth century. In 1900, only 18% of all Christians lived in the Global South (Asia, Africa, Latin America and the Caribbean, and Oceania). By 2020, this figure jumped to 67%, and it is expected to reach 77% by 2050. This is known as Christianity's shift to the Global South,

---

11. Brooten, "Early Christian Women," 83.

12. All subsequent statistics and tables are sourced from Johnson and Zurlo, *World Christian Database*.

where the majority of its adherents live today. Africa is home to the most Christians (667 million; 49% Christian), followed by Latin America (612 million; 92% Christian), and Europe (565 million; 76% Christian). Official data, sourced largely from governmental censuses, reveals that in most places, women claim only a slight majority of Christian affiliation over men. However, more localized studies reveal that women's share of congregations is much, much higher—in some cases, 90%!

Table 1. Christians by continent, 2020

Continent	Majority religion	Pop. female %	% Christian 2020	% Christian female 2020
Africa	Christians	50.0%	48.9%	52.1%
Asia	Muslims	48.9%	8.1%	51.0%
Europe	Christians	51.7%	76.6%	52.6%
Latin America	Christians	50.8%	92.2%	51.6%
North America	Christians	50.5%	73.1%	54.1%
Oceania	Christians	49.9%	67.1%	51.7%
Global total	Christians	49.6%	32.2%	52.1%

Table 1 compares the share of women on each continent to Christianity's gender makeup. For instance, Africa's population is overall 48.9% female, but according to available official census data, Christianity is slightly more female, at 52.1%.

Table 2. Countries with the most Christians, 2020

Country	Largest Christian tradition	Pop. female %	% Christian 2020	% Christian female 2020
United States	Catholics	50.5%	74.2%	54.3%
Brazil	Catholics	50.9%	90.8%	51.6%
Mexico	Catholics	51.1%	95.7%	51.7%
Russia	Orthodox	53.7%	82.2%	53.5%
China	Independents	48.7%	7.4%	52.6%
Philippines	Catholics	49.8%	90.6%	49.5%
Nigeria	Protestants	49.3%	46.2%	52.7%
DR Congo	Catholics	50.1%	95.0%	51.9%
Ethiopia	Orthodox	50.0%	59.1%	50.0%
India	Protestants	48.0%	4.8%	50.0%

Looking at the ten countries with the most Christians (Table 2), it is observed that most report higher percentages of Christian females than the overall population, except for Ethiopia, the Philippines, and Russia. These three countries, however, show greater gender parity between the general population and its Christian population because one Christian tradition makes up nearly the entire population (either Orthodox or Catholic).

Table 3. Countries with the highest % Christian female, 2020

Country	Largest Christian tradition	Pop. female %	% Christian 2020	% Christian female 2020
Mongolia	Protestants	50.7%	1.9%	63.2%
Israel	Catholics	50.2%	2.2%	63.0%
Estonia	Protestants	52.6%	37.3%	62.8%
BES Islands	Catholics	54.0%	92.1%	57.4%
Czechia	Catholics	50.8%	35.0%	57.0%
Botswana	Independents	51.6%	70.0%	56.0%
Barbados	Protestants	51.6%	94.9%	55.7%
Jamaica	unaffiliated Christians	50.4%	84.5%	55.4%
New Zealand	Protestants	50.8%	54.4%	55.4%
Bermuda	Protestants	51.4%	88.7%	55.2%

The highest recorded shares of Christian women are in Mongolia, Israel, and Estonia (Table 3). For each, particular dynamics drive the high share of women. Mongolia, for example, has a reverse gender gap due to the traditional herding lifestyle, where men travel with their flocks, leading women to outnumber men in many different institutions, including education and the churches.

Table 4. Largest denominations, 2015

Country	Denomination	Affiliated 2015	% Christian female 2015
Brazil	Igreja Católica no Brasil	148,550,000	50.0%
Russia	Russian Orthodox Church	110,850,000	53.5%
Mexico	Iglesia Católica en México	110,155,000	51.4%
Philippines	Catholic Church in the Philippines	78,271,000	49.3%
United States	Catholic Church in the USA	72,798,000	53.3%
Italy	Chiesa Cattolica in Italia	45,563,000	51.4%

Country	Denomination	Affiliated 2015	% Christian female 2015
DR Congo	Eglise Catholique au DR Congo	42,891,000	51.2%
Colombia	Iglesia Católica en Colombia	42,206,000	51.2%
Spain	Iglesia Católica en España	39,377,000	51.2%
Ethiopia	Ethiopian Orthodox Church	39,200,000	50.0%

Most of the world's largest denominations are either equally or more Christian than the general population of the country (Table 4). The greatest gap among these ten denominations is among Catholics in the United States (53.3% female). Removing Catholics from the equation reveals slightly higher shares of women in the world's largest denominations, such as the Evangelical Protestant Church in Germany (55% female) and the Assemblies of God in Brazil (55% female) (Table 5).

Table 5. Largest non-Catholic denominations, 2015

Country	Denomination	Affiliated 2015	% Christian female 2015
Russia	Russian Orthodox Church	110,850,000	53.5%
Ethiopia	Ethiopian Orthodox Church	39,200,000	50.0%
China	Three-Self Patriotic Movement	30,000,000	51.5%
Germany	Evangelische Kirche in Deutschland	24,450,000	55.0%
United Kingdom	Church of England	23,000,000	53.8%
Nigeria	Anglican Church of Nigeria	22,000,000	52.9%
Brazil	Assembleias de Deus	20,978,000	55.0%
China	Han traditional house churches	20,000,000	53.7%
China	Han house churches Big Five (rural)	19,510,000	53.7%
United States	Southern Baptist Convention	18,836,000	54.1%

Nuancing the Data

A common refrain in World Christianity studies is that churches around the world are majority female. Women were among the first converts to Christianity and in most places, women are the drivers of church life, whether in official leadership capacities or not. . Consider the following examples from Africa:

- On the Catholic Church in Benin: "Women are very active in the Church, [she boasted]. For instance, women are the majority in Church attendance everywhere. Women do everything! . . . Coming to the Church, you will find out that the population of women is greater. Women could be about 80%, while men would be something like 20% in attendance."[13]

- On the Brazilian Pentecostalism in Mozambique: "Based on fieldwork it is possible to affirm that nearly 75 percent of the visitors and converts at Brazilian Pentecostal churches in Maputo are women of varying age. . . . In general, women outnumber men in Christian churches . . . but in Mozambique Brazilian Pentecostalism appears to be a very 'female-oriented' religion as compared to Catholic and Protestant mission churches where I often counted that women made up about 60 percent of the visitors and men 40 percent."[14]

- On the International Centre for Evangelism, Burkina Faso: "Ouédraogo indicated that about 90 percent of their church members are women and they are far more dynamic than the men."[15]

And consider these examples from Asia:

- The Presbyterian Church in Korea (Tonghap) is one of the largest denominations in South Korea, with more than 2.7 million members. A study suggested that its membership is 70% female, much higher than the 52% reported in this chapter for South Korean Christianity.[16]

- The Chinese Catholic Church is reported to be 52% female in the *World Christian Database*, but a more on-the-ground approach revealed 62% female.[17] It is likely the case that these higher figures are more representative of women's share of churches in Asia, but, unfortunately, this level of detail is not available for every denomination in every country.

- In the 1970s and 1980s, the Chinese house church movement was primarily rural and upward of 80% female. In the 1990s and early 2000s, the movement emerged in the cities and among the middle class, and the gender dynamic began to change with more men joining the churches. In the early 2000s, more localized studies suggested women

---

13. Uchem, "Overcoming Women's Subordination," 101–2.
14. Kamp, *Violent Conversion*, 21.
15. Dah, *Women Do More Work*, 128.
16. Cho, "Equal Discipleship."
17. Yang, *Atlas of Religion in China*, 43.

were an estimated 80% of house church leaders and evangelists and 70%–80% of members.[18]

From the data that are available, two general trends appear to be true. First, surveys tend to report higher percentages of Christian females than government censuses. There are few surveys available for this kind of analysis, but some of the highest percentages of Christian females are from Argentina and the United States, both sourced from surveys, and neither country includes a religion question on its national census for comparison. In Argentina, the religion survey by the National Scientific and Technical Research Council reported 80% female for Evangelical Baptists and 62% for Pentecostals.[19] For the United States, the Pew Research Center reported 57% female for historically Black Protestants and 54% for evangelical and mainline Protestants. Second, denominations that fall under the Independent category tend to report higher shares of women in their memberships than other traditions, regardless of source. Examples include the Universal Church of the Kingdom of God (Brazil), 60% female; Jehovah's Witnesses (Brazil), 58% female; Church of the Lord (Prayer Fellowship) (Nigeria), 56% female; and the Assemblies of God (Zimbabwe), 56% female.

Social Norms

A wide diversity of gendered expectations exists within Christian traditions, movements, families, and denominations. Some ordain women, others do not; some have substantial gender imbalances in their memberships, whereas others are more equal; some actively encourage women's public participation, while others prefer women to have more supportive roles. Nevertheless, in all Christian traditions, women are finding ways to live out their vocational callings, make important contributions to the life of the church, and in many ecclesial contexts, are pushing boundaries for greater equality and influence. It is widely known that women are more likely to attend religious services, pray, and say that religion is important in their lives.[20] However, it was not known until very recently what percentage of the church in Africa, for example, is female (52% by membership, much higher by attendance and participation). Comprehensive data on women's activities in churches, their influences in congregational life, what kinds of leadership

---

18. Wommack, "Women House Church Leaders of China"; Aikman, *Jesus in Beijing*.
19. Mallimaci et al., *Second National Survey*.
20. Pew Research Center, "Gender Gap in Religion."

roles they have, and the extent of women's service to their churches and religious communities are not available.

Most Christian denominations collect data of all kinds, including church membership, detailed budgets, attendance, number of pastors, buildings, women's and children's ministries, tithes, and so on. However, precious few groups appear to collect data on the gender makeup of their membership. This is even the case for churches with robust statistical traditions, like the Roman Catholic Church and the Church of Jesus Christ of Latter-day Saints, both of whom produce annual statistical annals and have been collecting information on the demographic makeup and activities of their members for decades (or centuries!). Even for groups like these, gendered membership data are apparently unavailable to the public, and even unavailable by request. With ministry roles so gendered, one would surmise that churches would collapse without the women working behind the scenes. Without good data, good decisions cannot be made.

Women are preachers and evangelists, ordained or lay; teachers, deaconesses, elders, and missionaries; women run Mother's Unions, wives' clubs, ecumenical fellowships, national chapters of the Young Women's Christian Association, and other global entities. Women teach young girls life skills and ensure their education. They are involved in political activism and humanitarian work, speaking out for the oppressed and advocating for equal rights. Some women openly critique social norms in their churches and societies, while others quietly and effectively work within established systems. Women are increasingly elected to honored leadership positions within Christian organizations and denominations. Like in the first century of Christianity, women today are leaders of house churches and risk their lives to make disciples. Many have prominent roles in "hidden" Christian communities in North Africa and the Middle East, where it is illegal or dangerous to be a Christian.

Conclusion

The data gap in World Christianity hinders the ability of Christian organizations to make intelligent and well-informed decisions for the benefit of all constituents, not just women. Gender equality activists are fully aware that women and men are unlikely to be truly equal without buy-in from men. Otherwise, echo chambers are created where women are talking to women about "women's issues" and little actually gets done because men are still the primary decision-makers. Men and women together must believe that gender equity is good for *everyone*, not just women. Men don't lose when women gain. In fact, men gain when women gain! They gain more holistic ways of viewing the world, the church, and even the gospel. Perhaps they can better see the women among Jesus's disciples who did not leave him nor forsake him, unlike the twelve male disciples, who did. Women were the last at the cross, the first at the tomb, and the first evangelists to declare the risen Christ. Women are the majority of the world's Christians today and are critiquing social norms and power imbalances that render them voiceless. In doing so, they are demanding biblical justice in their societies, communities, and churches not only for the sake of women and girls, but for all of God's people.

Bibliography

Aikman, David. *Jesus in Beijing: How Christianity is Transforming China and Changing the Global Balance of Power*. Oxford: Monarch, 2006.

Braude, Anne. "Women's History *Is* American Religious History." In *Retelling U.S. Religious History*, edited by Thomas A. Tweed, 87–107. Berkeley: University of California Press, 1997.

Brooten, Bernadette. "Early Christian Women and Their Cultural Context: Issues of Method in Historical Reconstruction." In *Feminist Perspectives on Biblical Scholarship*, edited by Adela Y. Collins, 65–92. Chico: Scholars, 1985.

Cho, Han Sang. "Equal Discipleship in the Presbyterian Church of Korea (PCK)." DMin diss., Catholic Theological Union, 2011.

Dah, Ini Dorcas. *Women Do More Work Than Men: Birifor Women as Change Agents in the Mission and Expansion of the Church in West Africa*. Eugene, OR: Wipf & Stock, 2017.

Herr, Ranjoo S. "'Third World,' Transnational, and Global Feminisms." In *Encyclopedia of Race and Racism*, edited by Patrick L. Mason, 190–95. 2nd ed. Detroit: Macmillan Reference USA, 2013.

Johnson, Todd M., and Gina A. Zurlo, eds. *World Christian Database*. Leiden: Brill, 2022.

Kamp, Linda van de. *Violent Conversion: Brazilian Pentecostalism and Urban Women in Mozambique*. Woodbridge: Currey, 2018.

Mallimaci, Fortunato, et al. *Society and Religion in Transformation: Second National Survey on Religious Beliefs and Attitudes in Argentina*. Research Report No. 25. Buenos Aires: CEIL-CONICET, 2019.

Mohanty, Chandra. "Feminist Encounters: Locating the Politics of Experience." *Copyright* 1 (1987) 30–44.

Pew Research Center. "The Gender Gap in Religion around the World." *Pew Research Center*, March 22, 2016. https://www.pewresearch.org/religion/2016/03/22/the-gender-gap-in-religion-around-the-world/.

Robert, Dana L. *American Women in Mission: A Social History of Their Thought and Practice*. Macon, GA: Mercer University Press, 1996.

———. "World Christianity as a Women's Movement." *International Bulletin of Missionary Research* 30 (2006) 180–88.

Stark, Rodney. *The Rise of Christianity: A Sociologist Reconsiders History*. Princeton: Princeton University Press, 1996.

Trzebiatowska, Marta, and Steve Bruce. *Why Are Women More Religious Than Men?* Oxford: Oxford University Press, 2014.

Uchem, Rose N. "Overcoming Women's Subordination in the Igbo African Culture and in the Catholic Church: Envisioning an Inclusive Theology with Reference to Women." PhD diss., Graduate Theological Foundation, 2001.

Wommack, Timothy R. "The Women House Church Leaders of China: Interviews with a Muted Group." MA thesis, Liberty University, 2006.

UNDP. *Human Development Report 2019.* https://hdr.undp.org/system/files/documents/hdr2019pdf.pdf.

Yang, Fenggang. *Atlas of Religion in China: Social and Geographical Contexts.* Leiden: Brill, 2018.

Zurlo, Gina A. *Women in World Christianity: Building and Sustaining a Global Movement.* Hoboken, NJ: Wiley & Sons, 2023.

— 3 —

Church Mothers
The Leadership of African Christian Women in the Pre-modern Period

Vince L. Bantu

Before the modern period, the Christian church grew extensively across the continent now known as Africa. The early African church was built and sustained by the efforts of African women. Early African male theologians exhibited oppressive views of women and enacted systems of oppression that actualized these views. Despite challenges from outside of and within the church, African women found a variety of ways to exhibit agency within Christian structures as well as in broader society. This chapter surveys pre-colonial African Christianity and explore the stories of some of the most prominent African Christian women leaders in different regions and in different periods, with a focus on how these women exercised agency in patriarchal ecclesial structures.

Survey of Pre-colonial African Christianity

The story of Christianity has been embedded in the African continent from its very beginning. Fleeing King Herod's persecution, the Holy Family sojourned in Egypt during the earliest time of Jesus' lifetime (Matt

2:13–15). An African visiting Jerusalem helped Jesus carry his cross (Matt 27:32; Mark 15:21; Luke 23:26). Egyptians and North Africans were present at Pentecost and a Kushite eunuch was among the first among believers (Acts 2:10; 8:27–39). Indeed, the eunuch is said to be a eunuch of Candace (or Kandake), which was the title of the queens of the Kushite kingdom of Meroë.[1] Therefore, the first sub-Saharan African Christian mentioned in history was connected to African queens. Immediately after the New Testament period, Christianity was prevalent in Egypt and the provinces of Roman North Africa (Numidia, Cyrenaica, Byzencena, Mauritania, and Africa Proconsularis). Some of the earliest and most prolific theologians in the Roman Empire emerged from Egypt and North Africa—including Origen, Tertullian, Cyprian, Athanasius, Cyril of Alexandria, and Augustine of Hippo. Some of the earliest biblical fragments come from Egypt and North Africa hosted some of the earliest church councils.

Egypt housed one of the most prominent theological schools in the third century and popularized communal Christian asceticism in the fourth century. Egyptian patriarchs such as Athanasius and Cyril were among the most influential theologians in the entire Roman Empire during times of intense theological debate. Likewise, the North African theologian Augustine of Hippo was one of the most foundational theologians for the subsequent development of Christianity in the Western world. During the fourth century, theology became expressed in the native Egyptian language—Coptic—as was evidenced in the writings of theologians such as Pachomius and Shenoute of Atripe.[2] While Christianity in North Africa rapidly declined following the Islamic Conquest of the seventh century, Christianity continued to thrive in the Coptic church of Egypt until today.

Also during the fourth century, the Axumite Empire (modern Ethiopia) became a Christian empire when Emperor Ezana was converted by a Syrian missionary who was also the empire's first bishop. Other Syrian missionaries helped translate the Bible into classical Ethiopic (Geʿez) and build monasteries and churches. The Axumite Empire fell in the tenth century and the Christian Zagwe Dynasty ruled in the twelfth and thirteenth centuries. This dynasty built the famous rock-hewn churches in the capital city of Lalibela. Beginning in the thirteenth century and until modern times, Ethiopia was ruled by the Solomonic Dynasty, which claimed descent from the biblical King Solomon. The thirteenth, fourteenth, and fifteenth centuries

---

1. For more information on the role of Kandake in Kush, see Welsby, *Kingdom of Kush*.

2. Veilleux, *Life of Saint Pachomius*; Brakke and Crislip, *Selected Discourses of Shenoute*.

witnessed an unprecedented amount of Ethiopian literature, architecture, art, and political expansion.[3]

During the fifth century, Nubian people south of Egypt began to be converted to Christianity in mass numbers due to the efforts of Egyptian monks.[4] In the sixth century, the Nubian kingdoms of Nobatia, Makouria, and Alodia/Alwa embraced Christianity as their imperial religion. Soon after the Christianization of the Nubian kingdoms, invading Arab Muslim armies were defeated by Christian Nubia during their attempted conquest. The Nubians and Arabs made a peace treaty stipulating Nubians would continue to be independent and Christian. While Nubians eventually became predominantly Muslim in the fifteenth century, the thousand-year Christian period of Nubia witnessed vast amounts of Nubian Christian culture, architecture, churches, paintings, and writings. The majority of Old Nubian literature, wall paintings, and architectural structures that survive from this period were Christian in nature, demonstrating the centrality of the church in Nubian society and culture.

In sum, Christianity spread all across the civilizations of the continent of Africa long before the colonial period. The theological, ecclesial, and cultural contributions of African Christians formed the foundation of African civilizations for centuries and promoted African agency. A lamentable reality is that these African civilizations limited and marginalized the leadership of African women in many cases. Despite the oppression that African women endured, many of these pillars of the faith displayed significant agency and power in pre-colonial African Christian history. The balance of this chapter will survey some of the most prominent Christian women leaders across the various regions of the continent we call Africa. The focus will be on African women who lived free from Western colonialism, in order to underscore the expansiveness of African Christianity apart from European intervention, an often-neglected portion of history.

North Africa

One of the first Christian texts to center women leaders was set in the North African city of Carthage. Carthage was the center of the Punic Empire for centuries before the time of Christianity. After losing the Punic Wars, Carthage and its environs became a Roman colony called Africa Proconsularis. Christians were present in this area from the beginning of the church, as is evidenced in Scripture (Matt 27:32; Mark 15:21; Luke 23:26; Acts 2:10).

3. Tamrat, *Church and State in Ethiopia*.
4. Gabra and Takla, *Christianity and Monasticism*.

Soon after the time of the New Testament, one of the most famous Christian theologians—Tertullian—lived and wrote in Carthage. Another wave of persecution against Christians broke out at the turn of the third century under Septimus Severus. In Carthage, there was a group of Christians who were imprisoned and martyred for their faith in the colosseum of Carthage.[5] The central figures of this event were two North African women named Perpetua and Felicity. Perpetua is the central figure in the *passio* ("passion narrative" of the martyrs), and the introduction of the text states that "she herself narrated the whole course of her martyrdom, as she left it described by her own hand and with her own mind."[6] The text immediately turns to Perpetua's struggle with her father, who, because of "his affection" for her, tried to convince her to apostatize to save her own life. Perpetua understood his efforts as an attempt to "cast me down from the faith." Nonetheless, this Christian woman defied the wishes of her father and replied:

> "Father," said I, "do you see, let us say, this vessel lying here to be a little pitcher, or something else?" And he said, "I see it to be so." And I replied to him, "Can it be called by any other name than what it is?" And he said, "No." "Neither can I call myself anything else than what I am, a Christian." Then my father, provoked at this saying, threw himself upon me, as if he would tear my eyes out. But he only distressed me, and went away overcome by the devil's arguments. Then, in a few days after I had been without my father, I gave thanks to the Lord; and his absence became a source of consolation to me.[7]

The text presents Perpetua as the symbol of faithful courage while her father is abusive and under the influence of the devil. Perpetua demonstrates agency in that she receives and interprets visions from God that are exclusively given to her, rather than the Christian men in prison with her. In fact, the men beseech her to share these visions about their impending martyrdom with them. The servant Felicitas was imprisoned as well and was with child, which meant that she would not be martyred along with her fellow Christians while she was pregnant. Rather than fearing her own demise, Felicitas only desired that she give birth so that she would be able to die for Christ along with the other martyrs: "Now it is I that suffer what I suffer; but then there will be another in me, who will suffer for me, because I also am about to suffer for Him."[8] Felicitas gave birth in the prison and her child was

---

5. See Wilhite, *Ancient African Christianity*.
6. Wallis, "Perpetua and Felicitas," 699.
7. Wallis, "Perpetua and Felicitas," 700.
8. Wallis, "Perpetua and Felicitas," 704.

adopted by other Christians. On the day of their martyrdom, Perpetua led the Christian retinue into the colosseum, bravely singing songs of worship. After horrific tortures, Perpetua even guided the blade of the timid soldier to finish her martyrdom. Indeed, the martyrdom of Perpetua and Felicity displays the agency of African women throughout the text. At the beginning of the production of Christian literature, the voices of these African women emerge as ideals of Christian piety and leadership.

Egypt

Like the church of Roman North Africa, the Egyptian church also traces its history back to the New Testament. While the most well-known Egyptian Christian figures are men, there were yet many women who were pivotal in this ancient Christian tradition. Perhaps the most influential aspect of early Egyptian Christianity both inside and outside of Egypt was communal—or coenobitic—monasticism. While not invented in Egypt, the "Desert Fathers" of Egypt and the communities they organized influenced subsequent Christian monks in the Middle East and all across Europe. The *Apophthegmata Patrum* ("Sayings of the Father") is a collection of proverbs and monastic practices of some of the most famous Desert Fathers, such as Anthony, Macarius and Moses the Black.[9] However, there were also many "Desert Mothers" who provided the model of ascetic piety. Alongside the *abbas* ("fathers"), many of the *amas* ("mothers") provided wisdom to aspiring ascetics. Sarah was one such Desert Mother, whose gender was sometimes used as a pretext to challenge her authority:

> Another time, two old men, great anchorites, came to the district of Pelusia to visit her. When they arrived, one said to the other, "Let us humiliate this old woman." So they said to her, "Be careful not to become conceited thinking to yourself: 'Look how anchorites are coming to see me, a mere woman.'" But Amma Sarah said to them, "According to nature I am a woman, but not according to my thoughts."[10]

For many early Christians, being a woman was associated with weakness and spiritual immaturity while manliness evoked ideas of strength and piety. While Sarah challenged the attitudes of the male anchorites, it seems that her autonomy came at the expense of her identity as a woman. Indeed,

---

9. Wortley, *Sayings of the Desert Fathers*.
10. Swan, *Desert Mothers*, 38–39.

Sarah made the provocative statement to other male ascetics: "It is I who am a man, you who are women."[11]

The most prominent Desert Mother in the *Apophthegmata Patrum* was Amma Syncletica. Syncletica lived in the Egyptian desert during the fourth century and many of her teachings have been passed down through Egyptian and more broad Christian traditions. Syncletica's family was originally from Macedonia, but immigrated to Egypt because of their desire to be among the passionate Christian community. The biography of Syncletica says that when their family came to Alexandria, "they discovered an unmatched faith coupled with a sincere charity, they made their country of adoption their second home."[12] Therefore, while Syncletica was not Egyptian herself, she has been embraced by the Egyptian Christian community since the fourth century. Syncletica also taught indigenous Egyptian women extensively and engaged in theological dialogue with them. Therefore, the literature surrounding the life and ministry of Syncletica is an invaluable resource for understanding the voices of Egyptian Christian women. For example, many Egyptian Christian women ascetics flocked to Syncletica and desired to learn from and question her on various areas of Christian life:

> But they would say to her: "We also know that we have one source of instruction—Scripture—and the same teacher. But you have made progress in virtues by your ever-wakeful zeal; those who are in possession of what is good, since they are better able, must also help those who are weaker. And indeed our common teacher commands this." And on hearing these words, the blessed woman used to weep, like babies at the breast. But the women gathered there put aside their questioning once more and urged her to stop weeping. And when she had grown calm, there was again a long period of silence and again they began to encourage her. Since she was deeply moved and knew, moreover, that what she had said did not bring praise for herself but rather sowed helpful ideas among those present, she began to speak to them in the following vein.[13]

The Egyptian ascetics placed the highest value on humility. In true monastic form, Syncletica did not desire praise from people, as this was a stumbling block to godly humility: "[Syncletica] also said, 'Just as it is impossible to be at the same moment both a plant and a seed, so it is impossible for us to be surrounded by worldly honor and at the same time to

---

11. Swan, *Desert Mothers*, 41.
12. Bongie, *Life of Syncletica*, 10.
13. Bongie, *Life of Syncletica*, 19.

bear heavenly fruit."[14] As her biography displays, Syncletica was a leader to many Egyptian women despite her desire to stay out of the spotlight. Her biography is also an important window into the voices of indigenous Egyptian women ascetics. The questions and challenges they pose to Syncletica display a strong degree of agency and the biblical training that occurred for late antique Egyptian women.

Nubia

The various kingdoms of Nubia—Nobatia, Makouria and Alodia/Alwa—embraced Christianity as the imperial religion in the sixth century. This ushered in a one-thousand-year long period of Christian Nubia that also entailed a golden era of Nubian architecture, literature, and culture. The Nubian church was under the jurisdiction of the patriarchate of Alexandria and Christianity likely entered Nubia through contact with Egyptian monks. Because of this ecclesiastical relationship, as well as extensive trade with the broader Byzantine Empire, Nubian Christianity was largely influenced by Egyptian and Byzantine cultural influences. Indeed, the majority of inscriptions and texts from Nubia were written in Greek or Coptic, while the amount of literature written in the indigenous Nubian language (Old Nubian) was much smaller. Furthermore, the majority of literature that survives in Old Nubian is in the form of translations of Greek or Coptic material. Few Christian texts that are original to the Old Nubian language that have yet been discovered. However, one of the few Christian texts that was likely originally written in Old Nubian centers on an unnamed Egyptian woman. The Miracle of St. Mina is set in Egypt and is named for the third-century monastic saint Mina, of the monastic community at Scetis. The protagonist of the text is a woman who is wealthy and a practitioner of indigenous Egyptian religion. The woman, her servants, and her animals are barren and cannot reproduce. So, the first words uttered by the woman are a declaration of her desire for herself and her household to bear children and produce heirs: "Truly, if it is the God (*tillil*) of Saint Mina saying to one of my fowls to give birth, I will place the egg it has laid first in his church (*kisse*)."[15] It is of note that the first person to speak in this text is a woman and that she heard of the work of God from other "women speaking" (*eittil pesran*). Indeed, women's voices and perspectives dominate this text, one of the few works of Christian theology in the history of Nubian civilization. Soon after the woman's pledge, one of her birds laid an egg which she set out

---

14. Swan, *Desert Mothers*, 60.
15. El-Guzuuli and Gerven Oei, *Miracle of Saint Mina*, 24.

to place in the Church of Saint Mina, as she promised. However, when she attempted to charter a boat to the church, a dishonest sailor suggested that she entrust him to deposit the egg in the church. The sailor suggested he would be better suited to deliver the egg in a church, since he was a Christian and she was a "pagan." The woman believed the man and gave him the egg, but instead of doing as he promised, he ate the egg. Some time passed, and that same sailor went to the Church of Saint Mary. During the service, Saint Mina appeared on a horse holding a spear in front of the sailor. Terrified, the sailor ran to an icon of Mary and begged her to forgive him. Again, it is of note that the dishonest sailor seeks absolution from Mary, further exemplifying the role of women in Nubian Christianity. Saint Mina kicked the sailor and then a bird came out from the sailor. Saint Mina took the bird back to the woman and told her to release the bird among her other birds, who would become pregnant. Saint Mina also announced that the woman would bear a son, and to name him Mina. It happened as the Saint declared, and the woman took her husband, son, and servants to the church of Saint Mina to be baptized. The woman of this story is the central figure and displays the agency, rather than her husband or son. As has been stated, there is not much literary evidence illuminating the nature of Nubian Christianity. Therefore, it is important that one of the few Nubian Christian texts highlighted the agency and voice of women.

Another source that highlighted the voice and agency of Christian women in ancient Nubia was from an unlikely source. There are a number of documentary texts that illumine the social, economic, and political life of Christian Nubia. While these texts may not appear as "interesting" to the modern reader due to their practical dynamic, they are indispensable to reconstructing the day-to-day-life of Christians in the ancient world. There have been a sizable number of such documentary texts discovered in the Nubian city Qasr Ibrim. One of the most common types of documentary texts from ancient Nubia were land sale receipts. The selling of land in Christian Nubia was an important part of religious and civic life. Leaders from the civic and church sectors would gather for public rituals between buyers and sellers, with a grand feast provided by the seller for all in attendance. Scribes would record the event as an important aspect of recording Nubian history and proof of land ownership. While such texts may appear as mundane to some, it is of great significance to gain a rare window into ancient African practices of land ownership and transfer of ownership before a time when African autonomy of land was disrupted. What is of even greater significance for the purpose at hand, is that the longest and most elaborate land sale receipt from Qasr Ibrim actually centered a woman seller and woman buyer. This is extremely rare, as most land sales centered Nubian men. And again, not only was there a land sale that centered women, but this receipt was the longest and most elaborate. What is more significant, is that this land sale was unique in its inclusion of personal information and declarations of faith:

> With God. In the name of the Father, the Son and the Holy Spirit, Amen. This certified document is written in the year 907 (of the era) of the Martyrs, it being the 5th of the month of Hathyr, it being the 24th of the moon, King Moses George being King of Dotawo, Mari being Queen Mother.... I, Kapopi, daughter of Toungngesi, competent in my eyes, in my hands and in my feet, rejoicing and exulting, being barren in respect to daughter and son, not being subject to litigation, as regards all the land that I inherited from my mother, without denial I sell to Neuesi, daughter of Adama and Anenikoli, all the land that is mentioned in this document, and the house itself which is included.[16]

The inclusion of the phrase "competent in my eyes, in my hands and in my feet" and the additional personal information is rare in Nubian documentary texts from this period. The degrees of the rarity of this African Christian woman's voice cannot be over-emphasized: the history of medieval Africa from African sources is rare, literary evidence from Christian Nubia is rare, texts in Old Nubian are rare, texts in Old Nubian that feature the voice of women are rare, and documentary texts from Christian Nubia that include personal information are rare. This rare window into an African woman's autonomy—as she has said, competency—shows that nevertheless African women exercised agency and voice in Nubia.

Ethiopia

The Ethiopian nation and the Ethiopian Christian tradition are built upon the memory of women leaders. According to Ethiopian tradition, a Queen was the first leader to introduce monotheism into Ethiopia. The *Kebrä Nägäśt* is a fourteenth-century Ethiopian text that recounts the story of the biblical Queen of Sheba bearing a son from King Solomon and beginning a dynasty of kings in the Solomonic line.[17] Ethiopian women are an invaluable resource not only for the history of African Christianity but to world history. Indeed, Ethiopia produced the earliest-known biographies of sub-Saharan African women known to humanity. Many of the *gädl*—spiritual

---

16. Browne, *Old Nubian Texts*, 3:36. For a more recent translation and discussion on the land plots, see Gerven Oei, "For Sale," 89–112; Ruffini, *Medieval Nubia*, 1–3.

17. See the English translation by Budge, *Queen of Sheba*.

biographies—are written about Ethiopian women saints who performed miracles, led Christian communities, and fought for freedom.

One of the earliest-known Ethiopian women saints is Krestos Śamra. Krestos Śamra was a noblewoman from the Shewa province of Ethiopia during the fifteenth century. She was known to be very beautiful and was bestowed with wealth and servants from the emperor. The son of the famous Ethiopian ascetic—Iyasus Mo'a—became her husband. Iyasus Mo'a was the leader of the Istifanos Monastery at the famous Lake Tana, and he aided the founder of the Solomonic Dynasty, Emperor Yekuno Amlak. Iyasus Mo'a was greatly pleased to be the father-in-law of Krestos Śamra and prophesied that she would be a great leader. One day, Krestos Śamra became enraged with her servant and shoved a hot poker down her throat, killing her. Krestos Śamra then prayed and vowed that if the Lord saved her servant, that Krestos Śamra would dedicate her life to the Christian monastic lifestyle. God saved the servant, and Krestos Śamra left her family and lived at the famous monastic center of Lake Tana. Krestos Śamra started off as a solitary ascetic, spending years praying in the waters of Lake Tana. Eventually, she started a monastic community. Krestos Śamra received a visit from the biblical patriarchs Moses, Elijah, and John the Baptist. These men foretold that she would be a monastic leader whose renown would be known to many: "They said to me: 'In a few days, you will become the Mother of a monastery named Guangut. Daughters of kings and governors will come to you and will bow down at the footsteps of your feet. Many women without number—from far and near—will come to you and will dwell with you.'"[18] Krestos Śamra responded with statements of unworthiness for such adoration, a posture expected and typical for Ethiopian monastic literature. However, the patriarchs ascended to the "Garden of Joy" and she indeed became the head of a monastery in Guangut.

One of the most well-known events described in her *gädl*[19] was a supernatural conversation she had with Jesus. The encounter began when Krestos Śamra was in prayer and was reflecting on biblical passages discussing the finite nature of human existence. This caused Krestos Śamra to weep, as this section reveals her heart's desire for universal salvation. This aspect of the theology of the text is significant, as the desire for universal salvation and that none should perish highlights the unique perspective of women leaders. It is common that the perspective of women in Christian theology

---

18. Cerulli, *Atti di Krestos Samrā*, 43.

19. "Struggle," in the sense of a spiritual struggle. An Ethiopian genre of literature narrating the life of a saint.

is more centered on pursuing harmony rather than causing division.[20] The claims that Krestos Śämra was in severe mourning at the thought of humans who perish without the salvation of Jesus Christ. It is of great significance that, although the text was written by the male servant of Krestos Śämra named Filippos, that the conversation with Jesus includes first-person statements made by Krestos Śämra. It is when engaged in dialogue with the Lord Jesus that the voice of this African woman saint comes to the fore most poignantly. It should also be noted that Jesus frequently refers to Krestos Śämra as "my beloved," further demonstrating the sense of agency and intimacy that African women such as Krestos Śämra displayed in Christian space. Krestos Śämra asks Jesus why he created humanity in his image, thus displaying a significant degree of philosophical inquiry among Ethiopian women leaders. Jesus responded by claiming that it was for the sake of humanity that Adam was made in his image and that he died on the cross. Jesus continues, asking:

> Then He said to her: "Please tell me the desire of your heart, my beloved Krestos Śämra—that which is in your heart." At that moment, I responded to Him and I said to Him: "My Lord, I desire that you forgive the Devil and that all of humanity would be saved from being condemned to torment. For you do not desire the death of the sinner but rather his return and his restoration [Ezek 18:23]. It is for this reason that I say to You, 'Forgive the Devil.' May it not seem to You as if I enjoy saying all of this to You. Rather, it is for the sake of Adam and his children, for their flesh is my flesh."[21]

While the question of universal salvation was raised by a few Christian theologians prior to the time of Krestos Śämra, the prospect of forgiving even the Devil is a unique line of inquiry. The fact that this unique theological inquiry appears in the biography of this Ethiopian woman leader is but one of the reasons why this text and its hero should be more widely known. Jesus responded to the inquiry of Krestos Śämra by laughing and summoning the Archangel Michael to take her to Gehenna. Upon arrival at Gehenna, Krestos Śämra lamented the torment of souls and she was brought before Satan. Krestos Śämra announced that Satan had the opportunity to receive forgiveness of his sins. However, the devil snatched Krestos Śämra and took her to the depths of Sheol. Archangel Michael came to her rescue and smote the devil. As they fled Sheol, Krestos Śämra and Michael ransomed one-hundred thousand souls from Sheol and brought them to

---

20. Belcher, "Life and Visions of Krəstos Śämra," 81.
21. Cerulli, *Atti di Krestos Samrā*, 45.

Heaven. Jesus welcomed these souls into Heaven and commanded Michael that they be placed in the home of Krestos Śämra.

This unique story demonstrates several layers of agency that women displayed in Solomonic-era Ethiopia. Women such as Krestos Śämra were leaders of women and men in monastic communities. The intimacy with which she spoke with Jesus was unique in Christian texts of this period, demonstrating a sense of belonging in the body of Christ on the part of Krestos Śämra. The kinds of questions and theological agenda of Krestos Śämra was distinct from her male counterparts, who were often concerned with correcting false teachings or establishing ecclesial hierarchy. Ethiopian biographies about women such as Krestos Śämra, therefore, represent an important voice in Christian history and demonstrate unique examples of the autonomy of ancient African Christian women.

Another example of an Ethiopian woman saint was the life and ministry of Walatta Petros. This seventeenth-century figure was also a monastic leader as well as a freedom fighter. Walatta Petros was born to a noble family in the Dawaro region of Ethiopia to Christian parents named Bahir Sagaad and Kristos Ebayaa. Bahir had a divine vision of the future birth of his daughter and reported this to his wife Kristos. The agency of women is already established in the *gädl* of Walatta Petros in the parents, ensuring that Kristos also received this celestial vision. So Bahir and Kristos continued to pray together until she also received divine confirmation of their future daughter's birth. When Walatta Petros was born, Bahir embraced her while she was still covered in blood from childbirth, to the shock of the midwife. Bahir replied: "There is no unclean blood or filth on this daughter of mine."[22] Walatta Petros was baptized and grew in the love and dedication of the Lord. She eventually married a military official named Malkiya Kristos. The two lost three children together, and Walatta Petros desired to live the monastic life. She ran away from her husband to live in a monastery, which he then attacked. When he saw that she did not desire to stay married to him, he allowed her to become a nun according to her desire. This was prompted by Walatta Petros' displeasure with her husband due to her belief that he was involved in the assassination of the Ethiopian Abuna during the arrival of "European" Christianity in Ethiopia. Soon after her departure from her husband, Walatta Petros met Eheta Krestos, the woman Christian companion with whom she would spend the rest of her life ministering.

King Susenyos of Ethiopia (1607–32 CE) established an alliance with the Portuguese at this time, which entailed his embrace of the "filthy faith

---

22. Galawdewos, *Life and Struggles*, 89.

of the Europeans," as it was referred to in the biography of Walatta Petros.[23] The text focuses primarily on the difference in christology between Chalcedonian Christians of Europe and the Miaphysite Christianity of Ethiopia and Egypt. Since the Council of Chalcedon (451 CE), the patriarchate of Alexandria retained its own distinct christology, articulating one united nature in the incarnate Christ. The Council of Chalcedon, on the other hand, argued for two distinct "natures" in Christ—one human and one divine. Over one-thousand years later, this issue was the primary point of contention for Walatta Petros in rejecting her king's alliance with the "filthy European faith." Emperor Susenyos and Malkiya Kristos arrested Walatta Petros and brought her before the imperial court to stand trial. The tone of the text resembles earlier martyr stories of the late antique Christian period. Walatta Petros demonstrates bravery and willingness to die for the orthodox (i.e., Miaphysite) faith. In response to the allegation of defying the king, Walatta Petros is recorded as responding thusly: "However, our holy mother Walatta Petros did not respond or reply at all. Rather she listened with her head bowed and a critical smile, but humbly said, 'I have not reviled the king. Rather, I will never renounce my faith.'"[24] According to the text, the king does not kill Walatta Petros, and she lived in exile in a monastic community in an area called Zagé. However, the emperor sent a spy to keep watch over her.

Walatta Petros and her entourage escaped this spy through a miraculous journey along the lake where God rescued the group from ravenous hippopotamuses. Indeed, the *gädl* of Walatta Petros credits her with the ability to speak to and control animals. When Walatta Petros was told that she would be the founder of many monasteries, she doubted. The *gädl* reports that Jesus himself appeared to Walatta Petros and gave her a series of visions, confirming that she indeed would found monastic communities all throughout Ethiopia. The ensuing dialogue between Walatta Petros and Jesus is reminiscent of that between Jesus and Krestos Śamra. Jesus appears to Walatta Petros and causes doves and goblets to appear, likening them to the Christians that will come under her care. However, she "does not believe" Jesus and rejects this prophecy out of concern for not being able to properly care for monastic communities. Jesus prophesies that a lion will appear and kill one of her disciples due to her disbelief, which happens as Jesus said it would. Walatta Petros then accepts the visions and message as being authentic when she says: "Your will be done, O my Lord." The text continues and praises Walatta Petros for her discernment and scrutiny of the message: "This is the behavior of the wise: they do not immediately

---

23. Galawdewos, *Life and Struggles*, 119.
24. Galawdewos, *Life and Struggles*, 125.

believe (someone) when they are told what is going to happen."²⁵ Walatta Petros' resistance demonstrates her humility and a lack of desire for fame and power, which have been common motivations for many male Christian leaders in antiquity and modern times. Indeed, Walatta Petros' resistance could even appear to be imposter syndrome at first, an indication that she may have felt un-deserving of a leadership role. However, the text clarifies that she was motivated by a lack of desire to be deceived like Eve in the Garden of Eden. Her insistence on the demonstration of a sign is praised in the text as an example of her discernment. In this way, Walatta Petros is a powerful example of an African woman being sure of her leadership ability, rooted in humility, and empowered to the point of even questioning Jesus.

Walatta Petros was captured by the king again and she debated with many "Europeans" about their "filthy faith." The text presents Walatta Petros as deeply knowledgeable of biblical and theological matters. Instead of the male king, *abuna,* or monastic leader, it is the woman Walatta Petros who exegetes Scripture and refutes the European Chalcedonian christology: "She argued with them, defeated them, and embarrassed them."²⁶ This led to her imprisonment for her defiance of the king. When Walatta Petros was imprisoned, her prison guard attempted to sexually assault her and was stopped by an angel of the Lord. This portion of the text would likely have been read as a critique of sexual assault upon women in Solomonic-era Ethiopia. Indeed, the Lord's protection of Walatta Petros against abuse is yet another dimension that demonstrates the text's relevance for empowerment of women in modern times as well. The strength of this ascetic leader was elevated above male contemporaries: "Where is she among women who is equal to Walatta Petros? Who could have patiently born all this like her? Not only a weak woman, but even men who possess strength—they would not have been able to endure like Walatta Petros. However, the power of God that was upon her enabled her to endure and gave her strength."²⁷ King Susenyos eventually renounced the "filthy European faith" and re-embraced Ethiopian Orthodoxy as the imperial religion.

Walatta Petros rejoiced to hear of this news, but decided to remain at Lake Tana to encourage the monastic communities who had suffered due to the king's oppression. The *gädl* reports a variety of miracles and healings performed in the later years of her life. There is an anecdote about some "important men" challenging the authority of Walatta Petros in the monastic community: "They went to her with their spiritual elder and said

25. Galawdewos, *Life and Struggles,* 148.
26. Galawdewos, *Life and Struggles,* 155.
27. Galawdewos, *Life and Struggles,* 161.

to her, 'Who brought you here, and who has given this monastic settlement to you? Is it not ours? So, now we say to you, 'Leave, in peace!' or else we will use force with you and set your hut on fire.'"[28] However, Walatta Petros welcomed them and served them food, which changed their hearts. The text celebrates the humility of Walatta Petros but also vindicates the authority of her leadership. Walatta Petros enforced strict separation between the sexes in her monastic community. In one anecdote, she even refers to lesbian women in the monastic community and denounces sexual activity among members of the same gender.[29] This provides a fascinating window into the perspective of sexuality among African women leaders in the pre-modern period. After a long career of healing, founding seven monasteries, resistance and miracles, Walatta Petros died due to an illness and appointed a successor to her monastic community. The story of Walatta Petros is important for African history, Christian history, women's studies, and world history. Her name should become more commonplace in church history as her life represents one of many examples of the leadership of African Christian women in the pre-modern period.

Conclusion

This brief survey has provided some vignettes of some of the most influential women leaders in the early history of the church in Africa. Other African women like Doña Beatriz Kimpa Vita, Mary Prince, and Phyllis Wheatley encountered Christianity in the context of European colonialism and slavery. These women displayed remarkable resilience against White supremacy and hetero-patriarchy in the midst of unimaginable oppression. However, it is also important to remember that the story of African Christianity did not begin with colonialism. This is also true for the story of African Christian women's leadership. As we have seen in this brief survey, ancient African women still had to resist male patriarchy and social injustice prior to the modern period. However, the pre-modern period provides a window into an African Christian world that lived free of Western colonialism and that African women were integral in shaping. The modern church in Africa, the African Diaspora, and beyond would be well-served to remember the lives of these pre-colonial African Christian women and to honor their legacy through the empowerment of African and African-descended women today.

---

28. Galawdewos, *Life and Struggles*, 187.
29. Galawdewos, *Life and Struggles*, 255.

Bibliography

Belcher, Wendy Laura. "The Life and Visions of Krǝstos Šämra, a Fifteenth-Century Ethiopian Woman Saint." In *African Christian Biography: Narratives, Beliefs, and Boundaries*, edited by Dana Robert, 80–101. Pietermaritzburg: Cluster, 2018.

Bongie, Elizabeth Bryson, trans. *The Life and Regiment of the Blessed and Holy Syncletica by Pseudo-Athanasius*. Vol. 1, *The Translation*. Eugene, OR: Wipf & Stock, 2003.

Brakke, David, and Andrew Crislip. *Selected Discourses of Shenoute the Great: Community, Theology, and Social Conflict in Late Antique Egypt*. Cambridge: Cambridge University Press, 2015.

Browne, Gerald M. *Old Nubian Texts from Qaṣr Ibrīm*. Vol. 3. London: Egypt Exploration Society, 1991.

Budge, E. A. Wallis. *The Queen of Sheba and Her Only Son Menyelek*. New York: Routledge, 2010.

Cerulli, Enrico, ed. *Atti di Krestos Samrā*. CSCO 163–64. Louvain: Secrétariat du Corpus SCO, 1956.

El-Guzuuli, El-Shafie, and Vincent W. J. van Gerven Oei. *The Miracle of Saint Mina*. Milton Keynes: Lightning Source, 2012.

Gabra, Gawdat, and Hany N. Takla. *Christianity and Monasticism in Aswan and Nubia*. Cairo: American University in Cairo Press, 2013.

Galawdewos. *The Life and Struggles of Our Mother Walatta Petros*. Translated and edited by Wendy Laura Belcher and Michael Kleiner. Princeton: Princeton University Press, 2015.

Gerven Oei, Vincent W. J. van. "For Sale: Geography in Old Nubian Land Sales." *Dotawo* 6 (2019) 89–112.

Ruffini, Giovanni R. *Medieval Nubia: A Social and Economic History*. Oxford: Oxford University Press, 2012.

Swan, Laura. *The Forgotten Desert Mothers: Sayings, Lives, and Stories of Early Christian Women*. New York: Paulist, 2001.

Tamrat, Taddesse. *Church and State in Ethiopia, 1270–1527*. Oxford: Clarendon, 1972.

Veilleux, Armand. *The Life of Saint Pachomius and His Disciples*. Collegeville, MN: Cistercian, 1980.

Wallis, R. E., trans. "The Martyrdom of Perpetua and Felicitas." In *The Ante-Nicene Fathers*, edited by Alexander Roberts and James Donaldson, 699–706. Buffalo, NY: Christian Literature, 1885.

Welsby, Derek A. *The Kingdom of Kush: The Napatan and Meroitic Empires*. London: British Museum, 2002.

Wilhite, David E. *Ancient African Christianity: An Introduction to a Unique Context and Tradition*. New York: Routledge, 2017.

Wortley, John, ed. *The Anonymous Sayings of the Desert Fathers: A Select Edition and Complete English Translation*. Cambridge: Cambridge University Press, 2013.

— 4 —

In the Circle of God's Mission
Mission as Coming Home

Musa W. Dube

BACK THEN WHEN I was still a student in high school and a member of the Student Christian Movement, we used to sing the hymn,

> I have wandered far away from God
> Now I am coming home
> The Path of sin too long I have trod
> Lord, I am coming home.

Its chorus repeatedly said:

> Coming home, Coming home
> Never more to roam
> Open wide the arms of love
> Lord I am coming home.[1]

I joined the Student Christian Movement (henceforth SCM) because of the faith of my Mother, Mrs. Agnes Tafa, who held the Bible in high regard. On Sabbath day my mother would take a break from all work, sit under a tree, and read the Bible. When my elder sister, Pauline Opha Dube, went to high school and became a member of the Student Christian Movement, and

---

1. Kirkpatrick, "Lord, I'm Coming Home."

began to profess her own Christian faith, my mother spoke glowingly of her. She was so proud of my sister, so much so that I predetermined that when I got to high school, I would also join SCM and accept the Christian faith to make my mother proud of me. And so I did—a fact that brought my whole life to be dedicated to biblical studies! It was the faith of my mother—as it is the faith of many African women and millions of other women in the world—that brings us to faith in God. And so during those years, as a teenager, in high school, we used to sing the above hymn and repeatedly repent and reconcile ourselves to our Creator. Repentance (*metanoia*) is the art of having a total change in thinking and living. Although it is unclear to me now what we knew about sin and repentance, I think now more than ever we need to interrogate our alienation from God the Creator. Now, more than ever, we need to interrogate ourselves about the "path of sin that we have long walked upon." Now more than ever we need to interrogate ourselves about "coming home."

The concept of home for women and other marginalized groups is often complex and problematic, for many women find themselves occupying violent and marginalizing spaces in the so-called home.[2] The very art of "coming home" involves movement, crossing multiple boundaries, encountering new realities, and becoming dislocated in the urge to find home. And yet this also brings us to many other complex questions as we ask: What is home? Where is home? When do we know we have arrived home? and What if we find home strange and unwelcoming? These questions are critical to us today as people of faith, who identify with the divine power and seek to be consistent with the will of God the creator, wherever we have been placed upon Mother Earth. In this chapter, I contribute to the theme of *Power, Agency, and the Mission of God*, using the case study of the Circle of Concerned African Women Theologians' work and the vision they provide for understanding and carrying out the mission of God.

Coming Home: History of the Circle of African Women Theologians

In 1989, sixty-nine African women gathered at Trinity Theological Seminary in Legon, Ghana, under the leadership of Mercy Amba Oduyoye. She had spent more than a decade searching for women in religion or theology, be it in the academy, the faith spaces, or both. Oduyoye had noticed that while women were dominant members in religious gatherings and cultural practices, there were few women in the leadership of faith institutions and

2. Brah, *Cartographies of Diaspora*.

academic departments of religion. African archbishops, bishops, priests, deacons, professors, and academic doctors of religion were largely men. The church was a strange home for women. The absence of women from both the academic theological space and the leadership space of believers had consequences for the lives of women and the girl children. Male-generated interpretations of cultures and Scriptures were often used to oppress, exploit, and keep women in patriarchally designated space. Occupying the space of marginalization, silenced and disempowered women were not only unwelcome strangers in their faith homes, but they were also denied their God-given agency. They that are created by the Creator God; they that are made in God's image have been empowered and given agentic power to speak, create, lead, and empower others by the seal of the creator God that they bear upon their bodies. Yet, as African women were discovering, they were bound by the sins of patriarchy, colonialism, capitalism, corruption, gender-based violence, and poverty that silenced and denied them their God-given dignity.

In response, Mercy Amba Oduyoye, an African Ghanaian woman of Methodist background, gathered other African women from almost every country, from all religions/cultures, and from the African diaspora to challenge and change this scenario. It was the process of walking away from the path of sin, characterized by the launch of a transformative African female intelligentsia space with a clear agenda. The quest was to generate a theology that embraces and empowers all genders. Oduyoye wanted a theology that flies with both wings, an inclusive theology—one that includes and empowers all genders. Women from all religions and cultures were thus invited to enter the space of researching, reading, and interpreting the cultural and scriptural texts for interrogating and exposing oppressive aspects as well as to generate liberating interpretations that affirm all members of the community. The Circle was thus launched in 1989 with a clear agenda for women to research, read, interpret, write, and publish for the liberation and empowerment of African women in particular and the whole Earth community in general. Since women studying religion were seriously lacking, building capacity through mentoring became an important strategy for finding and empowering women to enter the academic space and leadership of faith institutions.

According to Isabel Phiri, "the Circle is a community of African women theologians who come together to reflect on what it means to them to be women of faith within their experiences of religion and culture, politics and social structures in Africa."[3] She highlights that "from the outset the Circle

---

3. Phiri, "Major Challenges," 106.

was inclusive in its membership and on the type of theology produced. African women were defined as women who belong to diverse classes, races, cultures, nationalities, and religions found on the African continent and in the diaspora. This also meant bringing women from various religions found in the continent.[4] She further underlines that "the Circle's very existence is a protest against exclusion and discrimination in faith communities and society as a whole";[5] and that it seeks to "empower African women to actively work for social justice in their communities and through their publications."[6] Phiri points out:

> The Circle, as a protest movement against any form of exclusion and discrimination, and promoter of fullness of life as intended by God, seeks to increase the number of women studying and teaching theology. It is for this reason that African women theologians have generated many well-researched articles to engage churches on the understanding of the humanity of women and the African understanding of the church.[7]

Weighing in on the formation, purpose, and impact of the Circle, Brigalia Bam, one of the founding members of the Circle, holds that "the idea of a Circle was not merely the creation of a safe space and a new institution for women, but rather the creation of a new model of church and society in Africa, the roundtable of the Circle is open and not discriminatory."[8] Bam underlines that "from the onset, the Circle was concerned not only as an exclusive space for Christian and Church women, but women of all religions in Africa. Ours is, therefore, an expanded notion of ecumenism. What we have, therefore, is a new model not only of church but also of religion and of society."[9] This new model became particularly central for traveling with faith-based organizations during the global HIV/AIDS pandemic. It became clear then, that any effective participation in healing the world required collaboration across denominations, ecumenical bodies, religions, developmental agencies, non-governmental organizations, and governments.[10]

The mission of the Circle is to serve all people of God and all members of the Earth community, through the various faith communities occupied by their members. The Circle is thus interdenominational, ecumenical,

4. Phiri, "Major Challenges," 106.
5. Phiri, "Major Challenges," 110.
6. Phiri, "Major Challenges," 106.
7. Phiri, "Major Challenges," 111.
8. Bam, "Women and the Church," 11.
9. Bam, "Women and the Church," 11.
10. Dube, "Let There Be Light!"

interreligious, and multicultural. Its theology is drawn from both engagement with various communities of faith as well as from various Scriptures and cultures of their members. Biblically, the book of Genesis and the earthly ministry of Jesus are very important for the Circle's understanding of the mission of God.[11] What is God's purpose and intention for the Earth community? In Genesis 1, God is depicted as creating the Earth and everything in it within six days. Even before the process of creation starts, Gen 1:1–2 states that "the Spirit of God was hovering over the waters."[12] During the creation process, God repeatedly pronounces every stage (and the created members) of creation as good. Repetition in biblical literature denotes emphasis. Ultimately the whole creation is pronounced as very good (Gen 1:31). Basically, all creation is sacred, in balance, interconnected, and was created good in its diversity. Genesis 1, therefore, presents the mission of God as the mission of dwelling in and with all creation and keeping the whole creation in its sacred goodness.[13] The mission of God is to keep the sacred and good Earth as home for all members of the Earth community.[14] Human beings together with all members of the Earth community are invited to participate in keeping God's Earth good, sacred, and interconnected. All oppression that denies the sacredness and goodness of all members, or any member of the Earth community, denies the image and breath of God embedded within God's creation. The act of worship, the act of being in God's mission, is the act of working in solidarity with God to keep all members of the Earth community in their God-given dignity.

The earthly (pre-Easter) ministry of Jesus is also important for understanding the mission or purpose of God for the Earth community.[15] The Circle and most sub-Saharan African people experienced Christian missions carried out primarily by Western missionaries who unfortunately in modern history worked hand in glove with colonialism. The missionary-oriented model of Christian Mission is a post-Easter model, which ignores the manner in which Jesus carried God's mission among his people and for his people. He proclaimed God's justice within his country—to his land and country people—teaching, healing, and being with the marginalized. Jesus confronted the powers that be in his own country, context, and culture. This was a difficult mission, for prophets do not have respect amongst their own people. Consequently, Jesus was crucified within a year of his work.

---

11. Berman, *Mother Earth*.
12. Biblical citations in this chapter are from the NIV.
13. Dube, "And God Saw."
14. Habel, *Perspective of Earth*.
15. Dube, "Praying the Lord's Prayer"

The post-Easter missionary model tends to equate the mission of God with sending workers to foreign nations. The missionary model of mission tends to equate sin with other cultures and religions. The model tends to equate sin with individuals, while ignoring structures that sin against the whole Earth community. The missionary model has gravely missed the opportunity to prophesy to structures of colonialism, capitalism, neo-colonialism, and neoliberalism that have sinned against the whole of God's creation.

The Circle of Concerned African Women Theologians embraces the pre-Easter mission of Jesus, which was most programmatically pronounced in Luke 4:16–22. Jesus began his mission in his own hometown by reading from prophet Isaiah where is said:

> The Spirit of the Lord is upon me,
> because God has anointed me to proclaim good news to the poor.
> God has sent me to proclaim freedom for the prisoners
> And recovery of sight for the blind,
> to set the oppressed free,
> to proclaim the Year of the Lord's favor.

The mission of Jesus as the mission of God is not only concerned with the restoration of broken and marginalized human beings, but also to mend the whole creation, that is, proclaiming the Jubilee. And so the Lord's prayer says God's will should be done *on Earth as it is in heaven*, thereby underlining the importance of Mother Earth as our home and the importance of Earth to God the creator. Perhaps the greatest miss in the modern missionary project of preaching the gospel was failure to realize that the good news must be preached for, to, and with all members of the creation community. The gospel must be the gospel to the whole Earth community, not just human beings. It goes without saying that sin is far much more than individuals' sin. Sin is first and foremost sinning against God's creation, through violating its goodness, its sacredness, and its interconnectedness. It is failure to uphold God's purpose for the Earth community. The Circle of Concerned African Women Theologians, with its focus on the oppressed, sick, and marginalized including the oppression of the Earth, sees itself in line with God's mission for the whole creation. Mark 5, which has been among the most important passages for the Circle's understanding of God's mission and participation in it, will be addressed at the end of the paper.[16]

---

16. Dube, "Talitha Cum!" (2004).

Mapping Thematic Research

Since its inception, the Circle has had three research themes and periods for its members to explore in their various contexts and in collaboration with one another. The first research period (1989–2002) of the Circle's was characterized by building its capacity and interrogating how religions and cultures construct and impact women as well as imagining ways of re-interpreting religions for the empowerment of women. In the second research period (2002–19) the Circle focused on religions, theology, cultures, and HIV/AIDS as well as capacitating Faith-Based Communities for constructive response, given the gravity of the HIV/AIDS epidemic on the African continent and its impact on African women and children. At its most recently ended Africa-wide conference (July 1–5, 2019), the Circle decided to adopt the theme of *Religions/Theology/Culture, the Environment, and Sustainable Development Goals*. This theme was built on the conference theme, namely, "Mother Africa; Mother Earth and Religion/Theology/Ethics/Philosophy." Nine volumes have been co-edited from the conference proceedings.[17]

The Circle of Concerned African Women Theologians is currently preparing for the Sankofa 2024 conference to be held in Ghana during July 1–4, 2024. The word *Sankofa* is drawn from the Ghanaian Adinkra symbols. It is often symbolized by a bird stretching its neck back to its tail feathers to pick something. Sankofa symbolizes the need to reconnect with one's own history or the past to move forward. Sankofa 2024 conference is therefore a process of returning to Ghana—to the place where the Circle of Concerned African Women Theologians was first launched in 1989—to reconnect with its mission, to assess the path covered in the journey towards home. The research theme of the Sankofa 2024 Conference is "Earth, Pandemics, Gender, and Religion." You are all invited to attend. Yet as part of the preparation to go back, the Circle is undertaking a Sankofa act—the act of looking back and evaluating what has been achieved since 1989. Various Sankofa evaluative book projects are being undertaken. These include books on:

- African women's biblical studies, which investigates and showcases methods developed by African women theologians
- Ethics of African women theologies, which investigates the various ethics of liberation proposed by African women in their engagement with the world and traditions of faith

---

17. Some of the volumes produced include: Matholeni et al., *Mother Earth*; Berman et al., *Mother Earth*; Chisale and Bosch, *Mother Earth*; Chirongoma and Kiilu, *Mother Earth*; Gudhlanga et al., *African Literature*.

- Creative theologies, which is a volume that uses poetry, prayers, psalms, stories, and letter forms to engage major issues pertaining to women, faith, and Earth. It is also a volume that sought to engage wider members of the Circle, beyond the academic ones, in writing and speaking
- Three volumes on regional theologies of East, West, South, and Central Africa
- African women engagement with African indigenous religions
- Earth, Literature, and Faith in the works of African women's literature, which interrogate eco-feminism articulated by African women creative writers

Seeking Home: Agency and Power

What then is agency and how is it linked to power and powerlessness? According to Joseph Childers and Gary Henzi, "the term is often used interchangeably with the similar yet distinct concept of the subject . . . the subject is capable of thought and critique, and thus is also capable of choice and action."[18] However, they note:

> The difficulty with this concept of agent and agency has to do with theorizing change, especially political and social change. If the individual is always subjected to ideological and discursive constraints, and all his or her actions—even the ones that seem oppositional—are always accountable in terms of those ideologies and discourses, how then is it possible that anything can change? Some new historicists, like Louis Montrose have argued that agents and their concomitant agency are both constrained and enabled by the interaction of these power structures.

Consequently, while Ian Buchanan, holds that "agency is the degree to which a subject is able to determine the course of their actions," he also points out that Karl Marx holds that "people make history, but not in conditions of their own choosing."[19] Karl Marx, in other words, puts suspicion into our so-called choices, as choices to do what we have already been socially constructed to choose and to do, according to our class, gender, race, and ethnicity. Similarly, Sarah Gammage, Naila Kabeer, and Yana van der

---

18. Childers and Hentzi, *Columbia Dictionary of Modern Literary and Cultural Criticism*, s.v. "Agent."
19. Buchanan, *Oxford Dictionary of Critical Theory*, s.v. "Agency."

Meulen Rodgers explain, focusing particularly on feminist activism, that "structure and agency are closely intertwined with manifestation of power." They point out, too, that, "feminists from all disciplines . . . locate agency in the context of structural constraints."[20]

In her classic article, "Can the subaltern speak?," Gayatri Spivak argues that, for the subaltern, the agency to speak and be heard can only occur at the expense of self-annihilation.[21] In so doing Spivak underlines the viciousness of the structures of oppression for those who seek agency. In the African discourse of the trickster, Hare the trickster, who is among the smallest animals in the world of powerful animals, must do all that there is in her or his power to exercise his/her agency despite the constraints of the powerful structures and the dangers that come with exercising one's own agency.[22] In the African trickster discourse, therefore, exercising agency is imperative, that is, no amount of constraints should lead the oppressed to give up the struggle for their rightful place and rights. This makes the art of exercising agency and the effort to observe it complicated, for it takes various subtle forms, including hidden forms. Alice Yafeh-Deigh has argued that agency can even be exercised in silence.[23] Touring this subtle form of agency, Saba Mahmood has studied Islamic women who remain within their faith communities and shown that they are nonetheless agentic subjects within their space.[24]

Similarly, in her novel *Purple Hibiscus*, Chimamanda Ngozi Adichie shows us a range of agentic paradigms.[25] Whereas Aunty Ifeoma, a highly educated academic woman and her daughter, Amaka, are openly articulate, resisting both patriarchy, colonial thinking, military violence, and gender-based violence at home, in the churches and cultures, Beatrice and her daughter, Kambili, seem to be on the opposite end. They seem to tolerate most unacceptable violence at home by the man who is supposedly a god-fearing husband and father. In the name of his Christian faith, Eugene has physically assaulted his wife and daughter in the cruelest manner leading to many miscarriages of his wife and hospitalization of his daughter, all under the full view of his church, which remains unable to counsel or indict him because he gave the church a sinful amount of money. Home for Beatrice and Kambili was a place of terror and a place of sin, but as the narrative progresses, they slowly begin to undertake resistance to Eugene's violence

---

20. Gammage, "Voice and Agency," 2.
21. Spivak, "Can the Subaltern Speak?"
22. Dube, "Subaltern Can Speak."
23. Yafeh-Deigh, "Liberative Power." See also Avishai, "Theorizing Gender."
24. Mahmood, "Feminist Theory."
25. Adichie, *Purple Hibiscus*. For discussion see Dube, "Purple Hibiscus."

and imposition of his colonial Christianity that denied them even the right to sing and pray in their indigenous languages.

The concept of agency is complex since agency is exercised within multiple constraints of ideological, structural, and social relations of power, especially for those on the margins of power. In my view, for those in the margins of power, exercising agency is the art of coming home and finding a strange unwelcoming place. It is the art of persistently making efforts to find a space to speak and be heard, where one's voice is persistently subjugated to silence. Agency is the art of insisting on a home space that welcomes and empowers all members. But such efforts often become ways of being since the powers that be are not always willing to give up power to those who need it. And thus, we have heard the slogan, "the struggle continues." The slogan underlines that the journey of coming home, of seeking a home, and of homemaking must always be sought, since the posture of being unsettled is in itself the refusal to settle in sinful spaces, that is, spaces that deny our God-given agency and dignity. As I have argued elsewhere:

> Change agents bring about change even within settings that obstruct them—and they are also themselves transformed by this agency. Change agency is, therefore, a process of expanding empowerment through tenaciously employing various strategies and at various levels, both individually and collectively, against structures that constrain women and other marginalized persons and groups in a variety of contexts. Agency is practiced in an array of forms and manifestations, such as in subtle bargaining, passive resistance, outright rejection, negotiation, and intentional moves to start a revolution—but always within constraints of structures and always towards the quest to increase or maintain representation and empowerment.[26]

In the Circle of Agentic Power

For founders of the Circle of Concerned African Women Theologians, exercising agency was clearly resistance against constraints of multiple forms of oppression and exercise of the insistence to speak. Brigalia Bam, one of the founding members of the Circle, narrates that, "Many years ago, Mercy Oduyoye and a few of us had a dream. It was a dream that one day, churchwomen in Africa would cease to be spoken about, spoken for, and spoken at. We were tired of listening to conversations about women, conversations on

---

26. Dube, "On Becoming a Change Agent," 16.

behalf of women, and we were tired of being talked at, so we embarked on a struggle to change these situations."[27] Bam insists "if ever there was going to be a theology of liberation for women, women had to construct it. It would not come automatically, even from the most radical of our theologies."[28] Be that as it may, Bam does not minimize the number of constraints facing African women, for she points out:

> The first challenge to mention here is that women bear the brunt of all crises facing African societies and African churches. Any crisis that African nations are faced with—HIV/AIDS, poverty, war, violence, and genocide—hits women hardest. In this sense, in Africa, women are the bearers of the cross alongside the crucified Lord. The first challenge facing church women in Africa is all the challenges facing the continent put together. This is a mammoth challenge.[29]

Given the fact that African nations are also carrying the burdens of colonialism, neocolonialism, corruption, disappointing independent governments, neoliberal economies, and global environmental crisis, African women's experience of their home spaces (both the public and private ones) is unsettling, necessitating intense quest for making home, and finding ways to home. Under these grave constraints, Mercy Amba Oduyoye, the founder of the Circle, invites African women not to remain nailed to the cross by all the forces that silence them, but to embark on their agentic power. In her poem entitled "Dream, Girl Dream" she invites women to occupy the resurrection space, to rise from the graves of oppression that deny them their God given humanity. The poem reads:

---

27. Bam, "Women and the Church," 8.
28. Bam, "Women and the Church," 9.
29. Bam, "Women and the Church," 14.

> Dream, Girl Dream
> What's the future going to be?
> Dream, girl dream.
> What we may become, that's what matters.
> Dream woman dream.
> Woman dream, Africa's dream.
> Dream of the least of the world,
> Permissible dreams.
> Dream, for the other is you turned inside out.
> Make the other strong and you will be strong,
> We shall all be strong together.
> Dream, girl dream.
> Be a woman, and Africa will be strong.[30]

In this invitation to the dream space, African women are urged to embark on their own agency. They are invited to envision and work for a different future: "What is the future going to be?" the poem asks. "What we may become, that's what matters," the poem states. With all the challenges confronting African women, as tabulated above by Bam, the poem still insists: "dream, girl dream, be a woman and Africa will be strong!" The African woman's dream has the power to birth a new Africa! Oduyoye unapologetically calls upon and insists upon African women's agency.

As if the challenges facing African women are not "a mammoth task," Oduyoye invites African women to take further weight. So, in this dream space, where African women are invited to dream "Africa's dream," their dream for the future must also carry with them dreams for "the least of the world." The Circle of Concerned African Women Theologians is called to dream in solidarity with the least of these of the world. As the poem asserts, if you "make the other strong, you will be strong. We shall be strong together." One gleans the Ubuntu philosophy in this call to dream in solidarity with the other.[31] In the Ubuntu worldview, "I am because we are," that is, we are only human through and with others.[32] Or, as Nelson Mandela once expressed it, "your freedom and mine, cannot be separated." Puleng Lenka-Bula elaborates that Ubuntu's call to solidarity with the other is a call to be in solidarity with the whole creation, with all members of the creation community including animals, plants, and inanimate members of the Earth.[33] According to Ubuntu Philosophy, one's humanity can only be measured by

---

30. Oduyoye, "Be a Woman," 35.
31. Dube, "I Am Because We Are."
32. Dube et al., "*Botho*."
33. LenkaBula, "Beyond Anthropocentricity."

one's capacity to welcome, care, and empower the other.[34] Given Ubuntu's emphasis on recognizing and empowering the other as the measure of our human dignity, Dumi Mmnualefhe argues that, "without *Botho* (Ubuntu), we cannot worship God, for *Botho* is an expression of God's image in us."[35] Our expression of our agentic power in solidarity with the least of these in the world, is, therefore, an expression of the God in us, the God with us, and the God who made us in God's own image.

In the Mission of God: Mark 5:21–43, *Talitha Cum*, Little Girl I Say Arise!

In addition to the African contexts, African women's experiences and African philosophies, what are the key biblical Scriptures that inspire African Women theologians to participate in God's mission? Above, I discussed Genesis 1, Luke 4:16–22, and Jesus' earthly/pre-Easter mission. At this point I want to turn to Mark 5, which is central to the Circle's mission and its participation in God's mission for creation as well exercising their agency. Mark 5 has been central to the Circle of Concerned African Women Theologians' work, inspiring many papers, books, and centers.[36] Indeed, its centrality has made it possible to name Circle work as *Talitha cum* theologies.[37]

In Mark 5, Jesus travels to the region of Gerasene, where he is met by a man who used to live by the graves. He was a demon-possessed man, who could not even be chained, for he broke all the chains, hurt himself, and spent time in the mountains day and night. When Jesus lands in the region of Gerasene, the man comes to Jesus, begging Jesus to leave him alone. Jesus speaks to the demon that is occupying and tormenting the man asking its name. The answer is Legion. A legion referred to the Roman army consisting of one thousand soldiers. The Legion demons beg Jesus to cast them out into the pigs that were grazing by. Jesus does, but the demon-possessed pigs run mad and drown in the sea. The formerly possessed man is seen sitting down composed after the exorcism of Legion. In the story, colonial occupation of people, lands, and their animals is portrayed as a demonic and dislocating experience, one that makes the colonized mad, hurt themselves, and find their own homes strange. The story depicts the experience of colonialism as equivalent to dwelling with the dead, for one's home has been taken by demonic forces of the empire. But above all, the story depicts Jesus as one

---

34. Dube, "Mother Economies."
35. Mmnualefhe, "Botho and HIV & AIDS," 26.
36. Oduyoye and Kanyoro, *Will to Arise*; Njoroge and Dube, *Talitha Cum*.
37. Dube, "Talitha Cum!" (2009); Yafeh-Deigh, "Mapping Chapter."

who confronts colonial oppression and whose presence brings salvation from colonial oppression. For African women, who have been subjugated to various colonial powers and have experienced continued neo-colonialism, there is no liberation if it excludes decolonization. Jesus is thus depicted as resisting the empire and liberating the colonized from the spirit of Legion.

The second part of Mark 5:21–43 features a woman who had been sick, bleeding for twelve years, and a twelve-year old young girl who was very sick. The woman had been seeking healing in vain until she heard about Jesus the healer being in town. At that same time Jairus, father of the twelve-year-old sick girl, also hears about Jesus, the healer, being in town. He seeks Jesus on behalf of his daughter. The bleeding woman finds Jesus surrounded by massive crowds, but decides to push from behind, to touch his garment so that she may be healed silently without speaking any words. Jairus, on the other hand, comes straight to Jesus, falls on his knees and begs Jesus to come to his house to heal his daughter. Jesus begins to walk with Jairus, but the bleeding woman, still pushing silently from behind, finally touches Jesus' garment. Jesus feels power leaving his body as the woman is healed. Jesus stops. He searches for the woman, he listens to her long story and finally declares, "Daughter, your faith has healed you!" Jesus then proceeds to Jairus' house where the sick little girl had already died. He enters the room where she lay, takes her hand and says, "*Talita Cum!*" that is, "Little girl, arise." She rises from death and comes to life.

This story has been celebrated by African women theologians and seen as validation for the mission of the Circle, which is seen as the mission of God. Not only does the number twelve, featured for both the adult woman and the girl, represent Israel's suffering under various empires, but Jesus is depicted as the liberator. African women who have been bleeding under various national and international structures of oppression, identify with the woman's desperate search for healing—a search that renders one poor, without delivering healing. Yet this bleeding woman is also celebrated for her agency. She faced several constraints: there was a huge crowd around Jesus, but she kept on pushing; there were cultural and religious beliefs that rendered her an unclean pollutant due to her health, one that should not be around teachers, but she was determined to find healing; she faced poverty and gender constraints that did not allow her to speak to teachers in public, but she did not give up hope on changing her situation. She decided that she is going to touch the garment for Jesus for her own healing, which she successfully does, without asking for Jesus's approval or permission. In so doing, the woman takes responsibility for her own healing. She decided to get power from the powerful with or without their approval. She is an agent of change in the midst of various constraints.

Moreover, Jesus and Jairus, who are both powerful male religious leaders, are celebrated for standing in solidarity with the bleeding woman and the dying daughter. To start with, Jesus could have walked on with Jairus even when he felt someone had taken his power, but he stopped and searched for her. In so doing, Jesus brings the woman from behind, where she was a silent agent and gives her the space to tell her story. He gives her the right to break the silence, to speak and to be heard. Jesus could have been angry with the woman, for taking power from her without asking, but he congratulates her, stating: "Daughter, your faith has made you whole!" This woman who has been treated as an outcast for her health status, is called "Daughter!" She is welcome home, she is no longer a stranger. In the context of where the lives of little girls did not matter due to their gender, both Jairus and Jesus are noted for their solidarity with the sick daughter. Jairus seeks Jesus and begs Jesus to come and heal his daughter. Jesus could have made this pronouncement of her healing from a distance, but he accompanies Jairus to his house. He finds the daughter dead, which now rendered her body a pollutant to a teacher, but Jesus still took her hand and called her to rise from death and to come to life. The Circle of Concerned African Women Theologians sees Jesus' mission as the mission to allow women to be agents of their own empowerment as well as to call those who have been locked into various forces of death to rise: "*Talitha cum!*" "Little girl, I say arise!"

Conclusion: Coming Home to God's Beautiful Earth

In conclusion, for the Circle of Concerned African Women Theologians, the expression of one's agency is the act of being in the mission of God—working out God's purpose for the Earth community. God's purpose is to be in solidarity with the whole creation community, hence God created all members of the Earth community good. By virtue of the Spirit of God having been in creation, and since all members were created by God, they are all sacred.[38] Sin is the art of missing God's purpose in creation. Sin is manifest when some members of the Earth community are marginalized, denied their goodness, denied their interconnectedness, and denied sacredness. This sin takes forms of oppression in forms of marginalizing and disempowering others based on such social categories as gender, race, class, religion, sexuality, ethnicity, and dis/ability among others. Home, as the place where God invited, empowered and placed us, becomes strange in the presence of sin, for we then experience ourselves as unwelcome. This is when the Earth's resources are plundered by economic greed expressed in

---

38. Dube, "And God Saw."

global economic structural forces of colonialism, neo-colonialism, capitalism, and neoliberalism, among others. The Earth is plundered, exploited, polluted, and taken out of its interconnectedness, goodness, and sacredness. We are all witnesses that sin has been worked upon the Earth, rendering the Earth a strange home to us, characterized by climate change, global warming, floods, droughts, snowstorms, melting icebergs, rising sea levels, raging veldfires, sinking islands, cities, and villages, among many others. Earth has become a strange home for us because much sin has been worked against God's mission of creating and keeping the Earth sacred, beautiful, and interconnected.

Yes, the path of sin for too long we have trod, now we are coming home in full repentance. Full repentance entails embracing our God-given sacredness to assume solidarity with God in keeping the Earth and everything in it good. It is the call to harken to Jesus calling us to rise from the forces of death, which makes home strange and the call to make our way towards the home that God desires for all members of the Earth's community. Coming home and embracing God's mission is knowing that the good news of Jesus Christ seeks to change the situations of the marginalized and oppressed. It is not God's will for any people to be oppressed (Luke 4:16–22). This good news is not only good news to people, it is also good news to the Earth itself—God news must observe the jubilee of the land (Luke 4:19). Good news to the land should bring us home to maintain the Earth as a sacred place for God the Creator and the created. Once more, singing that song of "coming home, coming home never more to roam" is the refusal to occupy the space of sin and being sinned against. It is the courage to assume agency in the midst of insurmountable constraints. It is the call to rise from the dead. It is the call to live in the resurrection power against powers that nail us to the cross. Yes, it is to hear Jesus saying, "*Talitha cum!*" Little girl, I say arise!

Bibliography

Adichie, Chimamanda Ngozi. *Purple Hibiscus: A Novel*. Chapel Hill, NC: Algonquin, 2003.

Avishai, Orit. "Theorizing Gender from Religion Cases: Agency, Feminist Activism, and Masculinity." *Sociology of Religion* 77 (2016) 261–79.

Bam, Brigalia. "Women and the Church in South Africa: Women Are the Church in South Africa." In *On Being Church: African Women's Voices and Visions*, edited by Isabel A. Phiri and Sarojini Nadar, 8–15. Geneva: WCC, 2005.

Berman, Sidney K., et al., eds. *Mother Earth, Mother Africa, and Biblical Interpretation: Interpretations in the Context of Climate Change*. Bamberg: Bamberg University Press, 2021.

Brah, Avatar. *Cartographies of Diaspora: Contesting Identities*. London: Routledge, 1996.

Buchanan, Ian, ed. *Oxford Dictionary of Critical Theory*. Oxford: Oxford University Press, 2010.

Childers, Joseph, and Gary Hentzi, eds. *The Columbia Dictionary of Modern Literary and Cultural Criticism*. New York: Columbia University Press, 1995.

Chirongoma, Sophia, and Ven Scholar W. Kiilu, eds. *Mother Earth, Mother Africa: World Religions and Environmental Imagination*. Stellenbosch: African Sun Media, 2022.

Chisale, Sinenhlanhla S., and Rozelle R. Bosch, eds. *Mother Earth, Mother Africa, and Theology*. Pretoria: Aosis, 2021.

Dube, Musa W. "And God Saw That It Was Very Good! An Earth-Friendly Theatrical Reading of Genesis 1." *Black Theology* 13 (2015) 230–46.

———. "I Am Because We Are: Giving Primacy to African Indigenous Values in HIV & AIDS Prevention." In *African Ethics: An Anthology of Comparative and Applied Ethics*, edited by Munyaradzi F. Murove, 178–88. Pietmaritzburg: University of KwaZulu-Natal Press, 2009.

———. "Let There be Light! Birthing Ecumenical Theology in the HIV and AIDS Apocalypse." *Ecumenical Review* 67 (2015) 531–42.

———. "On Becoming a Change Agent: Journeys of Teaching Gender and Health in an African Crisis Context." *Journal for Interdisciplinary Biblical Studies* 2 (2020) 13–28.

———. "Praying the Lord's Prayer in the Global Economic Era (Matt 6:9–13)." In *The Bible in Africa: Transactions, Trajectories, and Trends*, edited by Gerald O. West and Musa W. Dube, 611–32. Leiden: Brill, 2000.

———. "Purple Hibiscus: A Postcolonial Feminist Reading." *Missionalia* 46 (2018) 222–35.

———. "The Subaltern Can Speak: Reading the *Mmutle* (Hare) Way." *Journal of Africana Religions* 4 (2016) 54–72.

———. "Talitha Cum! A Postcolonial Feminist & HIV/AIDS Reading of Mark 5:21–43." In *Grant Me Justice! HIV/AIDS & Gender Readings of the Bible*, edited by Musa W. Dube and Rachel A. Kanyoro, 115–40. Pietmaritzburg: Cluster, 2004.

———. "Talitha Cum! Some African Women's Ways of Reading the Bible." In *Semeia Studies: Twenty-Five Years of Liberation Theology*, edited by Botha, 133–46. Atlanta: SBL, 2009.

Dube, Musa W., et al. "*Botho*, Community-Building, and Gender Constructions in Botswana." *Journal of ITC* 4 (2016) 1–22.

Dube, Musa W. "Mother Economies: Botho/Ubuntu and Community Building in the Urban Space, a Focus on Naomi/Laban, Bridal, and Baby Shower." In *Ubuntu and Women: Building Community in Urban Areas*, by Musa W. Dube et al., 21–58. Stellenbosch: African Sun Media, 2023.

Gammage, Sarah, et al. "Voice and Agency: Where Are We Now?" *Feminist Economics* 22 (2016) 1–29.

Gudhlanga, Enna S., et al., eds. *African Literature, Mother Earth, and Religion*. Wilmington, DE: Vernon, 2022.

Habel, Norman C., ed. *Readings from the Perspective of the Earth*. The Earth Bible 1. Sheffield: Sheffield Academic, 2000.

Kirkpatrick, William. "Lord, I'm Coming Home." https://hymnary.org/text/ive_wandered_far_away_from_god.

LenkaBula, Puleng. "Beyond Anthropocentricity: Botho/Ubuntu and the Quest for Economic and Ecological Justice in Africa." *Religion and Theology* 15 (2008) 375–94.

Mahmood, Saba. "Feminist Theory, Embodiment, and the Docile Agent: Some Reflections on the Egyptian Islamic Revival." *Cultural Anthropology* 16 (2001) 202–36.

Mmnualefhe, Dumi O. "Botho and HIV & AIDS: A Theological Reflection." In *The Concept of Botho and HIV/AIDS in Botswana*, edited by Joseph B. R. Gaie and Sana K. Mmolai, 1–29. Eldoret: Zapf Chancery, 2003.

Njoroge, Nyambura, and Musa W. Dube, eds. *Talitha Cum: Theologies of African Women*. Natal: Cluster, 2001.

Nobuntu P. Matholeni, et al., eds. *Mother Earth, Mother Africa, and African Indigenous Religions*. Cape Town: Sun, 2020.

Oduyoye, Mercy A. "Be a Woman, and Africa Will Be Strong." In *Inheriting Our Mothers' Gardens: Feminist Theology in Third World Perspective*, edited by Letty M. Russell et al., 35–53. Louisville: Westminster, 1988.

Oduyoye, Mercy A., and Rachel A. Kanyoro, eds. *The Will to Arise: Women, Tradition, and the Church in Africa*. Maryknoll, NY: Orbis, 1992.

Phiri, Isabel A. "Major Challenges for African Women Theologians in Theological Education (1989–2008)." *International Review of Mission* 98 (2009) 105–19.

Spivak, Gayatri C. "Can the Subaltern Speak?" In *Marxism and the Interpretation of Culture*, edited by Cary Nelson and Lawrence Grossberg, 271–313. Urbana, IL: University of Illinois Press, 1988.

Yafeh-Deigh, Alice Y. "The Liberative Power of Silent Agency: A Postcolonial Afro-Feminist-Womanist Reading of Luke 10:38–42." In *Postcolonial Perspectives in African Biblical Interpretations*, edited by Musa W. Dube et al., 417–40. Atlanta: SBL, 2012.

———. "Mapping Chapter: 30 Years of African Women's Biblical Studies." In *Mother Earth, Mother Africa, and Biblical Studies: Interpretations in the Context of Climate Change*, edited by Sidney K. Berman et al., 37–87. Bamberg: University of Bamberg Press, 2021.

Conversation 2

Sexism from Multiple Frameworks

— 5 —

Challenging Sexism for God's Sake
A Psychological Perspective

M. Elizabeth Lewis Hall

In the fascinating story told in the first chapters of Genesis, the major contours of the effects of sin in a fallen world are succinctly described. Of the handful of sentences that are used to describe these consequences, one of them has to do with disrupted power relations between the sexes. In just a few short words that have had varied and devastating consequences throughout human history, God tells Eve, "Your desire will be for your husband, and he will rule over you" (Gen 3:16).[1] And so began a form of distorted patriarchy that has endured through the ages, disrupting human relations and impeding our efforts to collaborate as men and women in accomplishing God's mission in the world. In this basic description, we find men and women both complicit in this twisted pattern. Women "desire" the men in their lives, turning to them to fill roles that should only be filled by God, while men "rule," taking advantage of the women in their lives.[2]

As a consequence, gender-based inequality is the norm. Historically and across cultures, men have more resources, power, and status than women. The World Economic Forum tracks gender differences in political empowerment

---

1. Biblical citations in this chapter are from the NIV.
2. Here I follow the interpretations of "desire" and "rule" by Kaiser, *Hard Sayings of the Bible*, 97–98.

and participation, economic participation and opportunity, educational attainment and health and survival. According to their most recent Global Gender Gap Report for 2021, the average distance completed to gender parity worldwide is at only 68%.[3] Because of the disproportionate impact of the COVID-19 pandemic on women, the 2021 gap is actually larger than the gap the year before; the estimated time to close the gap given current rates of progress has increased in one year from 99.5 years to 135.6 years.

My task as a psychologist, is to provide an overview of how this imbalance of power is played out, helping to lay out the scope of the unique barriers, challenges, and forms of oppression that women face. In the field of psychology, power imbalances between the sexes in all its forms is studied under the name of "sexism." I realize that this is a challenging word that for some may carry connotations that blame men and that suggest intentionality in harming others. However, as we will see, both men and women treat women unfairly, and much of the unfair treatment happens outside of conscious awareness, and in fact often happens with good intentions. In the following sections I will discuss ambivalent sexism, the most prominent contemporary theory of sexism, as well as structural sexism. I will also address how sexism plays out in Christian contexts. I will then outline five lessons learned from the research on sexism. Finally, I will turn to what we can learn from psychology about how to combat sexism.

Ambivalent Sexism and Structural Sexism

When unpacking the concept of sexism, it is helpful to distinguish between sexist attitudes, sexist beliefs, and sexist behaviors. Sexist *attitudes* can be both hostile and benevolent, which we will discuss in depth in the following paragraphs. Sexist *beliefs* include gender schemas (sometimes referred to as gender stereotypes), as well as gender ideologies. Sexist *behaviors* include all kinds of violence against women, as well as discrimination and its subtype, harassment.[4]

Ambivalent sexism is a theory that was proposed by psychologists Peter Glick and Susan Fiske to explain the ways in which sexism differs from other forms of prejudice, such as racism.[5] Generally, prejudice takes the form of antipathy toward the target, as in the case of racism. But in sexism, the power differentials are enacted in the context of relationships in which men and women need each other for companionship, sexual gratification,

---

3. World Economic Forum, *Global Gender Gap Report 2021*, 5.
4. Swim and Hyers, "Sexism," 407–22.
5. Glick and Fiske, "Ambivalent Sexism Inventory," 491.

and procreation. Consequently, sexism does not take only a hostile form, but is also complemented by a benevolent form of sexism. Benevolent sexism is experienced as subjectively benevolent by the perpetrator, and may even be perceived as benevolent in nature by the target. However, in reality it serves as a crucial complement to hostile sexism in that it helps to make societal gender inequality more palatable to women, recruiting them as unwitting participants in their own subordination. Together, hostile sexism and benevolent sexism serve as a coordinated system of control to limit women's power, not just in the interpersonal domain, but also in the larger economic, political, and cultural domains. Benevolent sexism is the carrot for conforming to patriarchal norms, and hostile sexism is the stick when women refuse to toe the line. Let me be clear that maintaining inequality does not require the conscious desire on the part of men or women to subordinate women. The general acceptance of ambivalent sexism ideologies and their role in shaping cultural customs and institutions perpetuate inequality outside of conscious awareness.

In the context of ambivalent sexism, hostile sexism refers to "an adversarial view of gender relations in which women are perceived as seeking to control men, whether through sexuality or feminist ideology." In contrast, benevolent sexism idealizes women as "pure creatures who need to be protected, supported and adored and whose love is necessary to make a man complete."[6] While on the surface this characterization of benevolent sexism may sound harmless or even laudable, in reality it implies that women are weak and incompetent. It also stereotypes women as having communal traits (e.g., nurturing, helpful, warm) that uniquely equip them for domestic, low-status roles. Consequently, even though benevolently sexist attitudes and beliefs sound positive, they reinforce women's lower status.

Benevolent Sexism and Its Consequences

Let me say more about benevolent sexism, as it is probably less familiar to you than hostile sexism, and because, as we will see, it plays an important role in religious contexts. Benevolent sexism includes three kinds of beliefs.[7] First, protective paternalism beliefs justify limiting women's access to resources and masculine roles by presenting women as being in need of protection; women are seen as less than fully competent to make their own decisions and manage their own lives. Protective paternalism might take the form of a man stepping in to verbally defend a woman, even if she can

---

6. Glick and Fiske, "Ambivalent Alliance," 109.
7. Connor et al., "Ambivalent Sexism," 298–99.

defend herself, or taking on additional responsibilities in order to spare her without consulting with her, or making a decision for her because it seems clear what is best for her, or telling her what to do rather than letting her find her own solutions.

The second kind of benevolently sexist belief involves complementary gender differentiation. Men and women are presented as being different from each other in stereotypical ways. Demarcating gender boundaries is necessary in order to preserve status distinctions by attributing to men characteristics necessary for high-status positions, and attributing to women characteristics necessary for low-status positions. The resulting complementarity is presented as being natural and inevitable. This might take the form of talking to male colleagues about work projects and hobbies but to female colleagues about their homes and children, or assuming that a woman will do the caregiving tasks such as getting coffee or taking notes, or only being able to think of men when asked to identify a candidate for a leadership role.

Finally, the third kind of benevolently sexist belief, heterosexual intimacy, idealizes a certain kind of Prince Charming and the Princess romantic relationship, preserving men's need for women's companionship and sexuality while also shaping the form that this intimacy takes. This can take the form of inappropriately introducing gendered romantic or appearance-based comments into conversation outside of the context of romantic relationships, such as complimenting a woman who is not a romantic partner on her appearance, calling her "sweetheart," "darling," "honey," etc., or focusing on the wardrobe or hairstyles of prominent women public figures rather than on job-related capacities. Or it might take the form of expecting a romantic partner to meet all of one's needs.

Benevolent sexism is particularly insidious because it is often seen as harmless, romantic, or even desirable (for example, in the form of chivalrous ideology). But abundant research has begun to track the ways in which benevolent sexism perpetuates inequality and harms women; in fact, research suggests it may be more detrimental than hostile sexism. To date, studies have demonstrated that women higher in benevolent sexism blame the victims more in cases of acquaintance rape and when victims violate gender stereotypes, and generally endorse rape myths more.[8] Benevolent sexism makes women more vulnerable to sexual violence, more prone to consume alcohol, and more willing to take unwarranted financial risks.[9] Ex-

---

8. Viki et al., "Stranger and Acquaintance Rape," 295–303; Masser et al., "Bad Woman, Bad Victim?," 494–504; Forbes et al., "First- and Second-Generation," 236–61.

9. Durán et al., "It's His Right," 470–78; Durán et al., "Benevolent Sexist Ideology," 1380–401; Hamilton and DeHart, "Cheers to Equality!," 675–84; Teng et al., "Counting on You," 580–94.

posure to benevolent sexism leads women to behave in ways that conform to gender stereotypes, even when they personally do not endorse benevolent sexism. The need to present oneself as sexually attractive to men is part of gender stereotypes and exposure to benevolent sexism increases women's self-objectification, self-surveillance, preoccupation with appearance, and body shame.[10] Suitability for primarily domestic roles is another part of gender stereotypes, and exposure to benevolent sexism leads women to ascribe less importance to competence and academic achievement, and to aspire less to leadership.[11] Stereotypes present women as being less competent and in need of protection, and exposure to this ideology increases women's intrusive thoughts of their incompetence and their recall of past situations in which they felt incompetent.[12] In couples, more benevolently sexist men tend to provide more dependency-oriented support, such as directly providing plans and solutions and neglecting the woman's own abilities; this also results in the women feeling less competent.[13]

Research has demonstrated that not only do women think they are less competent when exposed to benevolent sexism, benevolent sexism actually seems to make women less competent. It has been found to decrease women's cognitive performance by increasing self-doubt and by decreasing perceptions that one's actions will result in desired outcomes.[14] One interesting study also showed that after being exposed to benevolent sexism, women showed a cardiovascular response indicative of threat (lower cardiac output/higher total peripheral resistance), impacting their emotional well-being.[15] Benevolent sexism perpetuates inequality by reducing women's willingness to challenge gender discrimination,[16] and it increases women's acceptance of inequitable social systems.[17]

Benevolently sexist ideologies are often presented as romantic chivalrous ideals, and yet research shows that women who endorse benevolent

---

10. Calogero and Jost, "Self-Subjugation among Women," 211–28; Shepherd et al., "I'll Get That for You," 1–8; Oswald et al., "Experiencing Sexism," 1112–37.

11. Barreto et al., "How Nice of Us," 532–44; Montañés et al., "Intergenerational Transmission," 1112–37; Rollero and Fedi, "When Benevolence Harms Women," 535–42.

12. Dardenne et al., "Insidious Dangers," 764–79; Dumont et al., "Be Too Kind," 545–53.

13. Hammond and Overall, "Benevolent Sexism," 1180–94.

14. Dardenne et al., "Insidious Dangers"; Gervais and Vescio, "Patronizing Behavior," 479–91.

15. Lamarche et al., "Clever Girl."

16. Becker and Wright, "Yet Another Dark Side," 62–77.

17. Jost and Kay, "Exposure to Benevolent Sexism," 498–509.

sexism are also less likely to be satisfied with their marriages and more likely to seek divorce, and tend to be more psychologically entitled.[18] They are more vulnerable to relationship distress when facing relationship problems or undesirable behavior in their partners, and this is especially true in longer relationships.[19]

Structural Sexism

To this point we have been addressing ambivalent sexism as it occurs at the interpersonal level. But it's also important to recognize that sexism is perpetuated not only at the individual level, but also at the structural level. Sexist attitudes, beliefs, and behaviors combine to justify patriarchal systems in which there are systematic gender inequalities in power and resources that are reified through institutional practices, regulations, and even laws.[20] For example, the United States has no guaranteed paid leave for mothers of infants—the only wealthy country in the world in this situation.[21] The lack of adequate paid leave makes work-family balance difficult, contributing to employment inequities. Structural sexism also includes symbols and practices that are used to reinforce sexist stereotypes. For example, professional football reinforces stereotypes of both men and women by contrasting hyper-masculine aggression with sexualized displays by underdressed women that reinforce the idea that women are sex objects.

Evidence for the relationship between ambivalent sexism and structural sexism can be found in a large multinational study which showed that both hostile and benevolent forms of sexism are correlated with national measures of economic and political gender inequity.[22] Across nations, men's hostile and benevolent sexism scores correlated with United Nations indices of gender empowerment (women in high-status jobs and in government) and gender development (women's education, longevity, and standard of living, relative to men in the same country). In contrast, women's scores correlated marginally or not at all, supporting the idea that those in positions of power determine the distribution of resources.

---

18. Casad et al., "Real versus Ideal," 119–29; Hammond and Overall, "Endorsing Benevolent Sexism," 272–87.
19. Hammond and Overall, "When Relationships Do Not Live," 212–23.
20. Homan, "Structural Sexism," 486–516.
21. World Policy Analysis Center, "Is Paid Leave Available?"
22. Glick et al., "Beyond Prejudice," 763–75.

Sexism in Christian Contexts

Let's move now to how sexism is enacted in religious contexts, especially in Christian contexts. Let's begin broadly, with the research on religion and sexism. Religions can contribute to sexism in a number of ways: through shaping gender attitudes, beliefs, and roles; through structural inequities; and through influencing the ways in which sexism is experienced by women. One large-scale study with participants from ninety-seven countries found that, even after controlling for education and income, religiosity was strongly correlated with gender inequitable attitudes.[23] At the country level, overall religiosity was also negatively related to various indicators of gender equality in well-being, through the mechanism of gender norms and stereotypes. This study did not find differences between world religions on these results. This is a very sobering finding for those of us who believe that following Jesus is associated with abundant life (John 10:10).

If we focus more specifically on Christianity, research indicates that Christians are more conservative in their views about gender roles than the general population, but also show considerable variability in beliefs about women's roles, including leadership roles.[24] The most conservative segments of Christianity is where we find more of an emphasis on the "proper" role for women in the home and the control of women's sexuality through purity culture ideologies.[25] Fundamentalism, the tendency to hold beliefs in a cognitively rigid way, has been associated with sexism; other religious variables associated with sexism are the valuing of tradition and conformity, and the use of religion instrumentally to obtain other ends such as social connection or comfort.[26] In contrast, intrinsic religiosity, that is, the engagement in religion for its own sake rather than for the benefits it produces, is negatively correlated with sexism.[27]

The concept of benevolent sexism is particularly helpful in understanding sexism as it occurs in Christian contexts, as several studies show that benevolent rather than hostile sexism is more commonly used to justify patriarchal views.[28] Religions help sexism to be "accepted and imbued with

---

23. Seguino, "Help or Hindrance?," 1308–21.

24. Gallagher, *Evangelical Identity*; Burn and Busso, "Ambivalent Sexism," 412–18.

25. Rose, "Christian Fundamentalism," 9–20; Owens et al., "Purity Culture," 405–18.

26. Hannover et al., "Religiosity"; Mikołajczak and Pietrzak, "Ambivalent Sexism," 387–99; McFarland, "Religious Orientation," 324–36.

27. McFarland, "Religious Orientation."

28. Glick et al., "Education and Catholic Religiosity," 433–41; Maltby et al., "Religion and Sexism," 615–22; Mikołajczak and Pietrzak, "Ambivalent Sexism."

moral and even spiritual significance."[29] Consistent with this idea that religions promote sexism, a recent study found that even priming participants with Judeo-Christian concepts (such as faith, baptize, God, divine, and sacred) led to an increase in self-reported benevolent sexism, beyond the contribution of gender and religious belief—this effect occurred even among participants who indicated they did not believe in God.[30]

I noted earlier that religions influence gender ideologies, structural inequities, and the experiences of women. Thus far we've been primarily discussing gender ideologies. How do structural inequities come into the picture? Here we rely on a large-scale study by sociologists Patricia Homan and Amy Burdette, who explored structural sexism in religious contexts in nationally representative datasets.[31] They examined religious structural sexism by measuring whether women were allowed to serve on the governing board, to be the head clergyperson, to serve as a teacher in co-ed classes, or to preach at a main worship service. These served as indicators of the power and resources available to women in church contexts. Their results indicated that increased structural sexism was correlated with decreased self-reported health. In fact, women in the more structurally sexist churches had similar self-reported health as women who do not attend church. Although attending church is known to be beneficial to one's health, this benefit is only for women in less structurally sexist churches.

We have now discussed religion's influence on gender ideologies and on structural inequities. Let me now move into how religions influence the experiences of women who are subjected to sexism. Here I draw on my own research. In a study my colleagues and I conducted, we asked women whether they had witnessed or been subjected to a number of forms of both hostile and benevolent sexism.[32] We also asked if they thought the act had been motivated by the person's Christian beliefs and commitments. What we found is that perceiving that sexism was motivated by Christian beliefs potentiated the harmful effects of sexism on evaluations of the institutional climate. In other words, sexism in Christian settings can be particularly harmful to women because God is invoked in justifying the sexism, perhaps because the beliefs are then perceived as more immutable.

---

29. Jost et al., "Belief in a Just God," 56–81.
30. Haggard et al., "Religion's Role," 392–98.
31. Homan and Burdette, "When Religion Hurts," 234–55.
32. Hall et al., "Sanctified Sexism," 181–85.

Five Take-Home Points

This review of the psychology of sexism and its interface with mission has covered a lot of ground, so let me pause at this point to highlight some of the most salient points that I hope are takeaways from this essay. First, sexism is both a target of mission, as an important and pervasive way in which sin has influenced the world, and a barrier to mission, not just because it limits the opportunities women have to serve, but because it decreases women's emotional and cognitive resources for engaging in mission.

Second, sexism is not something that men do to women, but that men and women do to women, often outside of conscious awareness. The target when addressing sexism are patterns of relating and the structures resulting from those patterns, in which men and women are both complicit. In the large multinational study I mentioned earlier, men's and women's sexism scores correlated very highly with each other.[33] While women's hostile sexism tended to be a little lower than men's, their benevolent sexism levels were sometimes actually higher than the men's.

A third and related point is that sexism doesn't just hurt women; sexism against women also hurts men. While it might be assumed that holding to sexist gender ideologies would benefit men because of the power that it affords them, these gender ideologies come at a price. Systematic literature reviews show that men who endorse traditional masculinity ideologies (which are part of benevolent sexism) tend to experience increases in a variety of negative interpersonal and personal problems, including issues such as dangerous risk-taking, alcohol and substance abuse, hostility and aggression, self-esteem issues, depression, anxiety, marital and family problems, and problems with relationship satisfaction and intimacy.[34] Many of these problems can be traced to the fact that these masculinity ideologies serve as a kind of emotional and behavioral straightjacket.

A fourth point is that not all women are subjected to sexism in the same way. Other aspects of our identity deeply influence the ways in which we are discriminated against, a point made by intersectionality theory. Different aspects of our identity, such as gender, race, class, sexual orientation, parental status, etc., come together to influence our experiences, and these are not simply additive. For example, Black women do not experience discrimination merely as the sum of racism and sexism, but instead they experience discrimination as Black women, in which their gender and

---

33. Glick et al., "Beyond Prejudice," 771–72.

34. O'Neil and Denke, "Empirical Review," 62–68; Gerdes et al., "Content Analysis," 584–99.

racial characteristics intersect to produce unique ways of being discriminated against.[35] Black women may be subject to intersectional stereotypes that objectify, sexualize, or exoticize them, such as expectations of being a Jezebel or an angry Black woman.[36] In another example, parental status interacts with sex in that research demonstrates that discrimination faced by women in the workplace seems to primarily (though not exclusively) be directed at mothers.[37]

A fifth point is that, in general, Christianity seems to have made things worse rather than better. This statement, of course, should be nuanced. Problematic versions of Christianity are those that are more fundamentalist, that advocate for traditional gender ideologies, that justify sexism by appealing to religion, that are engaged in for personal benefit, and that are enacted in sexist structures. We must address sexism in all its contexts, but we must not neglect the log in our own eye.

The Way Forward

Sexism is clearly a serious and pervasive problem. How should it be addressed? Many good resources are available for addressing specific types of sexism such as physical abuse or sexism in specific contexts such as the workplace, so here I intend to focus on more big-picture issues. Let me suggest three strategies to keep in mind in moving forward.

First, we need to disentangle sexism from the good news about Jesus Christ. Much of the conflict around gender in Christian circles has centered around women in leadership in church contexts. Having women in leadership is an important issue, as evidenced by the research I reviewed earlier, but it is not the only issue. We need to pay more attention to the ways in which sexist ideologies have become entangled with the message of Christianity at all levels, including the messages we give about appearance and sexuality through purity culture beliefs, the messages about how marriages should function that impede intimacy and put women at risk for violence, and even the typical ways women and men related in both work and church-related contexts that leave women segregated and outside of informational networks and decision-making contexts. Sexism is a broader issue than who should be a pastor.

Second, we need to confront sexism when we encounter it. Cornel West wrote, "None of us alone can save the nation or world. But each of us

---

35. Crenshaw, "Demarginalizing the Intersection," 139–67.
36. Lewis, "From Modern Sexism," 391.
37. Sabat et al., "Working Mothers," 9–31.

can make a positive difference if we commit ourselves to do so."[38] This may sound very simple, but research indicates that most people remain silent in the face of sexism.[39] This may be because confrontation requires people to detect discrimination, decide it is worth confronting, take responsibility to confront, and decide how to confront.[40] Confrontation can be uncomfortable, but it is effective. When confronting sexism in Christian circles, we should lean into the motivational resources available to us, foremost of which are the concepts of love of neighbor, compassion, and putting the needs of others before one's own needs. My experience in this area is that many people who engage in sexist practices do so from the best of intentions. The best way to confront benevolent sexism in particular is to highlight its negative consequences.[41] When people are shown that their well-intentioned actions are actually hurting others, their sexist actions tend to diminish. Even outside of Christian contexts, research shows that confronting sexism when it occurs can reduce sexism by increasing perpetrators' awareness and reducing the likelihood that they will continue to act in sexist ways.[42] Research shows that assertive, nonaggressive confrontation may be challenging, as it involves controlling our anger at the sexism, but will have better outcomes than aggressive confrontation.[43]

Third, men and women should cooperate to confront sexism. Having men as allies can be very beneficial, as research shows that when men confront sexism, offenders experience greater self-directed negative affect, view the confronter more positively, and perceive the confrontation as more legitimate.[44] Men have more structural power, so are often better positioned to confront sexism. Whenever possible, men should support women in confronting rather than taking over, in order to avoid benevolently sexist paternalism.

Many of my comments here have highlighted how Christianity has been complicit in denying women access to power. Let me end on a more positive note by reminding us that many of the early pioneers in advocating for women's rights were motivated by their Christian faith. When we care about these issues, we are following in a well-trodden tradition of advocating

---

38. West, *Race Matters*, 109.
39. Swim et al., "Self-Silencing to Sexism," 493–507.
40. Becker et al., "Confronting and Reducing Sexism," 605.
41. Becker and Swim, "Reducing Endorsement," 127–37.
42. Czopp et al., "Standing Up for a Change," 784–803.
43. Becker and Barreto, "Ways to Go," 668–86.
44. Czopp and Monteith, "Confronting Prejudice," 532–44; Drury and Kaiser, "Allies against Sexism," 637–52.

for the dignity and well-being of all humans because all humans are made in God's image. These pioneers include people like Christine de Pizan, who wrote *The Book of the City of Ladies* in 1405 to combat misogyny by arguing that God loves men and women equally.[45] These pioneers include Quaker Margaret Fell Fox, who wrote a pamphlet in 1666 defending women's right to preach.[46] These pioneers include the many Christian men and women who launched first-wave feminism by meeting in the basement of a church and drafting a declaration addressing the role of women in society during the famous Seneca Falls Convention of 1848.[47] Christians began the movement to address power inequalities for women; let's continue challenging sexism for God's sake.

Bibliography

Barreto, Manuela, et al. "How Nice of Us and How Dumb of Me: The Effect of Exposure to Benevolent Sexism on Women's Task and Relational Self-Descriptions." *Sex Roles* 62 (2010) 532–44.

Becker, Julia C., and Janet K. Swim. "Reducing Endorsement of Benevolent and Modern Sexist Beliefs." *Social Psychology* 43 (2012) 127–37.

Becker, Julia C., and Manuela Barreto. "Ways to Go: Men's and Women's Support for Aggressive and Non-aggressive Confrontation of Sexism as a Function of Gender Identification." *Journal of Social Issues* 70 (2014) 668–86.

Becker, Julia C., and Stephen C. Wright. "Yet Another Dark Side of Chivalry: Benevolent Sexism Undermines and Hostile Sexism Motivates Collective Action for Social Change." *Journal of Personality and Social Psychology* 101 (2011) 62–77.

Becker, Julia C., et al. "Confronting and Reducing Sexism: A Call for Research on Intervention." *Journal of Social Issues* 70 (2014) 603–14.

Burn, Shawn M., and Julia Busso. "Ambivalent Sexism, Scriptural Literalism, and Religiosity." *Psychology of Women Quarterly* 29 (2005) 412–18.

Calogero, Rachel M., and John T. Jost. "Self-Subjugation among Women: Exposure to Sexist Ideology, Self-Objectification, and the Protective Function of the Need to Avoid Closure." *Journal of Personality and Social Psychology* 100 (2011) 211–28.

Casad, Bettina J., et al. "The Real versus the Ideal: Predicting Relationship Satisfaction and Well-Being from Endorsement of Marriage Myths and Benevolent Sexism." *Psychology of Women Quarterly* 39 (2015) 119–29.

Connor, Rachel A., et al. "Ambivalent Sexism in the Twenty-First Century." In *The Cambridge Handbook of the Psychology of Prejudice*, edited by Chris G. Sibley and Fiona Kate Barlow, 295–320. Cambridge: Cambridge University Press, 2017.

Crenshaw, Kimberlé. "Demarginalizing the Intersection of Race and Sex: A Black Feminist Critique of Antidiscrimination Doctrine, Feminist Theory, and Antiracist Politics." *University of Chicago Legal Forum* 1989 (1989) 139–67.

---

45. Pizan, *Book of the City of Ladies*.
46. Fell, *Women's Speaking Justified*.
47. McPhillips, "Contested Feminisms," 134–49.

Czopp, Alexander M., and Margo J. Monteith. "Confronting Prejudice (Literally): Reactions to Confrontations of Racial and Gender Bias." *Personality and Social Psychology Bulletin* 29 (2003) 532–44.

Czopp, Alexander M., et al. "Standing Up for a Change: Reducing Bias through Interpersonal Confrontation." *Journal of Personality and Social Psychology* 90 (2006) 784–803.

Dardenne, Benoit, et al. "Insidious Dangers of Benevolent Sexism: Consequences for Women's Performance." *Journal of Personality and Social Psychology* 93 (2007) 764–79.

Drury, Benjamin J., and Cheryl R. Kaiser. "Allies against Sexism: The Role of Men in Confronting Sexism." *Journal of Social Issues* 70 (2014) 637–52.

Dumont, Muriel, et al. "Be Too Kind to a Woman, She'll Feel Incompetent: Benevolent Sexism Shifts Self-Construal and Autobiographical Memories toward Incompetence." *Sex Roles* 62 (2010) 545–53.

Durán, Mercedes, et al. "Benevolent Sexist Ideology Attributed to an Abusive Partner Decreases Women's Active Coping Responses to Acts of Sexual Violence." *Journal of Interpersonal Violence* 29 (2014) 1380–1401.

Durán, Mercedes, et al. "It's His Right, It's Her Duty: Benevolent Sexism and the Justification of Traditional Sexual Roles." *Journal of Sex Research* 48 (2011) 470–78.

Fell, Margaret. *Women's Speaking Justified, Proved, and Allowed of by the Scriptures* London, 1666.

Forbes, Gordon B., et al. "First- and Second-Generation Measures of Sexism, Rape Myths, and Related Beliefs, and Hostility toward Women: Their Interrelationships and Association with College Students' Experiences with Dating Aggression and Sexual Coercion." *Violence against Women* 10 (2004) 236–61.

Gallagher, Sally K. *Evangelical Identity and Gendered Family Life*. Piscataway, NJ: Rutgers University Press, 2003.

Gerdes, Zachary T., et al. "A Content Analysis of Research on Masculinity Ideologies Using All Forms of the Male Role Norms Inventory (MRNI)." *Psychology of Men & Masculinity* 19 (2018) 584–99.

Gervais, Sarah J., and Theresa K. Vescio. "The Effect of Patronizing Behavior and Control on Men and Women's Performance in Stereotypically Masculine Domains." *Sex Roles* 66 (2012) 479–91.

Glick, Peter, and Susan T. Fiske. "An Ambivalent Alliance: Hostile and Benevolent Sexism as Complementary Justifications for Gender Inequality." *American Psychologist* 56 (2001) 109–18.

———. "The Ambivalent Sexism Inventory: Differentiating Hostile and Benevolent Sexism." *Journal of Personality and Social Psychology* 70 (1996) 491–512.

Glick, Peter, et al. "Beyond Prejudice as Simple Antipathy: Hostile and Benevolent Sexism across Cultures." *Journal of Personality and Social Psychology* 79 (2000) 763–75.

Glick, Peter, et al. "Education and Catholic Religiosity as Predictors of Hostile and Benevolent Sexism toward Women and Men." *Sex Roles* 47 (2002) 433–41.

Haggard, Megan C., et al. "Religion's Role in the Illusion of Gender Equality: Supraliminal and Subliminal Religious Priming Increases Benevolent Sexism." *Psychology of Religion and Spirituality* 11 (2019) 392–98.

Hall, M. Elizabeth Lewis, et al. "Sanctified Sexism: Religious Beliefs and the Gender Harassment of Academic Women." *Psychology of Women Quarterly* 34 (2010) 181–85.

Hamilton, Hannah R., and Tracy DeHart. "Cheers to Equality! Both Hostile and Benevolent Sexism Predict Increases in College Women's Alcohol Consumption." *Sex Roles* 83 (2020) 675–84.

Hammond, Matthew D., and Nickola C. Overall. "Benevolent Sexism and Support of Romantic Partner's Goals: Undermining Women's Competence While Fulfilling Men's Intimacy Needs." *Personality and Social Psychology Bulletin* 41 (2015) 1180–94.

———. "Endorsing Benevolent Sexism Magnifies Willingness to Dissolve Relationships When Facing Partner-Ideal Discrepancies." *Personal Relationships* 21 (2014) 272–87.

———. "When Relationships Do Not Live Up to Benevolent Ideals: Women's Benevolent Sexism and Sensitivity to Relationship Problems." *European Journal of Social Psychology* 43 (2013) 212–23.

Hannover, Bettina, et al. "Religiosity, Religious Fundamentalism, and Ambivalent Sexism toward Girls and Women among Adolescents and Young Adults Living in Germany." *Frontiers in Psychology* 9 (2018) no. 2399.

Homan, Patricia. "Structural Sexism and Health in the United States: A New Perspective on Health Inequality and the Gender System." *American Sociological Review* 84 (2019) 486–516.

Homan, Patricia, and Amy Burdette. "When Religion Hurts: Structural Sexism and Health in Religious Congregations." *American Sociological Review* 86 (2021) 234–55.

Jost, John T., and Aaron C. Kay. "Exposure to Benevolent Sexism and Complementary Gender Stereotypes: Consequences for Specific and Diffuse Forms of System Justification." *Journal of Personality and Social Psychology* 88 (2005) 498–509.

Jost, John T., et al. "Belief in a Just God (and a Just Society): A System Justification Perspective on Religious Ideology." *Journal of Theoretical and Philosophical Psychology* 34 (2014) 56–81.

Kaiser, Walter, et al., eds. *Hard Sayings of the Bible*. Downers Grove, IL: InterVarsity, 1996.

Lamarche, Veronica M., et al. "Clever Girl: Benevolent Sexism and Cardiovascular Threat." *Biological Psychology* 149 (2020) no. 107781.

Lewis, Jioni A. "From Modern Sexism to Gender Microaggressions: Understanding Contemporary Forms of Sexism and Their Influence on Diverse Women." In *APA Handbook of the Psychology of Women: History, Theory, and Battlegrounds*, edited by Cheryl B. Travis et al., 381–97. Washington, DC: American Psychological Association, 2008.

Maltby, Lauren E., et al. "Religion and Sexism: The Moderating Role of Participant Gender." *Sex Roles* 62 (2010) 615–22.

Masser, Barbara, et al. "Bad Woman, Bad Victim? Disentangling the Effects of Victim Stereotypicality, Gender Stereotypicality, and Benevolent Sexism on Acquaintance Rape Victim Blame." *Sex Roles* 62 (2010) 494–504.

McFarland, Sam G. "Religious Orientation and the Targets of Discrimination." *Journal for the Scientific Study of Religion* 28 (1989) 324–36.

McPhillips, Kathleen. "Contested Feminisms: Women's Religious Leadership and the Politics of Contemporary Western Feminism." *Journal for the Academic Study of Religion* 29 (2016) 134–49.

Mikołajczak, Małgorzata, and Janina Pietrzak. "Ambivalent Sexism and Religion: Connected through Values." *Sex Roles* 70 (2014) 387–99.

Montañés, Pilar, et al. "Intergenerational Transmission of Benevolent Sexism from Mothers to Daughters and Its Relation to Daughters' Academic Performance and Goals." *Sex Roles* 66 (2012) 1112–37.

O'Neil, James M., and Robyn Denke. "An Empirical Review of Gender Role Conflict Research: New Conceptual Models and Research Paradigms." In *APA Handbook of Men and Masculinities*, edited by Y. Joel Wong and Stephen. R. Wester, 62–68. Washington, DC: American Psychological Association, 2016.

Oswald, Debra, et al. "Experiencing Sexism and Young Women's Body Esteem." *Journal of Social and Clinical Psychology* 31 (2012) 1112–37.

Owens, Bretlyn C., et al. "The Relationship between Purity Culture and Rape Myth Acceptance." *Journal of Psychology and Theology* 49 (2021) 405–18.

Pizan, Christine de. *The Book of the City of Ladies*. Translated by Rosalind Brown-Grant. London: Penguin, 1999.

Rollero, Chiara, and Angela Fedi. "When Benevolence Harms Women and Favours Men: The Effects of Ambivalent Sexism on Leadership Aspiration." *Československá Psychologie: Časopis Pro Psychologickou Teorii a Praxi* 58 (2014) 535–42.

Rose, Susan D. "Christian Fundamentalism: Patriarchy, Sexuality, and Human Rights." In *Religious Fundamentalisms and the Human Rights of Women*, edited by Courtney W. Howland, 9–20. New York: Palgrave, 1999.

Sabat, Isaac E., et al. "Understanding and Overcoming Challenges Faced by Working Mothers: A Theoretical and Empirical Review." In *Research Perspectives on Work and the Transition to Motherhood*, edited by Christiane Spitzmueller and Russell A. Matthews, 9–31. New York: Springer, 2016.

Seguino, Stephanie. "Help or Hindrance? Religion's Impact on Gender Inequality in Attitudes and Outcomes." *World Development* 39 (2011) 1308–21.

Shepherd, Melissa, et al. "'I'll Get That for You': The Relationship between Benevolent Sexism and Body Self-Perceptions." *Sex Roles* 64 (2011) 1–8.

Swim, Janet K., and Lauri L. Hyers. "Sexism." In *Handbook of Prejudice, Stereotyping, and Discrimination*, edited by Todd D. Nelson, 407–30. New York: Psychology, 2009.

Swim, Janet K., et al. "Self-Silencing to Sexism." *Journal of Social Issues* 66 (2010) 493–507.

Teng, Fei, et al. "Counting on You: Benevolent Sexism Increases Women's Financial Risk-Taking." *Journal of Social Psychology* 162 (2021) 580–94.

Viki, G. Tendayi, et al. "Evaluating Stranger and Acquaintance Rape: The Role of Benevolent Sexism in Perpetrator Blame and Recommended Sentence Length." *Law and Human Behavior* 28 (2004) 295–303.

West, Cornel. *Race Matters*. New York: Vintage, 1994.

World Economic Forum. *Global Gender Gap Report 2021*. https://www3.weforum.org/docs/WEF_GGGR_2021.pdf.

World Policy Analysis Center. "Is Paid Leave Available for Both Parents of Infants?" https://www.worldpolicycenter.org/policies/is-paid-leave-available-for-both-parents-of-infants.

—6—

Women Rise Up
Power, Agency, and Christianity

Grace Ji-Sun Kim

Introduction

THE BIBLICAL DEPICTION OF women has not been kind, accurate, or just towards women. Biblical characters such as Eve, Hagar, and biblical patriarch's wives, have often been viewed and depicted as the sinner, the helper, the temptress, the powerless, or the weaker of the two genders. Women in the Bible are portrayed as second-class citizens who do not have their own initiative or agency. However, there are a few biblical women, like Mary the mother of Jesus, Dorcas, Mary Magdalene, and Mary from Bethany who stand out and offer power, hope, and agency for women today.

How power and agency are embodied by women in different cultural and organizational contexts is important to study. White women can garner more power and agency than women of color are able to because women of color are also subject to their own cultural biases, restrictions, marginalization, and subjugations. This chapter will explore strategies for challenging cultural and theological frameworks that hinder women as agents in their own lives and in the lives of their communities. It will also work towards women gaining agency and liberation as full members and participants of God's kin-dom.[1]

---

1. The traditional term "kingdom of God" has a patriarchal connotation as it is

Bible and Women

Scripture has not been favorable to women. In many Christian communities, women have been depicted as evil. Women are viewed as the one who brings evil into the world through the story of Adam and Eve in the garden of Eden. Eve tempts Adam with the fruit that God said not to eat. "So when the woman saw that the tree was good for food and that it was a delight to the eyes and that the tree was to be desired to make one wise, she took of its fruit and ate, and she also gave some to her husband, who was with her, and he ate" (Gen 3:6).[2] From this story of Eve tempting Adam, Christians have believed that the woman brought evil into the world. It is unfortunate that Bathsheba, who is a victim of King David's desires, is portrayed as a tempter and a seductress. "David rose from his couch and was walking about on the roof of the king's house, that he saw from the roof a woman bathing; the woman was very beautiful" (2 Sam 11:2). Christians have distorted this passage to portray Bathsheba as the evil one who tempted King David by bathing on her rooftop.

There are many reasons for this negative depiction of women. First the Israelites were living and habiting a patriarchal world. This world continues into the New Testament times and even into our present context. In a patriarchal world, women are subordinated and subjected to second class roles. Women are expected to be obedient to men and are even property of men, such as their father or their husband. The Israelite family was headed by a man and transmission of property was through males. Women were either aliens or transients within their family of residence and men had legal authority over women. Women were counted among men's possessions along with children, slaves, and livestock (e.g., Exod 20:17; Deut 5:21).[3] Thus women were presented and treated as subordinate to men.

We see a few examples of how women are the property of men in the story of Sarah and Abraham. In this story, Sarah takes an Egyptian enslaved woman named Hagar who becomes the property of Abraham. When Sarah couldn't give birth to a child, she asked Hagar to be with Abraham and bear a child for her. However, once Ishmael was born, Sarah became jealous of the child and of Hagar. Miraculously, Sarah at her ripe old age was able to give birth to a son named Isaac. Once Isaac was born, Sarah had no use for Hagar and her son Ishmael. When Ishmael was around thirteen years

---

referencing a king ruling over his land. To move away from this patriarchal notion of God and God's realm, many feminist theologians are using the term "kin-dom of God" which emphasizes equality and kinship rather than patriarchy.

2. Biblical citations in this chapter from the NRSVue.

3. Sauder, "Sexual Property and Personhood," 2.

old, he and his mother Hagar were both banished into the desert (Gen 21). There was no law to stop this banishment and they went into the desert with little food and water with the anticipation of facing death. It was by the grace of God that they survived the harsh desert, and Ishmael became known as the father of Arabs.

In Ezra 9 when the Israelites returned from exile, there were a lot of foreign women who also returned. The Israelites were concerned about the status of the foreign women and therefore held a meeting to decide what to do with them. The meeting concluded that they would send the foreign women away. Some of these foreign women were married with children, but the Israelites were afraid that these foreign women would end up taking their land. This is another example of how, in the Bible, men determine the fate of women and, if they wish, they can banish them or send them away.

There are other biblical examples of the mistreatment of women as both Testaments were written and read under patriarchy. Women are often viewed as the villain of the story and were often blamed for negative things such as bringing sin into the world. We see this in the story of the Garden of Eden where Eve is blamed for tempting Adam (Gen 2–3). Believing that women have brought evil into the world through Eve, the passage is misinterpreted to mean that all women then deserve to be punished, banished, or mistreated. This trope of treating and understanding women negatively still occurs in our churches, in biblical interpretations, and in the wider society.

Another more significant reason for the ongoing subordination of women in Scriptures is due to God being presented and perceived as a male God. Mary Daly famously wrote, "If God is male, then the male is God,"[4] which means that God's maleness has deep consequences on society and our faith. God's maleness implies that men are above women and men are the ones who hold power as men are closer to God than women. This perception of a male God puts lots of restrictions on women as men get to dictate what women are supposed to do and what women are not to do. There are many laws and commandments for women to show how they are to behave and act within the Old Testament and the New Testament. Most of these were defining laws which narrowed and limited the scope of women and their actions.

Dualism and the Subordination of Women

Christianity emerged and developed during the Roman Empire. Under this harsh empire, Greco-Roman philosophy was very influential and impacted

---

4. Daly, *Beyond God the Father*, 19.

society in many different ways. It even had a huge impact on Christian beliefs and teachings. This influential way of thinking enforced dualism within Christianity. Greek dualism separates and divides things and concepts into two opposed or contrasted aspects. In dualism, men and women are categorized and viewed as opposites. Men are viewed as good, and women are viewed as unfavorable. Other examples include heaven is good and earth is bad, or spirit is good and matter is evil. This strict dualistic way of viewing the world has reinforced women's status as subordinate and second-class.

Within Asian culture, the terms Yin and Yang also illustrate the dichotomous inclinations found in society. Within the traditional Chinese world view, the world has two complementary elements, Yin and Yang. Yin refers to the feminine or negative principle, and Yang is the masculine or positive principle in nature. Yin means shade which refers to the female symbolized by the moon which is dark, hidden, weak, and passive. On the other hand, Yang means sun and refers to male which stands for open, warm, strong, and active.[5] The dichotomy between Yin and Yang feeds into the subordination of women and continues to uplift men over women.

Popular children's stories and fairy tales help us understand how dualism comes into play and how it is still prevalent in our cultures. Dualism is embedded into our cultural narrative and hence it is at times difficult to notice or even object to it. Take for example a girl's popular story of *Sleeping Beauty*. The name of the main character is Sleeping Beauty, and she is found on or in a bed. She is a fragile woman and cannot do anything without a man. Sleeping Beauty is lifted from her bed by a man because women do not wake up by themselves and require men to intervene to even wake up. She is lifted up by the man who will lay her in her next bed so that she may be confined to a bed ever after, just as the fairy tale says. So, her trajectory is from one bed to another bed where she can dream even more. She sleeps, and first love becomes her dreams and then she dreams of love. In some stories, she can be found standing up, but not for too long. She is a passive individual. In this story, Kierkegaard views woman as a sleeper,[6] which implies she is passive, lifeless, and has no agency. She is presented as "useless" and a non-contributor to family and society since sleeping is regarded as 'useless' and an unimportant task for a person to engage in. This presentation of a woman impacts how women are viewed, since *Sleeping Beauty* is read by children all over the world. Little girls look up to this story of *Sleeping Beauty* and aspire to become like her. They want to be asleep and be woken up by a prince and live 'happily ever after.' But this is a false and

---

5. Gao, "Women Existing for Men," 115.
6. Cixous, "Castration or Decapitation?," 346.

a dangerous narrative which should not be told nor shared in our society as it perpetuates a patriarchal narrative of what a woman is supposed to be like—passive and unimportant.

Another popular children's story is *Little Red Riding Hood*. In this story, the girl is between two houses and between two beds. She is caught in-between and fixed in a chain of metaphors that organize culture and context. The huntsman is portrayed as active, upright, and productive while the girl is not. This opposition to woman is the classic opposition, dualistic and hierarchical view. This dualistic perception of woman automatically divides man and woman as great and small, superior and inferior, high and low, nature and history, and transformation and inertia. These views separate man and woman and put them in a dichotomous relationship. Theories of culture and society, together with discourses, art, religions, the families, and language, are "ordered around hierarchical oppositions that come back to the man" versus woman opposition. It is "an opposition that can only be sustained by means of a difference posed by cultural discourse as 'natural'—the difference between activity and passivity."[7] This dualistic understanding and separation between men and women can be very dangerous. It portrays men as great at the cost of women being useless and inconsequential. It paints a distinct line between men and women when instead there isn't a clear-cut line but rather a gray area where it is very difficult to know what the difference is between men and women. There is much overlap between men and women and therefore this dichotomy should be eliminated as it leads to essentialization which can lead to devastation and destruction.

There is no essence to women that defines women's identity and prescribes certain behavior to women. Essentialization misrepresents by falsely stating that something is essential to the whole. We cannot essentialize women as there are different kinds of women, such as White women, Black women, and Asian women—none of which has a fixed identity. Women can be subdivided into heterosexual women, lesbian women, bisexual women, and transgendered women, and each can be further subdivided into wealthy women, middle-class women, and poor women. No group is a homogeneous entity, but each contains similar divisions and subdivisions.[8] Each person has multiple identities which are intersectional. Women are complex beings and cannot be reduced to essentials.

This distinct differentiation between men and women has led to detrimental understandings not only of women but also of God, which in turn perpetuates patriarchy within society. God has been portrayed as

---

7. Cixous, "Castration or Decapitation?," 347.
8. Min, *Solidarity of Other*, 54.

masculine from the beginning of Christianity and as a fearful, all-knowing, and almighty God. As a result, men are shown to be always closer to God then women and therefore will be able to know better the will of God. This type of logic has pervaded the church and legitimized patriarchy within the church. Yet, this unequal view of women is not the intention of God, who created all people, male and female, white, yellow, brown, red, or black, all equally. Patriarchal cultures, the worship of a male God, and dualism have all contributed to the oppression of women world-wide. Oppression is not limited to women in North America, or in Asia; it is a global existence for all women. Therefore, this patriarchal depiction of women as the sinner, the helper, the temptress, the powerless, and the weaker of the two genders, which is culturally created and religiously reinforced, needs to be challenged and dismantled so that we can build new paradigms and understandings.

Power and Agency

Power and agency embodied by women in different cultural and organizational contexts look all differently. Some have power and agency, and some have less. Power and agency look differently to women in different cultural and organizational contexts. Due to cultural and religious restrictions, such as Confucianism, women in parts of Asia, Africa, and South America have less power and agency. There are additional cultural expectations and aspects which further contribute to women's subordination. If we look at North American and European women, they may appear to have more power and agency than other women around the globe. This is in part due to the women's movement and women's liberation. There have been significant women philosophers and leaders who have led the way to give women more power and more agency. We have thinkers such as Simone de Beauvoir and Mary Daly as well as feminist theologians such as Rosemary Radford Reuther, Letty Russell, and Elisabeth Schussler Fiorenza who have paved the way for White Western women to find more liberation and freedom from the bonds of patriarchy.

Many scholars have tried to understand the different dynamics of power and agency. Austrian neurologist Sigmund Freud tackled this by asking the question "what do women want?" in a rhetorical way. The answer is "she wants nothing" because she is understood to be submissive. The man asks, "without me, what could she want?"[9] Women are depicted as useless and having no agency as she desires and needs nothing apart from man. She desires nothing because man will give whatever she desires, and the man is

9. Cixous, "Castration or Decapitation?," 348.

also the object of her desire. In this view, women are powerless and passive. Woman is the Other and there does not exist between the sexes a reciprocal relation. She is not seen as a fellow being in a man's eyes. She has no power but constitutes a part of the property of a man and is under the guardianship of men. She is the intermediary of authority and not the one who possesses it.[10] It is only an illusion of power and authority that women seem to have in a marriage or family. Men move or take women in, and have the power to absolve it.

Women are also condemned to hold only uncertain power: slave or idol. She doesn't choose her own lot. French philosopher Simone Beauvoir looks at the work of James Frazer who states, 'Men make the gods; women worship them,' as men indeed decide whether their supreme divinities shall be female or male. Woman has been in a co-dependent relationship with man. Everything man gained, he gained against her. The more powerful man became, the more woman declined.[11] This co-dependent relationship puts women on the bad end of the relationship with less power and agency. A woman's place in society is always what men assign to her and "at no time has she ever imposed her own law."[12] This restriction on women gets translated into Christianity as it is a patriarchal religion and God is portrayed as male. Women cannot seem to rid themselves of this entrenched idea that men have created this religion to serve themselves. This keeps women in their place and to make them the Other. Religion is a powerful force in our society, and it can have devastating effects on women if religion is unchecked. It is important for all parties involved that this is recognized and that steps need to be taken to fix this problem.

Patriarchal notions, concepts, and ideas within Christianity need to be challenged as they continue to perpetuate negative ideas about women in society and within Christianity. Patriarchy affects women of different races and ethnicities. White Western Christian patriarchy can be very harmful to women from multiple levels as it teaches sexism as well as Western domination and colonialism. Christianity has become westernized and White, so that anything non-western sounds foreign, untrue, or even evil. Challenging this colonization of the East by Western ideas will work towards eliminating racism, prejudice, and subordination of non-white to White people. This notion of White Christian colonialism intersects with patriarchy and works against women of color around the globe. Colonialism, sexism, and racism intersect to perpetuate continued oppression against women of color.

10. Beauvoir, *Second Sex*, 70–71.
11. Beauvoir, *Second Sex*, 78.
12. Beauvoir, *Second Sex*, 77.

Power and agency are embodied by women in different ways and levels depending on the cultural and organizational contexts. In Asia, where most societies are male-oriented and male-dominated, militarism, neocolonialism, capitalism, and consumerism have contributed to the maintenance of traditional patriarchal culture at the expense of Asian women. Asian women struggle against not only dehumanizing economic and political conditions, but also demeaning and subjugating elements of the traditional cultural realities. Hence, sexism is prevalent and is often sanctioned by religion which includes Christianity.

Confucianism is very hierarchical. It orders society based on class and gender. In a Confucian society, women are at the bottom of the social ladder and are required to obey men. In this Asian context, when they are young, they are required to obey their fathers, when married their husbands and when widowed their sons. As such, women are always required to be obedient to men all throughout their life. Women are viewed as "inferior men" who are unable to communicate or understand. The *Book of Rites* teaches feminine virtues such as quietness, obedience, good manners, and respect for the husband's parents and brothers.[13] Therefore sexism and patriarchalism "have deep roots in the Confucianism of East Asian cultures"[14] and is deeply embedded within culture, religion, and society. For example, Asian American women lack power and agency due to the long cultural history and legacy based on Confucianism.

With this strong cultural norm of obedience, Asian women lack power and agency. Educational and employment opportunities for women are limited. In both the church and society, women are excluded from decision-making bodies, even when the subject they are considering affects women's lives and bodies directly. Without full control of their own bodies and lives, it becomes a depressing and oppressive situation for Asian women. Without their own agency and power to make decisions regarding their body and present/future lives, it drains women's enthusiasm, hopes, and desires.

Asian American women exist in the margins of society. Hence, it is crucial that we understand intersectional theology and how intersectionality plays a key role in understanding the different layers of oppression and the need to work towards justice. Asian American women live between two cultures, the Asian and the Western European culture. As such, they are caught in-between both cultures. As a result, they end up suffering from the oppressive aspects of both cultures. Within Asian American culture, there is still the high expectation to live by the strict "obedient" lifestyle.

---

13. Gao, "Women Existing for Men," 115.
14. Cheah, "Asian Women's Mariology," 77.

Furthermore, within the Western European culture, there is the double oppression of patriarchy and racism. Both forms of oppression intersect to add multiple layers of oppression and discrimination.

There is no stable place where one can definitively transcend power/knowledge effects and find a "pre-given entity" prior to or apart from these cultural and linguistic structures. Given that the individual is seen as constituted within a nexus of societal discursive conventions, even so-called private or personal sin is linked to collective structures. Power, even when it seems monolithic and centralized, turns out upon closer analysis to be a network of widely extended apparatuses. Power is dynamic and is tied to agency which women lack. Power is not just what my oppressor possesses as it is always a power relation that may have subjugating effects but also creates subjects. For example, capitalism creates a proletariat; patriarchy creates subservient women. Hence, power "produces discourse"—including discourses and practices of resistance.[15] In this way, women need to engage in resistance. Women need to resist patriarchal patterns and evils such as men wanting to control women's body and women's future. When sexist patriarchy exists, women must not succumb to it but must resist it.

This understanding of power has the potential to correct a tendency to employ more-or-less static oppressor-oppressed categories that view the sinned-against primarily as victims in relation to domination. Such categories are meant to express compassion for the downtrodden and outrage against injustice, but these categories are somewhat paradoxical because calls for liberation require that one envision agency for victims.[16] To move towards the liberation of women, theologians need to divorce theological thinking from dualism which separates such categories as totally distinct from one another. Rather, we should approach things intersectionally and recognize that nothing is clean cut but can be rather messy. In this way, we can then gain agency and fight back and resist systems of evil.

Agency can be achieved in different ways as identity is constantly negotiated and renegotiated at the nexus of multiple cultural discourses. In postcolonial theory, the concept of hybridity helps us understand the political agency of the "subaltern" subject to help describe the ways in which subaltern subjects sometimes both embrace and confront the "master's tools." What could look like complicity with the oppressor may in fact be a process of formulating subaltern agency in relation to colonialist as well as indigenous cultural practices, languages, attitudes, and religions. Hybridity is a pragmatic exercise of power and agency, reflecting a contextualized

---

15. Jones and Lakeland, *Constructive Theology*, 154.
16. Armour et al., "God," 54.

approach to cultural, economic, and political survival in contexts of pervasive structural evil.[17]

What Women Want

In a patriarchal world, men believe that women lack a lot of things. She lacks a phallus and without man she would be indefinite, indefinable, non-sexed, or unable to recognize herself. But if she has a man, he teaches her to be aware of lack, aware of absence, and aware of death. He will teach her that without man, she would not exist. Within him she remains in a state of distressing and "unpoliced" by the phallus. "Without him she would in all probability not be contained by the threat of death, might even, perhaps, believe herself eternal and immortal. Without him she would be deprived of sexuality."[18] Man works actively to produce "his woman."[19] Man has a constant need to define and redefine women. This is the same phenomenon as when the colonizer in the center redefines or speaks for the marginalized. Thus, women being in the margins are doubly marginalized and continuously oppressed.

Women need to resist the movement of reappropriation that rules the whole economy. Women need courage to understand that, in breaking away from patriarchy, women do not lose but can actually win. Women can organize this regeneration, this vitalization of the other, of otherness in its entirety. They have it in them to affirm the difference, their difference. "If women were to set themselves to transform history, it can safely be said that every aspect of History would be completely altered. Instead of being made by man, history's task would be to make woman. And it's at this point that work by women themselves on women might be brought into play."[20] It would be a strange new world. But a new world of equality and new birth.

Woman needs to speak up and should stop saying that she has nothing to say. We should

> stop learning in school that women are created to listen, to believe, to make no discoveries. We have to get rid of and also explain what all knowledge brings with it as its burden of power; to show in what ways, culturally, knowledge is the accomplice of power; that whoever stands in the place of knowledge is always getting a dividend of power; show that all thinking until now

---

17. Ray et al., "Sin and Evil," 156.
18. Cixous, "Castration or Decapitation?," 349.
19. Cixous, "Castration or Decapitation?," 349.
20. Cixous, "Castration or Decapitation?," 352.

has been ruled by this dividend, this surplus value of power that comes back to him who knows.[21]

Thus women need to study and learn and have knowledge. As Foucault and many others have noted, knowledge is power as the two are inexplicably intertwined. Therefore, women's task is to gain knowledge so that the tables of power can be overturned.

Biblical, Theological, and Faith Narratives about Women

There are some liberating biblical narratives surrounding women. For liberation, Christian women can draw on liberative biblical texts which show the equality of all genders under God. Jesus treats the Samaritan woman at the well as someone of importance, and not as an outsider. When a woman came to anoint Jesus' feet, Jesus told everyone that people will remember the good act that she has done to Jesus. There are other liberative biblical characters such as Deborah, Hagar the prostitute, Mary Magdalene, the Samaritan woman at the well, and the Syrophoenician woman who shows how God wants to liberate women from cultural and religious restrictions. They also promote women's power and agency to pursue shalom for their communities. It is essential that women's narratives be uplifted and emphasized as so many stories are centered around men as leaders and heroes while women are being pushed to the margins. The few stories that are in the Bible must be emphasized and lifted to encourage women to pursue power and agency.

Furthermore, there is the feminine dimension of God. God is described as a mother hen: "How often have I desired to gather your children together as a hen gathers her brood under her wings" (Matt 23:37b). In the Old Testament, God is compared to a mother eagle, "As an eagle stirs up its nest and hovers over its young, as it spreads its wings, takes them up, and bears them aloft on its pinions" (Detu 32:11). It is also very interesting to note that one of the names for God, *El Shaddi*, has been understood to mean "God with Breasts." The word is derived from Akkadian *shadu* (*shad* in Hebrew) which means breast.[22] Breasts are more often associated with women, not men, so this points to a feminine dimension of the divine. There are other feminine references as found in Jacob's blessing, "by the God of your father, who will help you, by the Almighty who will bless you with blessings

---

21. Cixous, "Castration or Decapitation?," 353.
22. Biale, "God with Breasts," 241.

of heaven above, blessings of the deep that lies beneath, blessings of the breasts and of the womb" (Gen 49:25).

The church has been focused on masculine terms and names for God. But Scripture also includes feminine words such as *Hokmah* (wisdom in Hebrew) and *Sophia* (Wisdom in Greek). Wisdom is feminine in both languages, and it is often associated with God. This makes a difference in how we view God and understand ourselves. These feminine words need to be emphasized and used in the church so that we can have a holistic understanding of God and not just a masculine understanding of God. We need to incorporate this in our languages, liturgies, prayers, hymns, and sermons so that it makes us rethink our long history of patriarchal languages.

Another aspect we need to emphasize is the notion of God as Spirit, which tries to move away from a gendered portrayal of God.[23] Spirit is beyond gender as the Spirit exists in the world and universe, and is often associated with wind, breath, and light which are all intangible and non-gendered. As such, Spirit can be a positive aspect within Christianity as a tool to dismantle patriarchy. Moving away from gendered language of God helps us work towards more equality and establishes a more equal understanding of church, family, and community. The patriarchal understanding of God as male has led to the subordination and subjugation of women throughout Christian history. Therefore, having a non-gendered understanding of God becomes an essential step to gain liberation of women. It will bring changes within the church that move away from patriarchy to a more egalitarian understanding of God.

Women's messages of power are found in the biblical stories of judge Deborah and prophetess Miriam. Their roles and work reinforce women's leadership and wonder, and motivate women to also seek religious leadership. That they can lead not just other women but also men. Women are strong, wise, and essential leaders, so biblical characters such as these two women should be highlighted and remembered. In the New Testament, we also see Mary Magdalene, who appears in the four gospels as one of Jesus' followers who witnessed the crucifixion and resurrection. She is mentioned by name twelve times in the gospels, more than most of the apostles or any other woman in the gospels other than Jesus' family. She was probably a wealthy woman as she supported Jesus' ministry. She is often known as the "apostle to the apostles." It was much later in history in 591 CE that she was viewed as a prostitute when Pope Gregory I conflated Mary Magdalene (Luke 8:2) with Mary of Bethany (Luke 10:39) and the unnamed

---

23. For more reference to gendered portrayal of God, see Kim, *Grace of Sophia*.

sinful woman who anointed Jesus' feet (Luke 7:35–50).[24] In 1969, Pope Paul VI removed the identification of Mary Magdalene with Mary of Bethany and the "sinful woman" from the General Roman Calendar. However, her misidentification as a prostitute continues today. We also have other role models for women today, such as Dorcas who was an early disciple of Jesus (Acts 9:36–43). She lived in Joppa, and she is known for her good works and acts of mercy as she sewed clothes for the poor. When she died, the widows in her community mourned her and sent urgently for Peter (Acts 9:38) who was in nearby Lydda. They showed him some of the clothes she had sewn, and he raised her from the dead. Dorcas was a much-loved woman in her community and someone whom Jesus cared about. Dorcas sets an example for many women today: that we can serve in different ways with whatever gifts God has given to us, whether it be sewing, teaching, leading, or caring.

Strategies for Challenging Cultural and Theological Frameworks

In my book, *Invisible*, I introduce a theology of Visibility to challenge cultural and theological frameworks that demean women. Women have been made invisible in the Bible and during biblical times due to patriarchy. Today, women in various cultures around the globe are made invisible in society by patriarchy and other social constraints. Asian American women are made invisible by the wider dominant white society and also by Asian cultural restraints. Within the kin-dom of God, everyone is equal, everyone is accepted, and everyone is visible. We are all created in God's image, and we are all beautiful and acceptable in the sight of God. Becoming invisible is not the way the kin-dom of God is created to be.

Four Asian terms can help us move towards a theology of Visibility: *Chi, jeong, han, and ou-ri*. These four things help us understand how we can lift the marginalized and the oppressed people in our society. *Chi* is an Asian term for Spirit which enlarges the White European Christian perspective of God. *Jeong* is a Korean term for love that emphasizes how love is unbreakable and binds us together. *Han* is a Korean term which conveys unjust suffering. *Ou-ri* is a Korean term which means "our." In the Korean language, the "ourness" is emphasized over the individual. Therefore, one does not say "my church," "my family," or even "my wife." In the Korean language, we say "our church," "our family," and "our wife" to emphasize the communal understanding of relationships and the world. This *ou-ri* concept has meaningful implications on Christianity, on how God relates to the world, and on

---

24. Covington, "Mary Magdalene."

how we are to relate to one another.[25] Within an Asian community, there is a communal understanding of belonging and possession. I don't exist without the "we." It is also worthy to note how the Western individualism is extenuated by the capital I in the English language. There other common languages do not capitalize the I as the English language does.

These four Asian terms, *Chi, jeong, han*, and *ou-ri*, help us move towards a theology of Visibility which is strategic in overcoming some of the marginalization, and oppression that women face. Integrating these four aspects of theology of Visibility can help us move forward. This can be part of the strategy for challenging cultural and theological frameworks that hinder women as agents in their own lives and in the lives of their communities. A theology of Visibility reminds us how the community is important and it is the community which defines the individual. It reminds us that everyone has the Spirit of God within them. This makes a difference in how we interact and treat one another. The *jeong* brings us closer to one another and to God through a love which seems unbreakable. Also *han* reminds us that there are unjust systems which create enormous suffering. As Christians, we need to work towards dismantling systems which cause unjust suffering so that we can work towards building a kin-dom of God which embraces us all.

Conclusion

To gain liberation, women need to draw on liberative biblical texts which illustrate the equality of women and men. Jesus treats the Samaritan woman at the well as someone of importance and not as an outsider. When a woman came to anoint Jesus' feet, Jesus told everyone that people will remember the good act that she has done to Jesus. There are other liberative biblical passages which show how God wants to liberate women from cultural and religious restrictions. Women can overcome some of the common social, cultural, and organizational barriers by recognizing their own intersectional identity and by also finding their own agency. Women need to empower other women to achieve the flourishing of everyone in the community as women's liberation also means men's liberation. Women need to gain agency so that they can work towards liberation as this is all part of the mission of God which is to liberate the oppressed and the subjugated. God wants the marginalized to experience and gain liberation. This is the message of the gospel. The work continues till all women of every ethnicity and background will gain liberation from God. A theology of Visibility is one possible way to help the oppressed overcome and be liberated.

25. See Kim, *Invisible*, 139, for more discussion.

Bibliography

Armour, Ellen T., et al. "God." In *Constructive Theology*, edited by Serene Jones and Paul Lakeland, 18–76. Minneapolis: Fortress, 2005.

Beauvoir, Simone de. *The Second Sex*. Edited and translated by H. M. Parshley. New York: Vintage, 1989.

Biale, David. "The God with Breasts: El Shaddai in the Bible." *History of Religion* 21 (1982) 240–56.

Cheah, Joseph. "Asian Women's Mariology in Christological Context." *Marian Studies* 46 (1995) 71–88.

Cixous, Hélène. "Castration or Decapitation?" In *Out There: Marginalization and Contemporary Cultures*, edited by Russell Ferguson et al., 345–56. New York: New Museum of Contemporary Art, 1990.

Covington, Richard. "Mary Magdalene Was None of the Things a Pope Claimed." *U.S. News*, January 25, 2008. https://www.usnews.com/news/religion/articles/2008/01/25/mary-magdalene-was-none-of-the-things-a-pope-claimed.

Daly, Mary. *Beyond God the Father*. Boston: Beacon, 1985.

Gao, Xiongya. "Women Existing for Men: Confucianism and Social Injustice against Women in China." *Race, Gender, & Class* 10 (2003) 114–25.

Jones, Serene, and Paul Lakeland, eds. *Constructive Theology: A Contemporary Approach to Classical Themes*. Minneapolis: Fortress, 2005.

Kim, Grace Ji-Sun. *The Grace of Sophia*. Eugene, OR: Wipf & Stock, 2010.

———. *Invisible: Theology and Experience of Asian American Women*. Minneapolis: Fortress, 2021.

Min, Anselm. *The Solidarity of Other in a Divided World: A Postmodern Theology after Postmodernism*. New York: T. & T. Clark International, 2004.

Ray, Stephen G., et al. "Sin and Evil." In *Constructive Theology*, edited by Serene Jones and Paul Lakeland, 117–60. Minneapolis: Fortress, 2005.

Sauder, Laura. "Sexual Property and the Personhood of Women in the Old Testament, New Testament, and the Mishnah." *Consensus* 33 (2011) 1–7.

—7—

The Transformed and Transformative Voice of Hannah in 1 Samuel 1–2

Jacqueline N. Grey

Introduction

WHEN LISTING THE GREAT women of the Bible who were valiant and brave, the figure of Hannah is not usually one that comes immediately to mind. Hannah is often dismissed as a sweet mother, whose purpose was fulfilled through the birth and dedication of her son Samuel to the Lord's work. Yet, there is much more to the story of this unassuming woman in the biblical narrative. While Hannah is introduced in 1 Sam 1 as voiceless and barren, her situation is reversed following her prayer to God in the tabernacle. Not only does Hannah give birth to a son, but she emerges in 1 Sam 2 to voice a prophetic song that announces both personal vindication and justice for the community in response to the corruption of Eli's priestly family. Drawing on the methodology of narrative analysis, this chapter examines closely the transformation of Hannah's speech throughout 1 Sam 1–2. It will focus on how her speech reflects her agency as a person. It will particularly explore how her speech functions as an expression of her agency as she is transformed through the narrative from being voiceless to using her voice to speak truth to power. The chapter will conclude by exploring how this narrative can be utilized by contemporary women to understand and address power for the sake of engaging God's mission in and for their communities. It will discuss how Hannah is a model for the empowerment of women's voices today, and a model of dismantling of competitive environments that promote rivalry between women.

It is important from the outset to ensure a clear differentiation between the concepts of agency and power, as these terms are notoriously slippery and often confused. The notion of agency primarily refers to the degree of autonomy that an individual person possesses, particularly in contrast to the potential constraint of social structures and social expectations.[1] This includes the capacity of women to use their voice to speak up and be heard. While there is a dimension of agency in every action, the focus on agency in this paper is on the ability of a person to express and meet their self-defined needs and desires, regardless of possible social constraints.[2] Similarly, power is connected to social status and refers to the capacity for a person to influence and effect change in their social setting. The two concepts are connected as a person's agency (that is, their ability to act to meet their needs) may potentially increase their ability to influence those in their community.[3] For the character of Hannah, this self-defined need is connected to her desire for a child. Barrenness is a common theme in the biblical narrative including, most notably, Sarah and Rachel in the Genesis narratives. The culture of ancient Israel was based on honor-shame, where the value and honor of a woman was determined by her fruitfulness, therefore barrenness was shameful and considered a curse.[4] This would underscore Hannah's desperate desire for a child. The culture of ancient Israel was also collectivist, in comparison to the individualist society of the modern Western world. So, while the concept of agency is helpful in this analysis to highlight the actions of Hannah to meet her need for a child, it does have limitations if used anachronistically to stress independence. Instead, culturally relevant evidence of agency in the character of Hannah will be highlighted through her speech acts, such as initiating conversations, vowing, naming, and voicing her views. This agency demonstrated by Hannah is for the purpose of meeting her felt need of a child and to provide an environment of justice for her community to flourish.

---

1. Campbell, "Power of Agency," 408.
2. Deomampo, "Surrogacy in India," 168.
3. Spencer and Doull, "Concepts of Power and Agency," 904.
4. Esler, *Sex, Wives, and Warriors*, 117.

Power Dynamics in Hannah's Story

The story of Hannah occurs in the context of corporate worship. The narrative of 1 Sam 1 begins by introducing Elkanah, Hannah's husband, and listing his impressive pedigree and noble heritage (1:1). The description emphasizes his important status as the male patriarch of the family. We are told that Elkanah had two wives: Hannah, who was barren, and Peninnah, who had children (1:2). Although Hannah is listed here as the first wife, we will see later in the narrative when the portions of the sacrifice are divided that Hannah is lower than Peninnah in the family hierarchy due to her infertility. The narrator then describes how year after year, the family would travel to worship and offer sacrifices at Shiloh (1:3). These sacrifices were overseen by the two sons of Eli, Hophni and Phineas. Under the supervision of Eli's sons, Elkanah would provide the meat portions to his wives and children, though a double portion was given to Hannah.

This initial setting in 1 Sam 1:1–5 establishes the hierarchies of power that exist within its narrative world. The sacrificial ritual described in 1 Sam 1 demonstrates the power dynamics and hierarchical rank of the characters (1:3–5). At the top of the hierarchy, within this story world, is the cultic leader Eli and his sons. As de Andrado writes, "As hereditary priests (2:27–28), Eli and his sons hold a permanent elite status denied to nonpriests. The priests enjoy social prestige among worshipers and conduct key rites, while prospering economically from offerings such as bulls, wine, and flour brought by pilgrims like Hannah and Elkanah (1:24)."[5]

However, later in the narrative (1 Sam 2:12–17, 22–25) we discover that this elite priestly family was oppressive, corrupt, and evil. The wickedness of Eli's sons, Hophni and Phineas, included abusing the sacrificial offerings and sleeping with the women who served in the tabernacle, suggesting the existence of a type of temple prostitution (2:22). In addition, the servants of these priests were threatening violence to any male worshipper who voiced opposition to the abuse of the sacrificial offerings (2:16). Yet, despite their depravity, the elite priestly family of Eli maintained control of the sacrificial system and thereby held power within the community. Even Eli, sitting on the seat "beside the doorpost of the temple of YHWH" (1:9 ESV), controlled access to the sanctuary and consequently held a form of power over others in the community.[6]

Following the priests in the social hierarchy, Elkanah, as the head of the household, received the sacrificial portions from the priests to distribute

---

5. De Andrado, "Hannah's Agency," 274.
6. De Andrado, "Hannah's Agency," 274.

to his family (1:4–5). As a lay participant in the sacrificial system, Elkanah's position was between the priests and his family.⁷ This emphasizes the chief status of the older male and husband within the household. As Elkanah divided the meat among his family (1:4), the first recipient was his second wife, Peninnah. Although a second wife, or *ṣaratah*, which can also be translated as "rival" or "enemy," Peninnah follows Elkanah in the family hierarchy due to her fertility.⁸ She is then followed by her sons and daughters. Peninnah's place of honor in the family hierarchy results from her production of children and the important provision of a male heir. Finally, the infertile Hannah received a portion, albeit more generous than that given to the other family members. This order reinforces the inferior status of Hannah in the family. Despite being loved by Elkanah, the shamefulness of her barrenness positions her as the lowest member in the family hierarchy. To add to Hannah's distress, we are told that she was barren because the Lord had closed her womb (1:6).

Hannah's barrenness was used as a weapon of torment by her husband's other more fertile wife. The narrative describes the situation that "her rival [*ṣaratah*] kept provoking her in order to irritate her. This went on year after year" (1:6–7 NIV). As Lilian Klein observes, the annual distribution of the portions both reinforces Hannah's shameful barrenness and emphasizes Elkanah's favoring of Hannah. The ordering of the narrative suggests that the preference for the infertile Hannah demonstrated by the elite male in his distribution of the portions incites the jealousy of Peninnah. Her tormenting of Hannah is only introduced *after* the distribution of the portions. Kleins notes that Elkanah's actions aggravate the tension between his wives, as one desires to bear his children and the other desires his love.⁹ The taunting seems to only occur at the public setting of the pilgrimage, suggesting this provocation by Peninnah may not occur in the privacy of their home but does occur at the public location of Shiloh in response to the favoritism shown Hannah in the distribution of the sacrificial portions (1:7). As Esler notes, Peninnah's taunting was probably similar to the response of Hagar when she learnt she was pregnant. It not only shifted the power dynamics between the two wives, but Hagar now "looked with contempt upon her mistress" (Gen 16:4 ESV).¹⁰ This taunting by her rival caused great grief to Hannah, which was expressed by her weeping and refusing to eat, resulting

---

7. De Andrado, "Hannah's Agency," 275.
8. Klein, *Deborah to Esther*, 44.
9. Klein, *Deborah to Esther*, 46.
10. Esler, *Sex, Wives, and Warriors*, 128.

in her voicelessness. Hannah's diminished agency is emphasized by her inability to voice her desire or to meet her need for a child.

Hannah's Voicelessness (1 Sam 1:1–8)

Throughout 1 Sam 1:1–8, prior to her seeking solace in the sanctuary, Hannah was silent. The pilgrimage experience at Shiloh was marked by torment from her rival. While Elkanah asked her questions, she did not respond. She was voiceless. Hannah's silent response to the tormenting underscores her social shame resulting from her barrenness and her powerlessness in this family dynamic.

Voicelessness before Peninnah

First, Hannah is publicly shamed by Peninnah at Shiloh (1:6). The narrative describes how Peninnah provoked Hannah bitterly in order to "irritate her"(NIV), and that Peninnah's provocation distressed Hannah. This uncommon term (*harimah*) not only means to irritate but also means to humble, humiliate, and oppress. Peninnah's public activity of highlighting Hannah's barrenness would have caused great shame and embarrassment to Hannah. This shaming was not just a one-off event, but an annual torment.

Hannah responded to such provocation with ceaseless weeping and ceasing to eat (1:7). She internalized her pain.[11] Yet, despite her weeping, Hannah remained silent. Any verbal reaction or response to Peninnah was not recorded, and seemingly unwanted in the narrative. Her thoughts were unknown and unspoken, expressed only through her tears and her abstaining from food. Hannah was not fasting for religious purposes, suggesting a type of depression rather than devotion. However, it is important to note that although Peninnah is presented as the antagonist in this account, both women are voiceless in the narrative. While Peninnah's tormenting of Hannah is described, she did not speak directly in the text, unlike Elkanah whose voice was privileged by being quoted directly in the next verse. In this patriarchal system, both women were voiceless.

Voicelessness before Elkanah

Second, the narrative records Elkanah's conversation with Hannah (1:8). Elkanah initiated the exchange by asking Hannah four questions. His speech

---

11. Klein, *Deborah to Esther*, 48.

was quoted directly, emphasizing his prestige in comparison to the lower-status women who were not quoted. He first asked Hannah why she wept. He did not wait for an answer as he launched into the next question, asking her why she did not eat, and why her heart was sad. He was either oblivious to Hannah's public shaming by his second wife, or he was insensitively goading Hannah to recover quickly from her ongoing mortification. Yet, each time Elkannah asked a question he did not allow Hannah to speak. Finally, under the guise of affection, he blamed Hannah for her distress as unjustified, and diminished her suffering: "Am I not more to you than ten sons?" (1:8 ESV).[12] Elkanah clearly understood that it was the shame of barrenness that was causing her such grief, yet he trivialized her suffering. Hannah's response to Elkanah's four questions is unrecorded and unknown. She remained voiceless.

Voicelessness before Eli

Third, as the narrative continues, after "they" had eaten the sacrificial meal at Shiloh, Hannah "rose" (1:9). That is, feisty Hannah moved to "take her stand" before Yahweh.[13] Hannah took the initiative to go to the tabernacle alone to confront God in private. She left behind her husband and her tormentor to seek answers from Yahweh in the tabernacle.[14] Yet, sitting by the entrance of the tabernacle was Eli the priest. Despite his role as gatekeeper, Eli ignored Hannah and did not speak to this woman worshiper, though he was scrutinizing her activity (1:12). Hannah, in her distress, poured out her heart to the Lord in prayer and wept bitterly (1:10). As it was God who had closed her womb (1:5–6), it was God to whom Hannah turned to remedy her situation. However, it is at this point in the narrative, in the place of worship that Hannah's voice is now heard for the first time as she verbally prays to the Lord. Her words were recorded for the first time as she makes a vow to God (1:10–11).

The Transformed Voice of Hannah

It is in the context of worship that Hannah is empowered to speak. A transformation occurs as Hannah's voice is heard. Interestingly, Hannah's speech was initially directed to God and heard by God. The narrative

---

12. Klein, *Deborah to Esther*, 50–51.
13. Auld, *I & II Samuel*, 29.
14. De Andrado, "Hannah's Agency," 280.

records her direct speech as she appeals to Yahweh to see her suffering and to reverse her situation. Hannah looked to Yahweh to turn her barrenness into fruitfulness and reverse her shame. As the narrative unfolds, it is this tabernacle experience that functions as a turning point as her voice is transformed. Hannah then speaks. Following her vow to God, her voice is heard addressing Eli, naming Samuel, instructing Elkanah, and dedicating Samuel.

Voicing Her Vow

The first words recorded as voiced by Hannah were a vow to the Lord in the sanctuary (1:11), albeit words whispered (1:13). Addressing God as the "Lord of Hosts," Hannah's soft but direct speech appealed to God to see her misery and "remember" her. Her words follow the same general pattern as a standard complaint prayer.[15] Hannah then boldly presented her request and articulated her need for God to provide her with a male child. This demonstrates an increase in agency. Hannah vowed that if the Lord would give her a son, she would dedicate him back to the Lord as a Nazarite (1:11). Despite desiring a male child, she would relinquish the child to the Lord.[16]

Three times Hannah referred to herself as an *'ama* "servant" or "handmaid'" of the Lord (1:11, 16). As Robin Branch observes, this self-descriptive term is significant in the narrative of Samuel and is used by influential people. Branch writes, "Throughout Samuel, subservient-sounding terms like 'servant' and 'maidservant' are loosely spoken by confident and powerful men and women when they seek to exert their influence."[17] In addition, the only other person reported to have prayed in the tabernacle in the book of Samuel is David (2 Sam 7:18–29), who is also connected to Hannah through the function of their prophetic speech providing book-ends to the overall narrative of 1–2 Samuel. Through the record of her prayer, Hannah is associated with this prophetic and powerful king. These associations point to the emerging voice and authority with which Hannah will speak to defend herself, and to her prophetic protest of the corruption of the house of Eli. However, at this point, while Hannah's agency is increased through her articulation of her needs in prayer, her words were heard only by her and Yahweh.

---

15. Brueggemann, *First and Second Samuel*, 13.
16. Klein, *Deborah to Esther*, 54.
17. Branch, *Jeroboam's Wife*, 72.

Responding to Eli

Because of her whispered prayer, Eli falsely accused Hannah of drunkenness (1:14). She had been praying silently. She spoke but was not heard by any person except God. As Jacqueline Lapsley writes,

> Hannah is literally whispering, and she represents all the other biblical women who, under constraints of various types, must whisper what they have to say. Attending carefully to women's speech means straining to hear those whispers, with an ear to the possibility that the whispers of women also bear a commingled whispering of the divine Word.[18]

Eli, the most elite and powerful male in this context, had seen her murmuring and assumed she was intoxicated. It is somewhat ironic that Hannah had just vowed that her unborn son would not drink wine when she was accused of drunkenness. Eli's speech was quoted directly as he wrongly accused her of intoxication (1:13–14). His speech was accusatory and dismissive. Interestingly, it is at this point, after Hannah had made her vow to God in the tabernacle and spoken of her needs to God, that she spoke up to defend herself and to articulate her needs to an elite male priest. Hannah refuted Eli by explaining that the only pouring out had been her "soul," and not wine (1:15).[19] She continued to voice her innocence: "do not take your 'ama ("servant") for a wicked woman" (1:16 NIV)—that is, for a temple prostitute associated with Eli's sons. It seems that Hannah's silent speech to Yahweh had emboldened her to use her voice to defend her innocence in response to the false accusation of Yahweh's priest.

Once Hannah had voiced her defense from the false accusations and associations, she was blessed by Eli. Preparing for her departure from the tabernacle, Hannah then responded to him by referring to herself as his "servant" (1:18), this time using the term *šiphah* ("servant") which suggests a lower social status. So, following her spirited self-defense she adopted a self-deprecating and socially inferior term for herself. This suggests an awareness as she was leaving the sacred space of the tabernacle of a return to her lowly social position. Interestingly, commentators such as Brueggemann and Evans emphasize the blessing (or benediction) of Eli as functioning as resolving Hannah's complaint. For example, Brueggemann writes, "The narrative conclusion indicates that the priestly assurance marks the decisive turn in the story. Hannah believes Eli."[20] He continues, "She is a new,

---

18. Lapsley, *Whispering the Word*, 21.
19. Auld, *I & II Samuel*, 31.
20. Brueggemann, *First and Second Samuel*, 13.

restored woman with a new chance in life, caused by a word of assurance authoritatively spoken. She believed the word!"[21] Mary Evans writes, "There is no evidence in the OT that the prayers of religious professionals are to be seen as more effective than those of any sincere believer. Nevertheless, it is possible that Hannah believed that Eli had exceptional powers. It is also possible that the peace she felt was a result of having expressed herself to God."[22] While the priestly blessing was certainly received by Hannah, her rejection of Eli's incorrect interpretation of her situation and use of the socially inferior šiphah ("servant") suggest that it was not his blessing that resolved her petition, although it may have contributed, but arguably her own pouring out of her soul to the Lord which she had confidently described to Eli that was decisive in her alteration. So, in the narrative, Hannah is progressively vocal and demonstrates increased boldness in speech, albeit using the language of obeisance expected for a woman speaking with a high-status male and reflective of her social status. There is an observable increase in her agency following her prayer to God. Hannah returned from the tabernacle back to her family quarters, now transformed. She ate, drank, and was no longer sad (1:18).

Naming Her Son

As the narrative continues, Hannah and family return to Ramah. The Lord "remembered" Hannah, as she petitioned in 1:11, and her barrenness was reversed as she gave birth to a son (1:19–20). Her faith-filled speech had transformed her situation. The text is very clear that it is Hannah (and not her husband) who named their son, Samuel (1:20). After all, it was Hannah who had "asked him of Yahweh," therefore she had the privilege of naming her son.[23] The emphasis is on what Hannah had said, that is, the vow she had made. Because she asked, she received from God and named her son.

---

21. Brueggemann, *First and Second Samuel*, 14.
22. Evans, *1 & 2 Samuel*, 17.
23. It is noted that Hannah's explanation for the naming of Samuel is somewhat controversial because the name "Samuel" does not align with the etymology of "to ask" (*sh'l*), but that name of "Saul" does align to the etymology. However, the argument in this chapter is that Hannah has the privilege of naming him because she asked, not that the name of Samuel derives etymologically from the verb "to ask." For further discussion on this, see Arnold, *1 and 2 Samuel*, 74.

Instructing Elkanah

After the promised son is born, Hannah refuses to join Elkanah and the household in their annual pilgrimage to Shiloh (1:21–22). She announced to Elkanah that she would not attend until the child was weaned, and only then would she bring the child to the Lord's presence and leave him there forever (1:22), according to her vow. Again, the emphasis on the Lord's presence as a euphemism for the tabernacle may suggest the importance of her own spiritual experience there. It is also significant to note that Hannah sent off her husband with her rival without hesitation, clearly as Klein observes, holding no jealousy of Peninnah.[24] Hannah's speech is transformed. It was Hannah who initiated the conversation with Elkanah, Hannah who set the agenda, and Hannah who instructed him as to her plans to which he acquiesced (1:22).[25] She was as attentive to her vows as Elkanah is to his own (1:21). She said to Elkanah: "I will offer him as a nazirite for all time" (1:22 NRSVA). The response of Elkanah to Hannah's speech was acceptance of her vow and support of her actions (1:23). Although according to Num 30:6–8, Hannah's husband could have nullified her vow, he did not. Hannah was transformed; no longer the barren and shamed woman, but confident and determined, as acknowledged by Elkanah in his reply. De Andrado writes, "The correlation between Hannah's agency and her articulateness is noteworthy. Increasingly, as she makes decisions and engages in activity, Hannah exhibits verbal skill in conveying her thoughts, persuading others, and explaining herself without being silenced by the male hierarchy."[26]

Once the child was weaned, Hannah took "her son" to Shiloh along with her own provisions for sacrifice.[27] The narrative is specific that it was Hannah who brought the boy to the house of the Lord. As Mary Evans writes, "Hannah took the lead in these ceremonies. Elkanah may have been included and was not opposed to the action she took, but it was her vow and the initiative in fulfilling it was hers."[28] Once at Shiloh, "they" brought the boy to Eli (1:24) to be dedicated to the Lord's service.

---

24. Klein, *Deborah to Esther*, 51.
25. Klein, *Deborah to Esther*, 51.
26. De Andrado, "Hannah's Agency," 283.
27. Klein, *Deborah to Esther*, 52.
28. Evans, *1 & 2 Samuel*, 17.

Dedicating Samuel

At Samuel's dedication, Hannah's direct speech was recorded once more, highlighting her increased agency and transformation from voiceless to vocal. Like her exchange with Elkanah noted above (1:22), Hannah initiated the exchange with Eli and confidently spoke to him. She articulately explained her need to dedicate the boy to the Lord's work. However, also reflective of her encounter with Eli in the tabernacle (1:18), Hannah adopted again the language of obeisance to address the high-status male priest (1:26–28). Hannah reminded Eli that "I am the woman" who had stood, praying to Yahweh, in his presence. She was the one who had taken her stand (1:9, 26), asking God for "this" boy who she was now presenting (1:27). The boy was the outcome of God's answer to her prayer and remembrance of Hannah. In her lowly status, Hannah had prayed to Yahweh, who acted. God was the provider and miracle worker who transformed her situation from barrenness to fruitfulness. Hannah was giving back the gift of her son to the Giver. As Bill Arnold observes, "Having come to God with nothing, she now returns to Shiloh to give back that which means everything."[29] Hannah had now fulfilled her vow and dedicated Samuel for all his life. She left the boy at Shiloh for the Lord's purposes.

The Transformative Voice of Hannah

Yet, leaving Samuel at Shiloh in the care of Eli was problematic, as this was the same location that the sons of Eli were administering the sacrificial worship. As noted above, their practices were known to be immoral and evil (2:22–24). While Hannah's personal situation had been reversed, the tabernacle and sacrificial worship at Shiloh continued to be barren due to the corrupt practices of Eli's sons. Thus, Samuel would "be inserted into a corrupt cultic establishment."[30] Therefore, it was this situation that Hannah addressed through empowered and prophetic speech in 1 Sam 2:1–10. The narrative continued with the statement: "Then Hannah prayed and said" (2:1 NIV). What follows is an extraordinary poem, commonly referred to as a psalm of vindication and thanksgiving. The psalm is accredited to Hannah in the text by the narrator or redactor.

---

29. Arnold, *1 and 2 Samuel*, 76.
30. De Andrado, "Hannah's Agency," 272.

Hannah's Song?

The song of Hannah in 1 Sam 2:1–10 announced a new work by God to reverse the current order and power structures of the community. The poem is filled with images of reversals, including military language. The poem ends with a remarkable reference to Yahweh giving strength to the king and exalting the horn of his anointed. There is much focus by scholars on this last verse of the psalm as it functions in the broader narrative of Samuel as a prediction of the rise of David as king (albeit anointed by a horn, and not a flask). Therefore, whether this psalm should and could be attributed to Hannah has been the subject of much debate. According to Tikva Frymer-Kensky, "This psalm does not seem like a poem that Hannah would have composed for the occasion of her weaning of Samuel and presentation to the temple. Much in this psalm seems alien to her situation."[31] Similarly, Walter Brueggemann writes:

> Hannah sings a very special song with reference to a concrete miracle. In doing so, however, she joins her voice to a song Israel has already long been singing. . . . Thus Hannah sings no new song; she appropriates a song already known in Israel. The "Song of Hannah" thus is likely to have been taken from Israel's repertoire of public hymns.[32]

Brueggemann suggests that because of the references to enemies (2:1), war (2:4), and eventually a king (2:10), that the song had a public and national function as a royal psalm rather than reflecting a domestic setting.

Yet, other scholars are not so quick to divorce the text from Hannah's domestic situation. Mary Evans observes:

> It is often assumed that the writers put a later psalm into the mouth of Hannah because the song is separate from the rest of the text, it interrupts the narrative, and, although it mentions barrenness, it is seen as more appropriate to a discussion of kingship than to the birth of a child. The psalm does form an appropriate introduction to the national history, but its exuberant tone of praise together with the reflection on power are appropriate as an expression of Hannah's feelings.[33]

Therefore, a closer analysis of this poem is needed to determine if it does indeed connect directly with the situation of Hannah and can be

---

31. Frymer-Kensky, *Women of the Bible*, 308.
32. Brueggemann, *First and Second Samuel*, 16.
33. Evans, *1 & 2 Samuel*, 21.

seen as evidence of her increased agency and power to influence others in the community.

The poem opens with a celebration of a victory over enemies (2:1–5). While various scholars argue that this poem has nothing to do with Hannah's personal situation, clearly within these opening verses there is much that may indeed reflect Hannah's experience. Hannah had been taunted by her husband's other wife (described as her "rival"), oppressed and bullied because of her infertility. Over many years, her rival taunted her to the point of tears and depression. But the poem announces that this long-term cruelty and provocation by her enemy because of her infertility has been answered by the birth of a son. In addition, Hannah had been falsely accused of drunkenness and association with temple prostitution by Eli, the highest spiritual authority in the land, when she had been praying in the tabernacle precinct. That Hannah should gloat over those that humiliated her is not beyond the realm of possibility. To return to Shiloh, the location of this oppression, and to then be vindicated by God from false accusations would have likely given any such victim a sense of exultation. It is argued that this poem does indeed reflect Hannah's rejoicing in victory over barrenness and relief from the oppression of her rival. This victory had only been achieved by Yahweh—the one to whom Hannah had appealed for this miracle. It is possible then that the poem does reflect Hannah's personal joy in her relationship with Yahweh: "*my heart rejoices,*" "*my horn is lifted high,*" "*my mouth boasts,*" and "*I delight*" (2:1–2 NIV).[34] The narrative is clear that her infertility was reversed by the One to whom Hannah had prayed and made her vow: Yahweh, her rock.

As the poem continues, the injunction to talk not proudly and arrogantly (2:3)—a feature of Hannah's rival in the narrative—could quite easily refer to the domestic politics of the house of Elkanah.[35] While Hannah had submitted to the verbal insults of her rival because of her powerlessness and lowly status in the household evidenced by the distribution of the sacrificial portions (1:4–5), she was emboldened in the Song by her changed status to no longer accept the bullying. While Hannah may not have sought revenge on Peninnah for her tormenting,[36] she sought and announced vindication in the Song. The reversal of Hannah's personal situation of infertility was also explicitly addressed in the poem: "She who was barren has borne seven children, but she who has had many sons pines away" (2:5 NIV). It is reported that Hannah later had five more children (2:21). The symbolism of

---

34. Arnold, *1 and 2 Samuel*, 92.
35. Esler, *Sex, Wives, and Warriors*, 133.
36. Klein, *Deborah to Esther*, 46.

the use of seven in this poem points to her sense of completion and wholeness. The barren, traumatized woman is made whole. The agent of this transformation is Yahweh.

That Hannah would use stereotypical language throughout the poem to express her feelings, such as the symbol of military victory (2:1, 4), is not impossible. The use of military language is used all throughout the psalms and the worship of Israel, so it would likely be language familiar to her. The psalms often use stereotypical language which arguably could be mimicked by those who valued the worship of Yahweh, such as Hannah and her husband. In fact, as noted above, this song attributed to Hannah was set in the context of corporate worship (1:28—2:1). Neither would it be considered unfeminine for a woman to sing a song of military victory, after all this was the domain of women singers. In 1 Sam 18:6–7, the tradition of women performing victory songs is referred to as already established (albeit in the context of actual warfare). Deborah and Miriam also sing songs of victory using military themes, emphasizing Yahweh as the victor. So, it is arguably conceivable for Hannah to utilize this tradition of women singing military victory songs to refer to her domestic situation. After all, if a male prophet can use the language of pregnancy to express his situation (Isa 26:17–18; 42:14), why cannot a female use the language of warfare to express her situation? To refer to how the bows of the mighty are broken (2:4), may refer to the weapon of her rival's taunt—Hannah's infertility—that had been shattered. All this suggests that it may not have just been a generic poem but that this Song reflected the personal situation of Hannah.

Yet, this song not only addressed the domestic situation of Hannah's household, it also addressed the national situation of the corruption of worship at Shiloh. Through this song, Hannah condemned the oppressive practices of the sons of Eli. As de Andrado observes, "Hannah plays a dynamic role in challenging the priesthood (as represented by Eli)."[37] She was the first to speak up against such corruption and oppression. Hannah spoke prophetically of their overthrow from power, which was soon fulfilled in 1 Samuel 4.

Singing Truth to Power

Hannah's song then continues the theme of reversal by addressing the national situation of corrupt worship. She sang that "Those who were full hire themselves out for food, but those who were hungry are hungry no more" (2:5 NIV). This arguably addressed her experience at Shiloh. As noted

---

37. De Andrado, "Hannah's Agency," 272.

above, the opening setting of Hannah's story occurs at Shiloh where the sons of Eli were priests and would oversee the sacrificial offerings. In 1:4–5, at the time of sacrifice, Elkanah would give meat portions to his family as part of their faithful worship. As the narrative continued in 2:12–17 the narrator elaborated on the wickedness of Eli's sons with a descriptive report, highlighting their "ruthless, cynical use of priestly power."[38] The narrator described at length how Eli's sons had been abusing the sacrificial offerings and taking meat portions for themselves. Eli's sons had been forcibly taking the choicest meat portions and treating the worship practices with contempt. The narrative in 2:14 revealed that "This is how they treated *all* the Israelites who came to Shiloh" (NIV). This arguably would have included Hannah, Elkanah, and Hannah's rival. Hannah's song is sandwiched (pun intended) between the description of Elkanah providing the meat portions for his family (1:3–5) and the description of the Eli's sons corrupting those meat sacrifices for their own personal gain (2:12–17). The text suggests the practice had been going on for some time, so most certainly these sons were officiating during the time of Hannah's earlier visits in chapter 1. So, if Elkanah distributed a double portion of meat offering to Hannah, and the sons of Eli had been grasping those portions, then Hannah and her family could well have experienced first-hand the corrupt practices of Eli's sons.

Therefore, in Hannah's song, when she denounced those who are "full" of bread (2:5), and those who are wealthy and exalted (2:7) she may well have had Eli's sons in mind. In fact, these words in the denunciation by Hannah in 2:5 were mirrored in the next section by the words of the "man of God" that came to Eli with a message of judgment. He predicted the fall of the House of Eli and a new priestly order whereby "everyone left in your family line will come and bow down before him for a piece of silver and a loaf of bread and plead, 'Appoint me to some priestly office so I can have food to eat'" (2:36 NIV). Hannah's poem continues in verse 6–9 to emphasize the revolutionary and social transformative work of Yahweh. Yahweh (in 2:9) will take care of his faithful ones, but the wicked will be cut off. This was also the message in 2:27–36 that the unnamed "man of God" delivered to the House of Eli and the message that Samuel, Hannah's son, delivered in chapter 3.

From this analysis we can see that Hannah's song highlights her transformation from voiceless to now speaking on behalf of the community to confront injustice. Hannah is transformed throughout this narrative from powerless to powerful. Yet, it is not just personal. The function of this poem in the broader narrative of the Samuel narrative is to bring change and

---

38. Brueggemann, *First and Second Samuel*, 22.

transformation to the community. Hannah announced that the current corrupt leadership of the tabernacle would be reversed. Hannah's song then was programmatic for the new, transformative work of Yahweh that would result in renewal and restoration.[39]

Conclusion: The Significance of Hannah's Story for Contemporary Women

With Hannah's story in mind, it is important to consider some implications this narrative might have regarding notions of agency and power for women in our contemporary world. How can women today draw on this passage to understand and address power for the sake of engaging God's mission in and for their communities? There are many issues this study on Hannah's narrative could inspire, however this concluding reflection will focus briefly on two implications: exploring how Hannah's story can first empower women's voices, and secondly dismantle competitive environments that promote rivalry between women.

Empowered to Speak

The narrative of Hannah encourages women to speak up. It encourages women today that their voice is valuable and can bring positive change. Hannah's voice was the first in her community to speak out against the injustices perpetrated by Eli's sons. Aimee Byrd refers to the book of Ruth as a "gynocentric interruption in Scripture."[40] Similarly, Hannah's song also functions as a gynocentric interruption to the status quo of the corrupt leadership of Eli's house. Her voice disrupted the power balance as she announced God's justice and future judgment. Her bold speech initiated the collapse of the oppressive leadership of Eli's sons and led to the restoration of proper worship of God for the benefit of the community.

Yet, how did Hannah find her voice? Interestingly, it is when Hannah sought solace in prayer in the tabernacle that she found her voice. In the narrative, she spoke for the first time in the tabernacle while praying to God. It was through the activity of speaking to God that Hannah found her voice and ability to articulate her own needs and thereby began the process of advocating for herself and others. Voicing her complaint to God empowered

---

39. The connection to Mary's Song in Luke 2:46–55 is noted beyond the scope of this discussion.

40. Byrd, *Biblical Manhood & Womanhood*, 49.

her to voice complaint against the false accusations and injustices in her community. This suggests a possible connection between prayer and the empowerment of women's voices. The sense of being seen by God, our surety in God's power to act on our behalf and on behalf of our community, and our subsequent actions in response to this revelation, can all be important sources of confidence for women as they seek to participate in God's work. As Robyn Wilkerson encourages, "As you focus on God's purpose for your life, you'll gain the traction to stay on mission."[41]

Hannah's story can inspire women to also be empowered to speak up to address issues of power. Their voice can be, like Hannah's, an unexpected and prophetic "gynocentric interruption" protesting issues of corruption and oppression in communities today. Hannah models how God can use women to speak powerfully and boldly to initiate change and to be harbingers of justice. It also encourages women to advocate for themselves. Like Hannah, women today can speak up to defend their dignity and reputation against false accusations and the diminishing of their gifted speech. This is particularly problematic in many contemporary cultures when women speak authoritatively. To speak powerfully is seen as unwomanly. It can result in criticism and a diminishing of a woman's confidence. Carolyn Moore refers to this as the "double bind" for women leaders. She writes, "If a woman acts like a leader—if she is assertive or aggressive in her style—she will not be as well-liked as her male colleagues. Yet if a woman leader behaves in more feminine ways—if she uses a softer tone of voice, demonstrates more feminine behavior, is less aggressive in meetings—she is less likely to be respected."[42] Like in Hannah's day, women leaders and influencers today are still sometimes marginalized, challenged, and misunderstood. Yet, notice how Hannah creatively used poetry and song to powerfully communicate her message. Criticism of our voice may require women to nurture creativity and seek new ways to speak truth to power. It also requires the fostering of internal resources and confidence for women to have the courage to verbally advocate for themselves boldly and wisely. That is, to speak up, like Hannah, against personal injustice, as well as to speak against the communal injustices we perceive in our communities today. This includes, at times, unjust treatment by other women.

---

41. Wilkerson, *Shattering the Stained Glass Ceiling*, 52.
42. Moore, *When Women Lead*, 25.

Dismantling Female Rivalry

It is sometimes the case in patriarchal contexts that women are pitted against each other and set up as rivals. Hannah demonstrated resistance to competitiveness. While she sought vindication from God from her rival, she did not seek retaliation or revenge. This is an important distinction. While Hannah initially avoided conflict with Peninnah in the narrative and responded with weeping and internalization of her pain, she voiced her pain to God. While such passive response to competitive taunting may not be the ideal, it was an acknowledgement of the reality of feminine rivalry, particularly in relation to male attention or promotion. As Kadi Cole writes,

> In the interviews and survey, the topics of "girl hate," "catfights," "Queen Bee effect," and "women eat their young" all came up. Assuming women will be competitive and work against one another is not helpful and not necessary, especially in the kingdom. This is a bad cultural reputation that we need to reinvent. In fact, new research is indicating that these competitive behaviors are less about being female and more about being in an environment in which opportunities are scarce and highly competitive.[43]

Hannah models a more mature response to the situation of competitiveness after she was no longer operating from a place of shame. Once her shame was reversed, Hannah bravely sent her husband to Shiloh with Peninnah without jealousy. By acknowledging and diffusing the sense of competitiveness, Hannah sought vindication but not revenge. In doing so, the structures of competitiveness can be dismantled. To see this become a reality, Cole suggests women leaders today should encourage one another that there is "room for everyone and that you support all women in pursuing the calling God has on their lives."[44]

In conclusion, Hannah's story offers women today a model of finding their voice and using their influence to bring change to their communities. As Hannah voices her desire for a child to God, she sees the power of God to provide. Similarly, through the narrative of Scripture we see Hannah participating in God's purposes through her powerful prophetic speech to bring change and restoration to the nation. Hannah's transformation from voicelessness to prophetic speech can inspire women today to address issues of power for the sake of engaging God's mission in and for their communities.

---

43. Cole, *Developing Female Leaders*, 160–61.
44. Cole, *Developing Female Leaders*, 161.

Bibliography

Arnold, Bill T. *1 and 2 Samuel*. NIVAC. Grand Rapids: Zondervan, 2003.

Auld, A. Graeme. *I & II Samuel*. OTL. Louisville: Westminster John Knox, 2011.

Branch, Robin Gallaher. *Jeroboam's Wife: The Enduring Contributions of the Old Testament's Least-Known Women*. Grand Rapids: Baker Academic, 2009.

Brueggemann, Walter. *First and Second Samuel*. Interpretation. Louisville: Westminster John Knox, 2012.

Byrd, Aimee. *Recovering from Biblical Manhood & Womanhood: How the Church Needs to Rediscover Her Purpose*. Grand Rapids: Zondervan, 2020.

Campbell, Colin. "Distinguishing the Power of Agency from Agentic Power: A Note on Weber and the 'Black Box' of Personal Agency." *Sociological Theory* 27 (2009) 407–18.

Cole, Kadi. *Developing Female Leaders: Navigate the Minefields and Release the Potential of Women in Your Church*. Nashville: Nelson, 2019.

De Andrado, Paba Nidhani. "Hannah's Agency in Catalyzing Change in an Exclusive Hierarchy." *Journal of Biblical Literature* 140 (2021) 271–89.

Deomampo, Daisy. "Transnational Surrogacy in India: Interrogating Power and Women's Agency." *Frontiers* 34 (2013) 167–88.

Esler, Phillip F. *Sex, Wives, and Warriors: Reading the Old Testament Narrative with Its Ancient Audience*. Cambridge: Clarke, 2011.

Evans, Mary J. *1 & 2 Samuel*. Understanding the Bible Commentary. Grand Rapids: Baker, 2000.

Frymer-Kensky, Tikva. *Reading the Women of the Bible*. New York: Schocken, 2002.

Klein, Lilian R. *From Deborah to Esther: Sexual Politics in the Hebrew Bible*. Minneapolis: Fortress, 2003.

Lapsley, Jacqueline E. *Whispering the Word: Hearing Women's Stories in the Old Testament*. Louisville: Westminster John Knox, 2005.

Moore, Carolyn. *When Women Lead: Embrace Your Authority, Move beyond Barriers, and Find Joy in Leading Others*. Grand Rapids: Zondervan, 2022.

Spencer, Grace, and Marion Doull. "Examining Concepts of Power and Agency in Research with Young People." *Journal of Youth Studies* 18 (2015) 900–913.

Wilkerson, Robyn. *Shattering the Stained Glass Ceiling: A Coaching Strategy for Women Leaders in Ministry*. Springfield: Influence Resources, 2017.

Conversation 3

Addressing #MeToo, #ChurchToo

— 8 —

"This Won't Be Our Undoing"
Sexual Violence, the Spirit, and the Work of the Church

Dara Coleby Delgado

Introduction

WHILE SCROLLING ON INSTAGRAM one evening, I saw a video by famed Contemporary Gospel artist Fred Hammond. Hammond, known for such hits as "Spirit of David," "We're Blessed," and "No Weapon," was addressing his challenges with depression. After viewing that video—now removed—another caught my attention. The second video featured a beautiful young woman, impeccably dressed in a blue suit complemented by a high-collared black and white polka dot blouse. Even at first glance, it was clear that Hammond, appearing in the upper left-hand corner, was not the focus. After scanning the caption, I learned that the woman was his daughter, BreeAnn Hammond.

Originally posted on February 12, 2023, the video tagged BreeAnn and included the following:

> Love you my darling always. #family in times like these I don't feel #Saved #Christian enough to say the politically correct thing, so it's best that I don't have a lot to say. But one thing I

will say, is we believe #God will help us. [praying hands emoji] @breeannhammond.[1]

While his page features the shorter version, her Instagram contains the original longer post. In both, BreeAnn discloses having been raped and sexually assaulted "more than once"—a point she makes repeatedly and emphasizes in the video with dramatic pauses. In the transcription of the extended version of the Instagram video, she says:

> I know this is supposed to be one of the happiest times of my life. Unfortunately, it isn't. I have been raped more than once, and sexually assaulted more than once.
>
> Each one of those times I took on the mental load myself. Back and forth to the doctor for Prozac, and Trazodone to sleep at night. I'm done taking the mental load myself.
>
> So, as best I know how, I'm trying to fight for myself . . . advocate for myself. I'm putting together a legal team. Attorneys, you must be licensed in Maryland, and I need you to have the time and energy to adequately represent me.
>
> If you're reading this, please spread the news. Please get the word out there . . . because . . .
>
> *[while fighting tears and as her voice cracks, BreeAnn sings]*
>   I'm no longer a slave to fear
>   I am a child of God
>   I'm no longer a slave to fear
>   I am a child of God
>   I am a child of God
>   I am someone's child
>   I am the wise God's child
>   I am a child of God.[2]

BreeAnn does not name the accused or associate her assailant(s) with the church. But BreeAnn is the daughter of a well-known Gospel artist identified with the Black charismatic-pentecostal tradition. Moreover, BreeAnn is an up-and-coming Gospel artist in her own right, even starring on a

---

    1. Fred Hammond (@realfredh), Instagram video, February 12, 2023, https://www.instagram.com/reel/ColwaiEvjgD/.

    2. BreeAnn Hammond (@breeannhammond), Instagram video, February 11, 2023, https://www.instagram.com/p/CoheQVwOhG2/.

reality television show entitled *Grown & Gospel*.³ In short, this is not merely a legal matter, as intimated by her post, which was purposed to solicit legal representation. It is also a church matter. Neither BreeAnn nor her father identifies it as such, and they do not construe her story as intertwined with the church broadly or the Black church narrowly. This is especially true of BreeAnn, who availed herself of the hashtag "me too" but not "church too." The omission of the latter is curious, given her affiliation with Christianity and pedigree in the Gospel music industry.

"Church Too," which emerged in 2017 when Emily Joy Allison shared her story of sexual abuse,⁴ is a derivative of the more prominent #metoo movement. As a result, #churchtoo's aim resembles that of #metoo, which is to provide survivors and their advocates with an affirming space to call out sexual predators and their allies for abuses in the church—across denominations and parachurch ministries—and demand accountability and reform. In many ways, disclosing what was already in plain sight but long ignored, #churchtoo is a clarion call to society writ large about the ubiquity of such abuses and the lengths churches will go to hide them.

Albeit pan-denominational—including churches that self-identify as nondenominational—the focus of the #churchtoo movement seemingly attends primarily to allegations reported about leaders in predominantly White Baptist congregations. The reason behind the attention to predominantly White Baptist churches, however, cannot be reduced to size. In short, arguments pertaining to size fail to acknowledge that while Baptists account for 15.4% of the adult US population, there are upwards of ten million self-identified Pentecostals and Charismatics in the United States.⁵ Although in matters of abuse and violence, there is no place for the proverbial oppression olympics, the underreporting of cases of sexual assault by pentecostal-charismatic women is noteworthy and alarming.

Despite her father's religious history, BreeAnn's denominational affiliation is unclear. However, because she identifies religiously as Christian,⁶

---

3. The show aired March 2023 on WeTV. WeTV very ambiguously describes *Grown & Gospel* as featuring "an energetic group of childhood friends navigate the ever-changing gospel World in the shadow of their celebrity parents. Dark secrets are revealed as they face the ups and downs of their friendships and personal relationships." WeTV, "*Grown & Gospel* Season 1 Trailer!"

4. See Allison, *#ChurchToo*; Joy, "#ChurchToo."

5. Delgado, "What Did Trump Know?"

6. In an Instagram video posted on March 22, 2023, BreeAnn named Forward City Church, a predominantly Black nondenominational charismatic church pastored by contemporary Gospel artist Travis Greene as her home church. BreeAnn Hammond (@breeannhammond), "Hearing my pastors @travisgreenetv and @drjackiegreene and 4wardcitychurch remind me . . . ," Instagram video, March 22, 2023, https://www.instagram.com/reel/CqGtevYjDmJ/.

and assuming that one or more of her abusers also has a connection to the church (even if only tangentially), I cannot help but wonder why she did not use the "church too" hashtag. Was it because she was unaware of the #churchtoo movement? Or was it because she had not found the #churchtoo movement particularly helpful? Truthfully, neither is a good option. The first speaks of the limitations of the movement's reach, especially among Black and Brown women. The second brings to the fore matters related to its overall effectiveness, e.g., resources, commitment, accessibility, representation, and cultural competencies. As a Black-identified woman, who is at least pentecostal-charismatic adjacent, BreeAnn Hammond exemplifies women in the US who sit in the cross-sections of gender violence, sexual abuse, and the church's complicity and/or impotence.

Whether #metoo, #churchtoo, or #pentecostalsisterstoo,[7] I contend that a religio-racial and cultural discussion, from a pneumatological perspective, provides a more generative response to our society's current moment. By turning my attention to Christianity in the US exclusively, I argue that a pneumatological exploration of personhood and self-actualization, as it pertains to sexual violence, provides practical and meaningful ways for the church to support survivors. Such an exploration can run counter to and even resist a culture of dissemblance that spurns disclosing the reality of these abuses within the church. Ultimately, I affirm the liberation and survival of survivors and their place in God's life-giving, life-changing, and life-sustaining pneuma. I conclude by admonishing the church towards (1) reminding survivors of the open invitation to participate in the divine life (imago Dei), (2) maintaining meaningful pathways to full personhood and self-actualization unobstructed (other-regard), and valuing the art of sitting in the ashes with survivors (radical sociality).

Theoretical Context: Pneumatology as *imago Dei*, Other-Regard, and Radical Sociality

Within the broader Christian tradition, a robust pneumatology must be subject to the doctrine of the Trinity. Despite its gradual development during

---

7. In 2018, Pentecostal scholars from various academic disciplines across denominational lines and affiliated with the Society of Pentecostal Studies (SPS) convened to initiate a robust response and thus begin the work many Pentecostal leaders failed to do. The result included a new hashtag (#pentecostalsisterstoo), gathering resources, publishing a special issue of Pneuma—the official organ of SPS—and planning a future annual meeting with the corresponding theme and papers addressing the issue. Nevertheless, #pentecostalsisterstoo remains a lesser-known subset of the larger #metoo and subsidiary #churchtoo movements in the United States.

the church's earliest years, the doctrine of the Trinity, which emerged with the Nicene Creed, was clarified at the first council at Constantinople. From these lengthy deliberations, the church concluded, "The Father, the Son, and the Holy Spirit have a single Godhead and power and substance, a dignity deserving the same honor and co-equal sovereignty, in three most perfect hypostases or three persons."[8] Even as the tradition has conceded that the Trinity is a sacred mystery—and one beyond total human comprehension—orthodox Christianity remains steadfast in its conviction that the doctrine of the Trinity is the most central of Christian claims and thus foundational to all Christian truth.[9]

As part of a larger doctrinal constellation on the nature of God, pneumatology does not stand alone as a theological category. Instead, as an extension of the doctrine of the Trinity—"the secondary support for christological and pneumatological claims"[10]—it is part and parcel of an interconnected theological system. In other words, by maintaining that the activity and power of the Holy Spirit are distinct from, but also related to, that of the Father and the Son, the Christian doctrine of the Spirit upholds broader yet equally essential claims about the perichoretic nature of the triune God. Because the three persons of the Godhead coinhere (*homoousion*—whatever the Father is, so too are the Spirit and the Son), they share in the divine activity. That point about a shared divine activity is essential to this essay because it establishes that the Holy Spirit, the Father, and the Son are the Lord and Giver of Life—a life that is constitutive of the *imago Dei*.

The privilege of humanity is an open invitation to participate in the divine life of God. This should not be misconstrued merely as an otherworldly reality. Instead, and more accurately, it is best-understood[11] as grounded—critically identified with and committed to all things pertaining to *terra firma*, and thus perceptible through materiality. Therefore, when faith is rightly construed as a conduit between the Divine and us and the thing that unites persons of shared religious identity, it reflects a communal self-understanding of the *imago Dei*. Specifically, a communal self-understanding that prioritizes the dignity of all persons and emphasizes the essentiality of mutual responsibility and other-regard. Said differently, to claim the image and likeness of God for oneself and others is to honor and actively facilitate

---

8. As quoted in Doyle, *What Is Christianity?*, 117.

9. Congar, *Holy Spirit*, 74–75. For more of a historical rendering, see Wilken, *First Thousand Years*; Gonzalez, *Early Church*.

10. Doyle, *What Is Christianity?*, 118.

11. For more on the interlocking relationship between the Spirit and the human spirit pertaining to materiality defined by creation/created order (the Earth), see Baker-Fletcher, *Sisters of the Dust*; Baker-Fletcher, "Breath of God."

the full (uninhibited) pursuit of realized personhood. Albeit parenthetical here, uninhibited is the operative word because it upholds the full pursuit of realized personhood and undergirds the human right to be a free and self-determining agent. Overall, the idea presumes a mutuality wherein no community member actively prevents or participates in actions that prevent another's self-actualization. In this essay, full personhood and self-actualization wholly depend on Spirit. Therefore, I affirm and treat Spirit as a life-giving agent of "otherwise possibilities."[12]

In his acclaimed book, *Blackpentecostal Breath: The Aesthetics of Possibilities*, Ashon Crawley considers the aesthetic practices of blackpentecostalism[13]—whooping, shouting, and glossolalia—as choreographic, sonic, and visual means of articulating otherwise possibilities. In other words, other worlds of being for Black bodies living in a cultural and sociopolitical context they were never meant to survive. Such otherwise possibilities led Crawley to consider and offer a revised construal of blackpentecostalism that is not institutionally static but rather religio-racially and socially fluid. For Crawley, this means that historically and predominantly Black Pentecostal organizations like the Church of God in Christ and the Pentecostal Assemblies of the World cannot claim exclusive rights to the aesthetics of blackpentecostalism. Instead, blackpentecostalism, as both an analytical lens and a lived experience, is a religio-racial and social response to the suffering, survival, and humiliation of Black persons in the US and abroad. Furthermore, blackpentecostalism, broadly construed, is not merely an extension of Black (Liberation) Theology. It is an articulation of Black difference via Black diversity, which does so by exchanging suffering and striving for flourishing and thriving.[14]

On the whole, pneumatology looks at the Spirit's role in the church's origin and acts of power. Such that in both cases—and whether implicitly or explicitly—pneumatology is invested in the dynamic between Spirit and flesh. Crawley's interest, however, is in *pneuma* (breath) and not pneumatology proper. His interest in *pneuma* establishes the parameters of his text and underpins his understanding of what he refers to as *black pneuma*. *Black pneuma* is the theoretical structure that necessitates possibility, animates the flesh, and shirks the static—even that which constitutes the coherent.

---

12. Crawley, *Blackpentecostal Breath*, 31.

13. Crawley's use of blackpentecostalism, one word, is an analytical lens, less for examining the larger Black religious tradition; and more for employing diverse theoretical approaches (e.g., black studies, queer theory, philosophy, sound studies, and performance studies) to explore the intricacies of Black modes of existence (being), Black modes of striving (otherwise possibilities) and Black modes of progress (flourishing).

14. Anderson, *Ontological Blackness*, 87.

Otherwise possibility, animation, and resistance make *black pneuma* particularly hospitable and thus given to other-regard.[15] Crawley writes:

> Blackpentecostalism, though excluded from the mainstream, was ever inclusive of those that would be excluded. It is an egalitarian mode of Spirit indwelling, wherein that which those filled with the Spirit have is immediately given away to others through aesthetic proclamation, through linguistic rupture that announces and enunciates expanded sociality.[16]

Crawley finds in *black pneuma* the literal and the metaphorical "black breath," and in black breath a "radical sociality" that shares in breath and breathing, *e.g., the vital thing on which life, and life more abundantly*, depends. Such that to be fully human, and thus made in the image and likeness of God, is to "share in the materiality of that which quickens flesh."[17] Here we might think of it as a radical sociality that emulates the love enjoyed between the Voice, the Word, and the Breath (the Trinity).[18]

The *imago Dei*, other-regard, and radical sociability are essential to the human project. Each is committed to the health and well-being of humanity and seeks to foster characteristics, qualities, and traits purposed to cultivate caring communities of faith and mutual responsibility. Therefore, when communities are disrupted by abuse, assault, and harassment intent on *undoing* God's handiwork (Eph 2:10) among God's people, both the radical sociality that mediates communal participation in the divine life *and* the meaningful pathways to full personhood and self-actualization are obstructed. All of this grieves Spirit (Eph 4:30).

Gender, Race, the Church, and Sexual Violence

In her 2018 book, *This Will Be My Undoing: Living at the Intersection of Black, Female, and Feminist in (White) America*, Morgan Jenkins's collection of essays offers cultural, social, and political critiques from her perspective as a Black woman. Within the ten independent yet interconnected essays, Jenkins critically examines how Black women are treated in the United States. She speaks poignantly about how society construes the Black female body

---

15. Crawley, *Blackpentecostal Breath*, 40.
16. Crawley, *Blackpentecostal Breath*, 38.
17. Crawley, *Blackpentecostal Breath*, 40.
18. @bythechurchedfeminist, "I heard someone refer to the Trinity as the Voice, the Word, and the Breath and I can't stop thinking about it," Instagram photo, October 18, 2022, https://www.instagram.com/p/Cj3KBKXOe_x/.

as a commodity for public consumption and pleasure. As a result, Black girls and women are readily rendered inhuman and thus wholly unworthy of the same respect, protection, and care enjoyed by their White counterparts.

Unquestionably, women broadly are woefully susceptible to every form of violence and abuse. But minoritized women and those from underrepresented ethnic and racial communities in this country are acutely and disproportionately vulnerable. According to the Sanctuary for Families website, "men are murdering Black women and girls at a rate almost three times higher than White women. For indigenous women and girls, the homicide rate is six times higher than it is for their White counterparts, and current or former partners are responsible for 94% of those homicides."[19] Even though the focus here is not homicide, abundant evidence links sexual violence with physical and psychological abuse. When ethicist and theologian Elizabeth Gerhardt reflects on this, she notes that gender-based violence is undergirded by a need to gain and sustain power. In a lecture where she discusses this in detail, Gerhardt notes that "all types of violence against women center around the idea that violence works!" In the same presentation, Gerhardt goes on to say, "By [using] coercion, physical, psychological, emotional abuse and/or withholding . . . what is needed by the victim, the perpetrator can best get what he or she wants/needs."[20]

The current essay's title derives from Jenkins's book title. The term *undoing* does not appear in the book; contextually, however, it functions as a literary tool. On the one hand, *undoing* attends to Jenkins's identity as a Black woman and her contention that neither her blackness nor her womanness is antithetical to her humanity. Within the text, this means that the collection of essays illustrates how these various extensions of culture, social constructs, and societal norms aided her journey to self-discovery, even when they were designed to make her hyper-visible Black body invisible. Concerning this, Jenkins reflects, "I had to be reminded of my blackness and womanhood because those two identity markers were supposedly the things that put me *in a bind* [emphasis mine]."[21]

On the other hand, what Jenkins discovered eventually was that those identity markers—her blackness and womanness, especially—were, in fact, critical disruptions that, ironically, made space for her in the world. Against the predeterminations of American society, Jenkins learned to lean wholly into the restrictive seams of Black womanhood. In doing so, she

---

19. Sanctuary for Families, "Silent Epidemic of Femicide," para. 7.
20. Gerhardt, "Gender Violence." For a full treatment on this, see Gerhardt, *Cross and Gendercide*.
21. Jenkins, *This Will Be My Undoing*, 251.

inadvertently loosed (*undid*) herself from the social structures designed to restrict and silence her. Ultimately, Jenkins found herself entering and being fully present in a world that never intended for her overall success—much less her survival and well-being. Therefore, Jenkins claims to live intentionally as someone set on shifting heterogender expectations, racial stereotypes, and misconceptions about universality and diversity so that others might be freed—*undone*.

Jenkins's focus on the Black female body is invested in Black women's hyper-visibility. Jenkins's examination of this aspect of the Black female experience roots hyper-visibility in objectification and expendability. Specifically, she highlights forms of objectification and expendability wherein Black women are involuntarily and often unwillingly in service to the sexual pleasure and domination of men, regardless of race. Even as she deals with issues about sexual harassment and diverse forms of sexual abuse, Jenkins does not discuss Black women rape survivors beyond a brief analysis of Black enslaved women. Unquestionably, the topic exceeds the scope of her work. However, the overall absence of such stories is consonant with the general culture of silence around Black women survivors of sexual violence.

The lack of stories about and by Black women survivors of sexual violence means our collective understanding of race, gender, and class is underinformed. Even more, it is another opportunity for Black women to be a forgotten and overlooked demographic. Elsewhere, one victim of sexual violence, only known by her alias "Ruth," spoke on behalf of Black women and about rape culture in general. Setting her reflections on the state of Black women in the United States within the context of sexual assault, Ruth bemoaned how society continuously disregards Black women rape survivors. In her view, society does not take Black women seriously. It does not see or value Black women as human beings—at least not "to the same degree that other people are valued." Ruth maintains that in the United States, Black women are "a very disposable people," a view she counters with the positive affirmation: "I—as a Black woman—have feelings. I get angry; I feel delight; I cry myself to sleep. We have a whole range of emotions that anybody else does."[22]

Ruth's words appear in Charlotte Pierce-Baker's 1998 text, *Surviving the Silence: Black Women's Stories of Rape*. Pierce-Baker, a devout Catholic, a professor, and a sexual assault survivor, opted against the culture's pathological silence to rape and the concomitant ways it makes Black women more invisible and less human. Appealing to her craft, Pierce-Baker responded by writing. *Surviving the Silence* is Pierce-Baker's attempt to provide Black

---

22. Pierce-Baker, *Surviving the Silence*, 92.

women rape survivors a space to share their individual and collective experiences. The book is a compilation of stories from women who felt they *had to remain silent*. The scarlet thread unifying each of these harrowing accounts is not sexual violence narrowly but rather *a rationale that convinced them that their silence was necessary* to protect themselves and their race. Pierce-Baker writes, "All of the women who have told their stories in these pages have chosen to live in some degree of secrecy, to protect themselves, from censure, to stave off family discomfort and worry, or to protect those they have been conditioned to believe are African-American 'brothers.'"[23]

Elsewhere in the text, she states more directly,

> For black women, where rape is concerned, race has preceded issues of gender. We are taught that we are first black, then women. Our families have taught us this, and society in its harsh racial lessons reinforces it. Black women have survived by keeping quiet, not solely out of shame, but out of a need to preserve the race and its image. In our attempts to preserve racial pride, we black women have often sacrificed our own souls.[24]

The prioritization of the race, specifically the acute need to ensure the safety and protection of Black men, also comes up in Jenkins's work. Recalling an incident while visiting a local corner store in her Harlem neighborhood, Jenkins takes the reader on a deep dive into the internal struggle of whose safety and well-being to privilege. In this case, she had to choose between herself and the Black community. While in the store, Jenkins was approached by a Black man. Although posing no perceptible or identifiable physical threat, the verbal harassment and infringement on her personal space were more than enough to shake her and leave her feeling acutely violated. At that moment, Jenkins contemplated whether to call the police on the man but ultimately chose to do whatever was necessary to get out of the situation and avoid confrontation.

Jenkins's thick description of the event draws the reader into the episode so intimately that one feels right there with her and shares the overwhelming sense of uncertainty and dread. Yet, most palpable is the post-traumatic stress Jenkins experiences later that evening. Her decision not to solicit aid from the police meant that she held the trauma and attending fear in her body. What Jenkins's account conveys is the precarity of Black womanhood in the United States and the audacity of Black trauma. Her internal struggle, involving self and community, functioned as a critical testament to the ongoing negotiations that Black women must make daily.

23. Pierce-Baker, *Surviving the Silence*, 19.
24. Pierce-Baker, *Surviving the Silence*, 84.

Journalist Rachelle Hampton made a similar observation in her review of Jenkins's text. Echoing Pierce-Baker, Hampton wrote, "[Jenkins's] reluctance touches on a fraught particularity of black womanhood: the experiences we bury to protect someone else at our own expense."[25]

Although race is a major aspect of this essay, we cannot reduce violence against women solely to that. Without question, violence against women is not solely a race issue. It is a human rights issue. Full stop. Sadly, it is also a longstanding issue. Phyllis Trible's groundbreaking book, *Texts of Terror: Literary Feminist Readings of Biblical Narratives*, has critically shown that even biblical traditions affirm the pervasiveness of this grotesque and, might I add, anti-God reality—because any action so deliberately fashioned to destroy one-half of the human population cannot be anything other than anti-God at its core. Its active and ongoing presence in the church has prompted some biblical scholars to respond by looking at how the Bible has been misappropriated to validate dehumanizing teachings on authority, headship, and submission. In his chapter essay entitled "Some Biblical Reflections on Justice, Rape, and an Insensitive Society," New Testament scholar Craig S. Keener does not merely name the devastating reality of gender violence and the misuse of the Bible as ubiquitous. He treats the presence of gender violence in Scripture as a critical resource for the church to develop a carefully-crafted biblical response. He writes,

> Various sociological, psychological, and theological approaches to abuse are vital in seeking solutions to the crises facing people whose pain is often neglected by our society. In addition, an examination of biblical texts addressing abuse can provide insights both to encourage Christian victims of abuse and to call the Christian Community as a whole to a more concerted and vocal stand against abuse.[26]

Keener's essay is, by design, not a practical how-to guide for responding to sexual violence. Through his scholarship, Keener offers hope to those working towards recovery and personal (read spiritual) development following their sexual assault. A point he expresses in his closing paragraph:

> It is not wrong for the rape victim to seek justice or to cry out to God for vindication; no court in this land takes rape as seriously as God does. But the Bible also offers a deeper hope to victims of rape and other major traumas: if they continue to cultivate their relationship with God, *God can turn their pain into healing for*

---

25. Hampton, "Poetic Profanity," para. 6.
26. Keener, "Justice, Rape, and an Insensitive Society," 117.

themselves and for others. What others have wounded, God and time can put back together. We must let the victims of rape and other crimes know that God is on their side, and that we are on their side too. Like God, we must walk through their pain with them, that our love and compassion may reflect in some small way the infinite love and compassion God feels towards his daughters and sons violated by others' spite, selfishness, and insensitivity.[27]

Arguably, Keener's conclusions are more pastoral than prophetic. In many ways, his take reflects the era in which he was writing. Because the original essay is over thirty years old, it does not bear the stubborn, no-nonsense approach now common to contemporary treatments of rape culture—in the church or elsewhere. Unquestionably, the essay is more suggestive and deferential, whereas contemporary works are often direct and challenging. Because current scholarship feels obligated neither to defend God (because God is not the perpetrator) nor to protect the church (an effort to value individuals over institutions), it has embraced a set of prophetic discursive practices that speak truth to power and work towards effective change. Such areas of reformation include but are not limited to (1) assailant accountability, (2) survivor recovery, (3) restitution, and (4) institutional reform.

Treating this topic more broadly and in ways more reflective of a prophetic approach that acknowledges spousal and child abuse as part of the church's long and complexly knotted story, Elizabeth Gerhardt has responded through a constructive theological ethic that centers survivors' overall well-being while challenging ecclesial commitments to silence and dissemblance. Her book, *The Cross and Gendercide: A Theological Response to Global Violence Against Women and Girls*, attends to a "theology of the Cross," wherein Gerhardt names violence against women—in all its forms—as sin that is an unquestionable evil and antithetical to the character, nature, and will of God. Through the theology of the cross, Gerhardt procures the theological latitude needed to propose a holistic framework that treats gender violence as an issue belonging to the community of faith, *in toto*, and not just women.

Gerhardt's sentiments around mutual responsibility, through other-regard and radical sociality, also appear in Nyasha Junior's essay "Jephtah's Daughter and #SayHerName." In this piece, Junior reads the account in "Judges 11 through the prism of the #SayHerName campaign and similar efforts in support of black women and girls."[28] In this essay, Junior is intent on taking the road less traveled. Unlike many of her colleagues, she opts against

---

27. Keener, "Justice, Rape, and an Insensitive Society," 130.
28. Junior, "Jephtah's Daughter and #SayHerName," 48.

the standard comparative lens that reads Judges 11 in light of Genesis 22. Junior argues that it is more generative to read Judges 11 as "highlighting issues of naming, victimizing, and possibilities for resistance."[29] Reading the text through the contemporary social-political lens of the #SayHerName movement prompts her to ask several questions about class, race, and gender violence. One driving question, in particular, is, "why don't we know the name of these black women and girls?"—those women victims of state-sanctioned violence.[30]

More than anything, Junior's work is an admonishment to the church. She calls on the church to read, preach, and teach accounts like Judges 11 and not ignore or avoid them because they make people uncomfortable. Moreover, she invites Christian leaders and laity to engage in such writings as prophetic. According to Junior, because these texts deal with the fragility of the human condition, they "could assist readers by increasing their ability to substantively address concerns associated with sexual politics—including public health crises, hate crimes, and social and theological equality—both within their congregations and in the broader society."[31] Much like Gerhardt, Junior prods the church to assume a posture of mutual responsibility. But for Junior, that work includes reflecting on "whose lives and deaths matter in our lives, neighborhoods, and faith communities."[32]

Whether through biblical studies or moral theology/ethics, trusted scholars have had the difficult but necessary task of indicting the church. The primary charge: instead of taking the position of Jesus, it appears that the church has adopted a stance that favors silencing survivors. To that end, it has marginalized the plight of victims by treating the problem as a private family matter that does not require the involvement of legal authorities or trusted professionals. It has also resorted to victim blaming and used spiritual manipulation to shame survivors and redeem offenders[33]—all while failing to hold abusers accountable.

---

29. Junior, "Jephtah's Daughter and #SayHerName," 48.
30. Junior, "Jephtah's Daughter and #SayHerName," 48.
31. Junior, "Jephtah's Daughter and #SayHerName," 48.
32. Junior, "Jephtah's Daughter and #SayHerName," 48.
33. The account in Pierce-Baker's *Surviving the Silence* names the church repeatedly as a complicit in either hiding the truth of gender violence in the home or prioritizing the offender over the victim. A matter of particular import to "Ruth," (an alias), who commented, "I think the better educated and more middle class we become, our attitudes will change as black women because we will realize that we have a right to a nonviolent life and we have a right to say to a black man that what you're doing isn't right instead of the African-American church telling our rapists, 'We'll forgive you,' and being so outrageously indignant when the rapist goes to prison." Pierce-Baker, *Surviving the Silence*, 91.

Undoubtedly, the propensity to redeem offenders while failing to hold them accountable for their crimes is the poisonous fruit of patriarchy. However, it also intimates the relational proximity of many victims to the accused. A point implied, but not often explicitly stated in many accounts, is that many survivors of gender-based violence know their abusers. In 2004, the Bureau of Justice Statistics reported that in the United States, (1) intimate partners murdered 1,218 women during 1999; (2) from 1993–99, intimates killed 45% of all female murder victims ages 20–24; (3) women age 35–49 were the most vulnerable to intimate murder; (4) females age 16–24 were the most vulnerable to nonfatal violence; and (5) women separated from their husbands were victimized by an intimate at rates higher than married, divorced, widowed, or never-married women. Moreover, of all intimate partner female homicides in 2018, 92% of victims were killed by a man they knew, and 63% were killed by current husbands, boyfriends, or ex-husbands.[34]

Another issue, of course, is intimate partner or domestic violence. Although the statistics vary, the numbers resonate with those related to femicide, e.g., one in three to four women are battered by an intimate partner (25–33%), making domestic violence one of the nation's most expensive healthcare issues (around $5–10 Billion a year)—with the ages of victims ranging between 15–44. Additionally, one in four girls is sexually abused before age eighteen.[35] Despite shame and fear that they will not be believed or supported, which often leads to underreporting, we know that one in six women has experienced attempted or completed rape. Even as power is at the root of these staggering and unsettling statistics, the takeaway is that women are victims of gender-based violence simply *because* they are women.

In acknowledging that comparatively, sexual violence is more complicated to measure than femicide or domestic violence, organizations like the Rape, Abuse, Incest National Network (RAINN) compile and report data available through the *National Crime Victimization Survey (NCVS)*, Justice Department studies, as well as data from the Department of Health and Human Services to provide critical insight concerning women and children victims of sexual violence. Namely, (1) every sixty-eight seconds, another American is sexually assaulted; (2) one out of every six American women has been the victim of an attempted or completed rape in her lifetime (14.8% completed, 2.8% attempted); (3) from 2009–13, Child Protective Services

---

34. Gerhardt, "Gender Violence."

35. Linda Crockett, "Why Are Churches Silent about Family Violence," cited in Gerhardt, "Gender Violence."

agencies substantiated, or found strong evidence to indicate that sixty-three thousand children a year were victims of sexual abuse; and (4) a majority of child victims are twelve to seventeen. Of victims under the age of eighteen: 34% of victims of sexual assault and rape are under age twelve, and 66% of victims of sexual assault and rape are age twelve to seventeen.[36]

Even more, according to RAINN, survivors like Charlotte Pierce-Baker, who was raped during a home invasion while watching television with her husband, are often engaged in the most mundane tasks when assaulted. Some 48% were sleeping or performing another activity at home. While reportedly 29% were traveling to and from work or school or traveling to shop or run errands. Another 12% said that they were working at the time.[37] If they were like "Renee," the alias of a teen rape survivor from Philadelphia, they make up the 7% attending school. Renee's story, which appears in *Surviving the Silence*, recounts her attack and subsequent hospital visit where she met Pierce-Baker, then a volunteer with Women Organized Against Rape (WOAR). In the text, Renee, who at the time of her rape was merely fourteen, notes that her assailant was also a high school student (himself fifteen years old) but already a repeat rapist and sex offender who had never been "caught, suspended, [or] arrested."[38]

The challenge to Christians in the United States, especially, is not to read these statistics as "of the world" and thus separate from the life of the church. Instead, the church must respond to this information as a prophetic mandate to wrestle with the fact that gender-based violence against women is part and parcel of the community that claims to align with the One who is the Lord and Giver of life and invites humanity to participate in the Divine life of God. On a more practical level, the church, writ large, must take seriously the fact that, arguably, if women victims in the church were to report their assaults at the same rate as those outside of the Christian tradition—even as low as such reportings might be—or even disclose assaults that take place while attending church or a church event, the numbers above would increase exponentially.[39]

---

36. RAINN, "Scope of the Problem."
37. RAINN, "Scope of the Problem."
38. Pierce-Baker, *Surviving the Silence*, 18.
39. Although it would be really helpful to this work to have some data for women of faith or even reported assaults against women within the church/Christian tradition, at this time, such data is very difficult to find—if not altogether unattainable. It is my hope that this will change as more survivors find courage and support within the #metoo and #churchtoo movements.

Confession as a Means to Overcome

In an interview with the Associated Press (AP) and reprinted in *US News and World Report*, Emily Joy Allison notes that while denominations like the Southern Baptist Church (SBC) need to overhaul extant policy and theology, she is fully aware that this type of radical change is not only unlikely but altogether unrealistic. In her own words: "They need to undergo a transformation so radical they would be unrecognizable at the end. And that will not happen."[40] At this stage, she recognizes that reform work focused on "harm reduction" is more realistic.[41] Here, Allison gestures towards changes in victim engagement—specifically, the deplorable tendency of many religious communities to force victims toward unconditional forgiveness. Through spiritual and emotional manipulation, survivors often are cajoled into moving on by forgiving their offenders and avoiding law enforcement interference.

Despite such predatory behaviors, there is a growing constituency inclusive of survivors and advocates who collectively agree that contrary to the attitudinal implications of the existing and problematic approaches to victim support, gender-based violence against women is life-alternatingly serious; it cuts to the core of human integrity and dignity. This is why the church has a vital role to play. Because Christians affirm and maintain that sin is that which fails to glorify God as God, the church must lead the charge in unapologetically naming gender-based violence against women a human rights violation with individual and communal implications. Even more, the church must confess not only its sins of omission and commission as they pertain to sexual violence. It also must confess Christ.[42] While this last point might seem like a given, the church must not presume anything. By confessing Christ, churches assume a posture of radical humility. Having confessed that gender-based violence is a sin that violates the rights and dignity of women as persons created in the image and likeness of God while acknowledging the ways it has been complicit and/or silent, the church is then better positioned to thoroughly examine how and when its failure to act like Christ has caused it to subvert and even undermine the *power* of the gospel. At issue is a critical self-examination of how the church of Jesus Christ has actively or passively hindered the effective proclamation of the gospel and, thus, obstructed meaningful pathways to full personhood and self-actualization.

---

40. Smith and Meyer, "#ChurchToo Revelations Growing," para. 23.
41. Smith and Meyer, "#ChurchToo Revelations Growing," para. 23.
42. Gerhardt, *Cross and Gendercide*, 120–32.

As noted above, confessing Christ is invoking God's full Trinitarian reality. Specifically, the Trinity evokes the otherwise possibilities for survivors and the church. Should the church take seriously the proposed triad of the *imago Dei*, other-regard, and radical sociability as essential to the human project, it would find itself better positioned to facilitate caring communities of faith invested in mutual responsibility. In this instance, caring faith communities committed to fundamentally disrupting cultures of abuse, assault, and harassment intent on *undoing* one-half of the population.

Similarly and consequently, to confess Christ is also to confess that all power belongs to God. God, who in their generosity and omniscience, has provided humanity with a means to move into preventative and restorative action through the gospel.[43] Therefore, the church's work cannot end with confession alone. After confession, the church must state in no uncertain terms that there is no redemptive suffering in violence against women. Such flawed theology lies against the will of God for all humanity and violates God's desire for the human family. Love and fidelity should not be tested and/or proven on victims' literal and proverbial backs. Violence against women is a sin. And as Gerhardt reminds us, it cannot be construed as a perverse penitential sacrifice that should be offered up to God.[44]

Lastly, the church must confess a commitment to upholding Christ's proclaimed liberty (Luke 4:18–19). Following the spirit of Christ, Christian liberty makes no concessions for ecclesial, cultural, or family norms that violate the will of God manifested in the freedom of Christ. Indeed, Christian liberty unabashedly seeks the preferential option for the poor and abused, preaches truth via the gospel, aids all victims of injustice, and actively resists evil in all its structural forms. Ultimately, the more the church adopts a pneumatology that boldly proclaims where the spirit of the Lord and Giver of Life is, *there* is liberty, it also will find increased opportunities to participate in the divine life through the *imago Dei*, other-regard, and radical sociality. Only from such a place can churches develop and uphold sexual assault policies and theologies that acknowledge (1) the devastation and suffering experienced when the church fails to lead in areas of gender justice; (2) the work of the Spirit as *empowering* women but also calling and

---

43. Here, I mean preventative and restorative action that resists evil, speaks truth to power, and stubbornly stands on the side of the oppressed—over and against the cultural or ecclesial semblance of propriety and the desire to save face.

44. Gerhardt, *Cross and Gendercide*, 122. For more on redemptive suffering, see John Paul II, *Salvifici Doloris*. See also Orsi, *Thank You, St. Jude*; Orsi, *Between Heaven and Earth*. In both works, Orsi examines the popular belief in the redemptive power of suffering among mid-century American Catholics, most especially those who identified as Italian-American women.

convicting; and (3) the invitation for humanity to partner with the Spirit to construct ecclesial spaces of empathy, healing, and solidarity.

This Won't Be Our Undoing

For author Morgan Jenkins, *undoing* is an agentive act. She actively releases herself from the ties that bind and restrict her. Amid everything she endured and continues to endure as a Black woman, the reader finds Jenkins discovering new ways to live fully as an unrestricted human being. In sum, Jenkins is free; and as her book title suggests, *she* obtained her freedom. *She* is the primary agent behind her liberation.

Contrary to the book, *This Will Be My Undoing*, this essay has thought about *undoing* as less a liberative act and more an assertion of otherwise possibilities made possible through Spirit. Here, the relentless desire *to be*, e.g., survive and, when possible, flourish is an affront to whatever was purposed to bring about the *undoing* of [Black] woman survivors of gender-based and sexual violence. Said differently: the acts designed to obstruct meaningful pathways to their emotional, mental, and spiritual well-being did not work. "This won't be our undoing" does not claim certainty; rather, it is prophetic. It intimates the already-and-not-yet necessary for survival. It is intended to remind survivors that they are not victims relegated to the horrors of their circumstances. And it is purposed to remind women that they are daughters fashioned in the image and likeness of God, who are part of the communal fabric that makes up the seamless body of Christ. A body wherein they share in the life-giving, life-changing, and life-sustaining *pneuma* of God.

As partners and advocates in this prophetic declaration, the church's task is important but simple. First, the church must be present to remind survivors of the open invitation to participate in the divine life (*imago Dei*). Then, it must keep the meaningful pathways to full personhood and self-actualization unobstructed (other-regard). Lastly, the church will need to value the art of sitting (radical sociality); namely, sitting in the ashes with survivors while the *breath* of God does her perfect work of mending broken hearts and wounded bodies.

A Final Word

As of April 26, 2023, BreeAnn Hammond had not returned to Instagram with any updates about her sexual assault. In fact, since the original post, BreeAnn's activity has been limited to selfies, professional photoshoots, promotional material for the show *Grown & Gospel*, and her latest business venture (matchmaking). Although updates about her sexual assaults and the concomitant legal proceedings are unavailable, she and her story are representative of the concerns raised in this essay. For one, BreeAnn and her story affirm that the church is not immune to gender-based sexual violence. Moreover, BreeAnn and her story illustrate the disconnect between the #churchtoo movement and Black women and other women of color. Ultimately, BreeAnn and her story exemplify society's pathological indifference toward Black women sexual assault victims—even those from privileged and well-known families.

In the end, BreeAnn and her story, brief though it may be, confirm the importance of a pneumatological exploration of personhood and self-actualization as it pertains to sexual violence. As a Black woman sexual assault survivor, BreeAnn and her story are included among the innumerable Black women victims whose names go unsaid, stories go untold, and whose marginalized status often results in them being forgotten and among those that society has left for dead. For this reason and others, it must be the church's business to act earnestly to support survivors by acknowledging (1) the devastation and suffering experienced when the church fails to lead in areas of gender justice; (2) the work of Spirit as empowering women but also calling and convicting; and (3) the invitation for humanity (namely the church) to partner with Spirit to construct ecclesial spaces of empathy, healing, and solidarity.

I believe such an acknowledgment by the church runs counter to and, therefore, actively resists a culture of dissemblance that spurns disclosing abuse within the church and the Black community. Moreover, I believe such support of those society has forgotten and left for dead discloses the Spirit as a life-giving agent of otherwise possibilities. Finally, I believe a pneumatological exploration of personhood and self-actualization, as it pertains to sexual violence, insists that survivors not only have access free access to "the materiality of that which quickens flesh"[45] but also the restorative love found in the perichoretic life of the Voice, the Word, and the Breath.

Bibliography

Allison, Emily Joy. *#ChurchToo: How Purity Culture Upholds Abuse and How to Find Healing*. Minneapolis: Broadleaf, 2021.

Anderson, Vincent. *Beyond Ontological Blackness: An Essay on African American Religious and Cultural Criticism*. New York: Continuum, 1995.

---

45. Crawley, *Blackpentecostal Breath*, 40.

Baker-Fletcher, Karen. "The Breath of God." In *Dancing with God: The Trinity from a Womanist Perspective*, 52–74. St. Louis: Chalice, 2006.

———. *Sisters of the Dust, Sisters of the Spirit: Womanist Wordings on God and Creation*. Minneapolis: Fortress, 1998.

Congar, Yves. *I Believe in the Holy Spirit*. New York: Crossroad, 1997.

Crawley, Ashon T. *Blackpentecostal Breath: The Aesthetics of Possibility*. New York: Fordham University Press, 2017.

Delgado, Dara Coleby. "What Did Trump Know? The Presidency, Prosperity, and Pentecostals." *Political Theology Network*, August 26, 2021. https://politicaltheology.com/what-did-trump-know-the-presidency-prosperity-and-pentecostals/.

Doyle, Dennis M. *What Is Christianity? A Dynamic Introduction*. New York: Paulist, 2016.

Gerhardt, Elizabeth L. *The Cross and Gendercide: A Theological Response to Global Violence against Women and Girls*. Downers Grove, IL: IVP Academic, 2014.

———. "Gender Violence: International Dimensions and a Theological Response." Presentation for course "Christian Social Ethics," Northeastern Seminary, October 10, 2022.

Gonzalez, Justo. *The Story of Christianity*. Vol. 1, *The Early Church to the Dawn of the Reformation*. Rev. ed. New York: HarperCollins, 2010.

Hampton, Rachelle. "Poetic Profanity." *Slate*, February 26, 2018. https://slate.com/culture/2018/02/morgan-jerkins-this-will-be-my-undoing-reviewed.html.

Jenkins, Morgan. *This Will Be My Undoing: Living at the Intersection of Black, Female, and Feminist in (White) America*. New York: Harper Perennial, 2018.

John Paul II. *Salvifici Doloris*. https://www.vatican.va/content/john-paul-ii/en/apost_letters/1984/documents/hf_jp-ii_apl_11021984_salvifici-doloris.html.

Joy, Emily. "#ChurchToo." https://emilyjoypoetry.com/churchtoo.

Junior, Nyasha. "Jephthah's Daughter and #SayHerName." In *The Sexual Politics of Black Churches*, edited by Josef Sorett, 41–49. New York: Columbia University Press, 2022.

Keener, Craig S. "Some Biblical Reflections on Justice, Rape, and an Insensitive Society." In *Women, Abuse, and the Bible: How Scripture Can Be Used to Hurt and Heal*, edited by Catherine Clark Kroeger et al., 117–30. Grand Rapids: Baker, 1996.

Orsi, Robert A. *Between Heaven and Earth: The Religious Worlds People Make and the Scholars Who Study Them*. Princeton: Princeton University Press, 2006.

———. *Thank You, St. Jude: Women's Devotion to the Patron Saint of Hopeless Causes*. New Haven: Yale University Press, 1996.

Pierce-Baker, Charlotte. *Surviving the Silence: Black Women's Stories of Rape*. New York: Norton, 1998.

RAINN. "Scope of the Problem: Statistics." https://www.rainn.org/statistics/scope-problem.

Sanctuary for Families. "Silent Epidemic of Femicide in the United States." March 10, 2023. https://sanctuaryforfamilies.org/femicide-epidemic/.

Smith, Peter, and Holly Meyer. "#ChurchToo Revelations Growing, Years after Movement Began." *AP News*, June 12, 2022. https://apnews.com/article/entertainment-health-baptist-religion-c7c5f62a5737b3aee20ceaa3f99ab603.

WeTV. "*Grown & Gospel* Season 1 Trailer!" https://www.wetv.com/shows/grown-and-gospel/videos/grown-and-gospel-season-1-trailer--1061966.

Wilken, Robert Louis. *The First Thousand Years: A Global History of Christianity*. New Haven: Yale University Press, 2012.

— 9 —

#MeToo, #ChurchToo
A Pentecostal-Charismatic Response to Sexual Violence against Women

Christian Tsekpoe

Introduction

THE HORROR OF VIOLENCE against women, including sexual violence, cuts across culture, ethnicity, and age. In both developed and deprived economies, violence against women has been and continues to be a scourge. It is estimated that more than 50% of women have, in one way or another, experienced some form of domestic violence.¹ Similarly, one form of domestic violence, sexual violence, is a global problem that has kept many women in pain for years. Sexual violence is defined as "any sexual act, attempt to obtain a sexual act, unwanted sexual comments or advances, or acts to traffic, or otherwise directed, against a person's sexuality using coercion, by any person regardless of their relationship to the victim, in any setting, including but not limited to home and work."² Since many of the perpetrators are people of power, society seems to have protected them whilst the victims remain silent in the face of these gruesome abuses for self-preservation and

---

1. Tenkorang et al., "Factors Influencing Domestic and Marital Violence," 771–81.
2. Jewkes, "Sexual violence," 149.

in fear of stigmatization and shame. The pervasive and debilitating nature of sexual abuse makes it a concern that must not be disparaged.

Takyi and Lamptey argue, "Despite the substantial gains women have made in education, health, and the political arena in recent years, studies indicate that they continue to be victims of sexual, physical, and emotional intimate partner violence (IPV) throughout the world."[3] In recent times, the increasing social media awareness that has coalesced through the #MeToo, #ChurchToo movements has heightened the need for the church to be concerned about the menace, to find ways of mitigating it within its fold, and to serve as the light of the world, expelling the darkness of sexual abuse in society. Indeed, the emergence of the #MeToo, #ChurchToo movements have sounded wake up calls and placed critical demands on the church to take up the issue of sexual violence against women more seriously.

This is especially crucial for the church in Africa in general, and Ghana in particular. Research has shown that between 33% and 37%, representing a third of Ghanaian women, have experienced a form of violence either physically, emotionally, or sexually.[4] After the establishment of the Domestic Violence and Victim Support Unit (DOVVSU), formerly known as Women and Juvenile Unit (WAJU) of the Ghana Police Service in October 1998, reported cases of sexual violence against women have begun to increase in the country.[5] Scholars have identified rape (including gang rape), forced marriages, defilement, incest, and indecent assault as prevalent forms of sexual violence against women in Ghana.[6]

Meanwhile, little research has been carried out on this menace in Ghana from Christian perspectives. This chapter, therefore, discusses how the church's missional role can be improved to provide healing, restoration, and refuge for victims of sexual violence from a Ghanaian Pentecostal-Charismatic perspective. The chapter also proposes the need to intentionally introduce the subject into the curriculum of Pentecostal-Charismatic theological education in Ghana as a way of training and equipping pastors and lay leaders, not only to mitigate the prevalence of sexual violence among Pentecostal-Charismatic leaders, but also to equip them to deal effectively with issues of sexual abuse against women in Ghana in general and in their congregations specifically.

---

3. Takyi and Lamptey, "Faith and Marital Violence," 26.
4. Takyi and Lamptey, "Faith and Marital Violence," 26.
5. Osei-Tutu and Ampadu, "Domestic Violence," 109.
6. Sossou and Yogtiba, "Abuse, Neglect, and Violence," 422–27; Quarshie et al., "Clergy-Perpetrated Sexual Abuse," 3028–57.

Defining the Pentecostal-Charismatic Movement in Ghana

It must be admitted that defining the Pentecostal-Charismatic movement is a daunting task because of the dynamism and variegated character of the movement globally.[7] In Ghana, for example, there are about five different waves of Pentecostal-Charismatic innovations within the country.[8] This notwithstanding, Pentecostalism has been generally considered as a movement concerned with the experience and manifestation of the power and gifts of the Holy Spirit.[9] I, therefore, defined the Pentecostal-Charismatic movement elsewhere as "a Holy Spirit-empowered community."[10] An all-embracing definition of this nature makes it possible to accommodate the variegated waves of Pentecostal-Charismatic innovations within the movement and offer opportunities for the various waves of the movement to provide reciprocal influence for each other to possibly obviate some of the abuses and manipulations within its fold while strengthening the current successes.

The #MeToo Movement

In recent times, many women have broken the culture of silence and have courageously spoken about their experiences of sexual violence to provide a community of solidarity for those who have experienced similar abuses. This community of solidarity coalesced through a social media movement popularly known as #MeToo. Although the term MeToo was coined by Tarana Burke in 2006, it became a popular and powerful movement in October 2017 when the USA actress Alyssa Milano used it in a tweet to express her experience of sexual abuse.[11] The response to Milano's tweet coalesced into a movement that produced collective courage for other women who have been raped, assaulted, groped, stalked, or harassed sexually, to open-up and either share their stories or just indicate #MeToo. According to Rebecca Leung and Robert Williams,

> The crux of the #MeToo movement has challenged gender norms and the roles they play in sexual assault and harassment.

7. Asamoah-Gyadu, *African Charismatics*; Anderson, *To the Ends of the Earth*.
8. Tsekpoe, "Navigating the Shades," 27–46.
9. Anderson, *To the Ends of the Earth*; Asamoah-Gyadu, *Sighs and Signs*; Ma and Ma, *Mission in the Spirit*.
10. Tsekpoe, "Navigating the Shades," 27.
11. Boyd and McEwan, "Viral Paradox," 1–18; Suk et al., "#MeToo," 276–94; Barnes, "Trace Publics," 1305–19.

Overall, perceptions of victims and what role they play in a sexual assault or harassment incident are often weighed heavily by observers who use social and gender norms to form a public opinion about how to treat victims and those accused of sexual assault and harassment.[12]

This movement has led to other revelations of sexual abuse in religious or sacred spaces, including the church, thereby generating the hashtag #ChurchToo.[13]

The #ChurchToo Movement

As an offspring of the #MeToo movement, the #ChurchToo movement also coalesced on social media to provide opportunity for women to share their experiences of sexual harassment, abuse, and assault within church communities. The movement seeks to encourage victims of church abuse to speak about their experiences on such issues without fear. This movement seeks to provide a voice for survivors of sexual violence, whose side of the stories have either not been heard at all, or have been heard but not treated satisfactorily by the church. #ChurchToo also became popular in 2017 when Emily Joy Allison decided to share her story and invited others who were abused to do the same. She later published her story into a book in 2021.

In this publication, Allison described how her youth pastor groomed her for sexual abuse, and how the church and her family shamed and traumatized her by making her carry the guilt of a coerced relationship she was too naive to handle. She insisted that "the very specific theological and cultural aspects of many of our churches, schools, and other ministries both enable and traumatize survivors."[14] Allison's story and other stories the book uncovers corroborate the gruesome pains and trauma experienced by survivors of sexual abuse, especially because of the church's failure to provide a place of refuge and restoration for them. What makes it even worse is the fact that because some of the perpetrators are church leaders and people of influence and power, there is no effective system in many of the churches to deal with these perpetrators. I could imagine the pain of the numerous voiceless teens and women who have suffered, and those who continue to

---

12. Leung and Williams, "#MeToo and Intersectionality," 352.

13. Ambrose, "Pentecostal Studies Face the #MeToo Movement," 1–7; Suk et al., "#MeToo," 276; Leung and Williams, "#MeToo and Intersectionality," 349–71.

14. Allison, *#ChurchToo*, 22.

suffer similar ordeals in the Ghanaian context without a trusted systems of help within the church community.[15]

#Pentecostalsisterstoo

In 2019, a special issue of *Pneuma: The Journal of the Society for Pentecostal Studies* was dedicated to the theme, *Pentecostal Studies Face the #MeToo Movement*.[16] In the introduction to this special issue, Linda Ambrose presented a series of stories of sexual abuse in the church, including Pentecostal churches. Corroborating Rachael Denhollander's sexual abuse allegations, Ambrose contends,

> The church is not a safe place for victims of sexual abuse, and not only because of a lack of help offered to survivors. Recent news of allegations of assault and serial abuse perpetrated by prominent evangelical leaders, and especially the reports of how those allegations have been, in many cases, dismissed and the victims discredited, point to this disturbing fact: the church may be unsafe because of the power differential at work.[17]

She made this statement after chronicling some sexual abuses within the context of the United States starting with the historical exemplar of Recy Taylor's gang rape at the age of twenty-four in 1944 and how the six perpetrators were left unpunished, Rachael Denhollander sexual abuse by Larry Nasar at age fifteen, the protest against Paige Petterson, the president of the Southern Baptist Theological Seminary, and the sexual abuse allegations against Bill Hybels, the founder and Senior Pastor of the Willow Creek Church.[18]

Ambrose argues that Pentecostal churches are not immune to the sexual abuse experienced within other faith communities. She points out the deafening silence of Pentecostal church leadership concerning the issue of sexual abuse allegations against Pentecostal churches.[19] She noted that "to date, no formal resolution or statement has been offered on the part of leadership in [P]entecostal denominations or institutions."[20] Although the #MeToo, #ChurchToo, and #PentecostalsistersToo movements all originated from the USA, the waves went viral on social media, became a nascent

---

15. Here too, the Ghanaian context will be discussed later in this chapter.
16. Ambrose, "Pentecostal Studies Face the #MeToo Movement," 1–7.
17. Ambrose, "Pentecostal Studies Face the #MeToo Movement," 7.
18. Ambrose, "Pentecostal Studies Face the #MeToo Movement," 7.
19. Ambrose, "Pentecostal Studies Face the #MeToo Movement," 3.
20. Ambrose, "Pentecostal Studies Face the #MeToo Movement," 3.

movement, and spread across the globe. Some African countries including Ghana, Nigeria, Kenya, South Africa, and Namibia among others, have engaged the #MeToo and #ChurchToo movements in different ways.

#MeToo, #ChurchToo in Ghana

Sexual abuse is pervasive in Ghana to the extent that there are abusers on the streets, in the job markets, and in the basic schools, high schools, and the universities. There are abusers in the homes and there are abusers in faith communities, including churches. The presence of these predators make women very vulnerable in the country, as the case has been globally.

Elizabeth Ardayfio-Schandorf contends that "in Ghana, like many African countries, the status of women today has been determined by the kind of girlhood they have had. Traditional values, cultural norms, as well as socializing processes, all appear to bestow a low status on the girl child and low status on Ghanaian women."[21] This low status of women in Ghana makes them vulnerable to sexual violence in society. The perpetrators may promise help, then take advantage of women's vulnerability and abuse them. There are stories of sexual harassment at the offices, where some male employers demand sexual favors from prospective female employees before employing them. The Home and Urban Missions (HUM) Committee of the Church of Pentecost (CoP) has recently rescued some vulnerable young ladies who have been trafficked from nearby African countries to Ghana under the pretext of securing lucrative jobs for them then forcing them into commercial sex work upon arrival.[22] Rev Emmanuel Agyei Kwafo, the national coordinator for HUM of the CoP in Ghana, noted that trafficking young ladies to Ghana and forcing them into commercial sex work is now seen as "a big business" by the pimps.[23] HUM is therefore developing a strategy to respond to the situation.[24]

Furthermore, there are stories of close family members including uncles, fathers, stepfathers, and siblings who sexually abuse young girls within the home. There are allegations and countless stories of teachers and lecturers who prey on vulnerable students with the promise of giving them better

---

21. Ardayfio-Schandorf, "Violence against Women," 2.

22. Rev. Samuel Ofori-Gyimah, a pastor of the CoP and the coordinator for HUM in the Ashaiman Area of the CoP in Ghana, in conversation with author, October 7, 2022; Rev. Emmanuel Agyei Kwafo, an Apostle of the CoP and the coordinator for CoP's HUM worldwide, in conversation with author, September 17, 2022.

23. "Pimps" is used in this context to describe both the males and females who solicit clients for commercial sex workers.

24. Rev. Emmanuel Agyei Kwafo, in conversation with author, September 17, 2022.

grades in exchange for sex or forcefully abusing them in the schools. The recent exposé both at the University of Lagos, Nigeria, and the University of Ghana, Legon, by investigative journalists are typical examples. In this exposé, dozens of young girls reported being abused by lecturers in Nigeria and Ghana.[25] In Ghana two lecturers were among the accused. The first is Dr. Kwame Butakor, a lecturer in the College of Education, University of Ghana, and the second is Professor Ransford Gyampo, a political scientist, an outspoken commentator and a former director of the Centre for European Studies of the University of Ghana.[26]

Again, the media is replete with stories of pastors who promise to help vulnerable women out of their spiritual predicament but eventually abuse them, compounding their problems and leaving them in desolation. From January 2000 to March 2019, Emmanuel Nii-Boye Quarshie and others collected and analyzed seventy-three local media reports about clergy-perpetrated sexual violence in Ghana.[27] According to this report, there were 105 survivors and seventy-seven perpetrators out of these seventy-three reports. Ninety-nine of the survivors, representing 94.3% were females whilst only six, representing 5.7%, were males. The perpetrators were all males between the ages of twenty and thirty-nine.[28]

The gender distribution of the survivors corroborates the vulnerability of Ghanaian women and how sexual abuse is largely gender based. Another worrying revelation in this report is that the age distribution of survivors ranged between three and fifty years with the majority of them (54.8%) between the ages of ten and nineteen. It is unthinkable that a clergyman could abuse a three-year-old child! The research also revealed that 23% of the perpetrators belong to the Pentecostal-Charismatic movement while 34% belong to the neo-prophetic movement.[29] Following my earlier definition of Pentecostal-Charismatics in Ghana, both categories belong to the broad categorization of the Pentecostal-Charismatic Movement, adding up to 57%. This report shows a disturbing trend of sexual abuse perpetrated by

25. Mordi, "Sex for Grades."
26. Mordi, "Sex for Grades."
27. Quarshie at al., "Clergy-Perpetrated Sexual Abuse."
28. Quarshie et al., "Clergy-Perpetrated Sexual Abuse," 3034.
29. The term "Neo-Prophetic Movements" is used to describe prophet-led churches that emerged within Ghana's Pentecostal-Charismatic movement in the early 1990s. The leaders of these churches lay much emphasis on giving what they call "spiritual" or "prophetic directions" to their clients. They attract large adherents who are mostly women who are interested in hearing such prophetic utterances from the prophets. These churches are also known as New Prophetic Churches. See Quayesi-Amakye, "Prophetism in Ghana," 162–73; Quarshie et al., "Clergy-Perpetrated Sexual Abuse," 3028–54.

the clergy that demand the immediate attention and action of the Ghanaian churches, especially those of the Pentecostal-Charismatic tradition.

Already, the #metoo, #churchtoo discussions are beginning to gather momentum in Ghana. Apart from their social media presence, there have been television discussions, workshops, and thousands marching against sexual violence. Reports of many of these are published both online and in local newspapers. On January 22, 2021, Phinehas Nana Osei hosted a #ChurchToo discussion on GracedLife TV.[30] In this discussion, Pastor Bartimus Neequaye, who was the guest on the program, lamented the prevalence of sexual abuse against women in Ghana. He asserted that sexual abuse seems to be a major problem of sin in the Ghanaian churches.[31] Prior to this, the Ghana News Archives reported about a workshop held by the Webster University, Ghana, to discuss #MeToo.[32] Furthermore, on September 25, 2019, it was reported on the official website of VoA Africa:

> Dozens of women have marched in the capital of Ghana to protest impunity surrounding attacks on women and girls in the West African country. The activists added their voices to the global conversation on justice for victims of sexual abuse, and holding abusers accountable. Protesters marching through Accra—a sign that Ghana's #MeToo movement is gaining strength here. Victims of domestic and sexual violence are publicly naming abusers, while authorities are being criticized for not making the safety of Ghana's women and girls a priority.[33]

Other related news headings include, "Women in Ghana March Against Sexual Violence,"[34] "Bolgatanga: Women Protest against Sexual Violence at Work,"[35] "The Current Generation Marches against All Forms of Sexual and Gender-Based Violence,"[36] "Thousands March against Sexual Assault,"[37] and "16 Days of Activism against Gender-Based Violence Launched."[38]

Notwithstanding this increasing spread of the #Metoo and #Churchtoo movements in Ghana, the culture of silence on matters of sexual abuse

---

30. Osei, "#ChurchToo."
31. Osei, "#ChurchToo."
32. Webster University, "Webster Ghana Panel."
33. Kosma, "Sexual Rights."
34. Knott, "Women in Ghana March," para. 1–2.
35. Emmanuel, "Bolgatanga."
36. UNFPA Ghana, "Current Generation."
37. Ghana Broadcasting Cooperation, "Thousands March."
38. Ministry of Gender, Children, and Social Protection, "16 Days of Activism."

is still prevalent in the country for several reasons. These include cultural beliefs and family ties, lack of trust in the legal system, and lack of trust in some church leaders. According to Kofi Boakye, cultural factors contributing to non-disclosure of sexual abuse in Ghana include "patriarchal nuances, (child) rape myth acceptance, and a 'collective shame problem.'"[39] Indeed, many women do not report sexual violence to the police because they fear of being blamed, not believed, or mistreated.[40] The vulnerable state of women in Ghana is reminiscent of some biblical stories of power, rape, and vulnerability. A brief discussion of how the Ghanaian context relates to the world of the Bible is considered in the next section.

Biblical Stories of Sexual Abuse against Women and the Ghanaian Contexts

Both the Old and New Testaments of the Bible provide stories of abuses, where power imbalance made way for abusers to prey on vulnerable women. A typical example is King David's sexual abuse of Uriah's wife, Bathsheba, leading to the subsequent killing of Uriah and David's marriage of Bathsheba (2 Sam 11). While some commentators claimed that it was a consented agreement between David and Bathsheba because of the latter's perceived silence, others contend that it was sexual abuse.[41] One needs to better understand the power play within the patriarchal context of the Old Testament to appreciate the vulnerability of Bathsheba. Reading the pericope in context reveals the power imbalance between the powerful King David and the powerless Bathsheba. Within an equally patriarchal society like Ghana, the silence of Bathsheba mirrors the ordeal of many voiceless Ghanaian women who remain silent in the midst of abuse for fear of being misunderstood by others. Here the role of the Ghanaian theological academy to contextually empower Ghanaian women by highlighting the sinfulness of patriarchal oppression and abuse as revealed in David and Bathsheba story.

Another sad biblical story of sexual abuse was the case of Amnon and Tamar (2 Sam 13). This time, David's son, Amnon, raped his own half-sister, Tamar. It is not surprising that David, their father, could not take any action against Amnon or deal with the issue. David himself was morally bankrupt and guilty of sexual abuse, so could not handle this circumstance ethnically and with justice. This story also speaks to the Ghanaian situation where

---

39. Boakye, "Culture and Nondisclosure," 951.

40. Jewkes et al., "Sexual Violence," 150.

41. For scholarly debate on Bathsheba's ordeal, see Grey, "Prophetic Call to Repentance."

vulnerable women have been abused in some churches, but church leaders refuse to call the perpetrators to account. As discussed earlier in this chapter, the research on Ghanaian clergy's involvement in sexual abuse suggests that, just like David, many of the clergy in Ghana lack the moral courage to deal with cases of sexual violence reported to them since they might be guilty themselves.

Similarly, we read in the New Testament about the woman who was caught in adultery and brought to Jesus. Notably, she was brought to Jesus without the man with whom she allegedly committed the adulterous act (John 8:1–11). This story suggests how the issue of patriarchal power and the powerlessness of women was a problem in New Testament times. As discussed earlier, the problem of patriarchal power in Ghana has led to biases in dealing with sexual abuse against women. For example, in many Ghanaian institutions such as schools and offices, men occupy decision making positions and are expected to handle issues of sexual abuse of which some of them are guilty. Jesus' response to the issue of the woman caught in adultery provides an important example for Pentecostal-Charismatic churches in Ghana to challenge the status quo in the light of the #MeToo, #ChurchToo crisis.

A Pentecostal-Charismatic Response to the #MeToo, #ChurchToo Crisis in Ghana

The need for Pentecostal-Charismatics in Ghana to break the silence and respond swiftly to the crisis of sexual abuse within its fold is evident. There have been a few attempts by Pentecostals to engage this issue as indicated earlier. An example is the video discussion on GracedLife TV.[42] The guest speaker, Pastor Bartimus Neequaye, is a minister of the Pentecostal-Charismatic tradition. Pent TV, the official television channel of the CoP has been discussing spousal abuse on the *Mawarie*[43] show of which I was invited as a panelist on June 20, 2022. In terms of scholarly research, Ebenezer Kpalam's PhD dissertation is one of the very few comprehensive works on the subject from a Ghanaian Pentecostal-Charismatic perspective. As a response to child sexual abuse, he argues for using the relational view of the Trinity to provide a foundation for pastoral anthropology for understanding children and church, where mutuality, equality, and interconnectedness are emphasized, with the aim of destroying power imbalances and providing equal worth.[44]

42. Osei, "#ChurchToo."

43. *Mawarie* (meaning "my marriage") is a weekly marriage education program on Pent TV.

44. Kpalam, "Pastoral Response to Child Sexual Abuse in Ghana."

Despite these attempts, it is not an exaggeration to indicate that the loud silence of Pentecostal-Charismatics in Ghana concerning sexual abuse against women still dominates. Consequently, as a theological educator in one of the leading Pentecostal theological institutions in Ghana, I began to search extensively for a curriculum that directly aims at equipping pastors on sexual violence against women, especially within Pentecostal-Charismatic theological institutions. I have yet to find one. I, therefore, propose the need to urgently respond to this by introducing courses that deal with violence against women into the curriculum of Pentecostal theological education in Ghana.

Furthermore, as a pastor of the CoP for the past eighteen years, my experiences and conversations with women who have been sexually abused reveal to me the lack of appropriate models of dealing with the menace among Pentecostal-Charismatic leaders in Ghana. Out of my personal observations and conversations with survivors of sexual abuse through these years of interactions, I propose the need for the church in Ghana to assume the role of a redemptive community, a disciplined community, a transforming community, and an empowering community, as pastoral responses to the menace. These responses have been briefly discussed as follows.

The Church as a Redemptive Community

Christopher McMahon argues that an obstacle to authentic religious faith and practice is that the contemporary church presents itself as paradoxical.[45] This is particularly because, whilst the church is meant to be a redemptive community, there are too many reports of violence against the vulnerable. Pentecostal-Charismatics in Ghana should redefine the church as a place of healing and restoration, and refuge for victims of sexual abuse. The church must work hard to redeem her integrity and trust through consistency and genuineness to enable victims to have the confidence to share their challenges. Such victims should not be stigmatized. Rather, they should be provided with counseling and support, capable of redeeming and restoring their self-esteem, dignity, and confidence to face life in its fullness. McMahon insists that "It is the role of theology to redefine the scandal of the Christian church's redemptive role in a world torn by sin and religiously sanctioned violence—even as the world looks on with suspicion and disbelief."[46] The need to rethink Pentecostal-Charismatic ecclesiology in the public sphere comes to the fore. Efforts should be made by Pentecostal-Charismatic

---

45. McMahon, "Theology and the Redemptive Mission," 781.
46. McMahon, "Theology and the Redemptive Mission," 781.

theological institutions in Ghana to adequately equip the pastors as well as lay leaders to effectively work at reclaiming the church's image as a redemptive community in Ghana.

The Church as a Disciplined Community

The multiplicity of meanings assigned to the word "discipline" in different contexts makes the concept of church discipline almost anachronistic within contemporary ecclesiology.[47] Following Duncan, the term is used in this chapter to signify "the whole range of nurturing, instructional, and training procedures that disciple making requires. . . . It also has an element of chastisement and correction. . . . It refers to approaches that emphasize character formation, the teaching of self-discipline and acceptable behaviour."[48] The church should, therefore, be very intentional to nurture and train its members to be self-disciplined and treat women with dignity. Self-discipline should be a Christian virtue that should be encouraged and inculcated in the members of the believing communities. Additionally, the church should not cover up for abusers or perpetrators of sexual abuse. Rather, the church should be bold to expose offenders to disciplinary machineries, irrespective of their status, position, power, or wealth, to be chastised to serve as a deterrent for others. This will help the church to redeem its image as a disciplined community.

The Church as a Transforming Community

This approach has the potential to deal with the problem from the root. When Zacchaeus was converted, he decided to stop cheating and oppressing his victims. He even promised restitution for those he has cheated. This conversion story is not only good news for Zacchaeus, but also, good news for the people he oppressed (Luke 19:1–10). The church's missional discipleship mandate must be deliberate in working towards transforming selfish, heartless, and wicked people into disciples of Christ who love their neighbors as themselves (Matt 22:39). According to Michelle Rodino-Colocino, the empathy attracted by the #MeToo movement is transformative in nature. She contends that "'Transformative Empathy' promotes listening rather than distancing or looking at speakers as "others." It requires self-reflexivity and potential transformation of one's own assumptions."[49] If the church can

---

47. Duncan, "Church Discipline," 1.
48. Duncan, "Church Discipline," 2.
49. Rodino-Colocino, "Me Too," 97.

work intentionally towards the transformation of its members, the problem of sexual violence could be mitigated from the roots.

The Church as an Empowering Community

Power imbalance between men and women has been identified as a cause for sexual harassment.[50] The missional engagement of the church should be holistic enough, aiming at empowering women spiritually, economically, professionally, socially, and in all aspects of their lives. Power and empowerment are common themes within the Pentecostal-Charismatic tradition. For Pentecostals, to be empowered "is to be resourced or made capable of achieving aims and accomplishing feats that would otherwise have remained difficult or impossible to undertake."[51] The Pentecostal understanding of empowerment should not be limited to being empowered to heal the sick or exorcise demons. It should also embrace social empowerment, especially to empower women to take their rightful place in society against abuses. It should include the power to "exorcise" perpetrators without covering them up. Veli-Matti Kärkkäinen contends that "Pentecostalism is also characterized by a commitment to social justice, empowerment of the powerless, and a 'preferential option for the marginalized' tracing back to its roots at Azusa Street as a kind of paradigm of marginalization."[52] This should encourage Pentecostals in Ghana to resource women to be socially, economically, and spiritually empowered above their current predicaments.

Conclusion

It has become obvious that Pentecostal-Charismatic denominations in Ghana are not immune to sexual abuse against women. The current image of Pentecostal-Charismatic churches in the country is a paradox. Whilst on the one hand, the church is believed to uphold moral integrity and fight sexual abuse, on the other hand, there are too many regrettable reports about the church in Ghana being guilty of sexual abuse. Meanwhile, the curriculum of theological institutions that train Pentecostal-Charismatic pastors and lay leaders in Ghana does not seem to have consciously considered sexual violence against women as a crucial issue. There is an urgent need for these institutions to find ways by which their curricula can be

---

50. Miazad, "Sex, Power, and Corporate Governance," 8.
51. Asamoah-Gyadu, "You Shall Receive Power," 46–47.
52. Kärkkäinen, "Pentecostal Understanding of Mission," 38.

more intentional about equipping pastors, theologians, pastors' wives, and lay leaders who go through training, not only to be in the position to help survivors of sexual abuse, but also to deal with the perpetrators more appropriately. With the huge demographic growth of Pentecostal-Charismatic Christianity in Ghana, a pragmatic approach of these churches as a redemptive community, a disciplined community, a transforming community, and an empowering community, will go a long way to mitigate the problem of sexual abuse against women in the nation.

Bibliography

Allison, Emily J. *#ChurchToo: How Purity Culture Upholds Abuse and How to Find Healing*. Minneapolis: Broadleaf, 2021.

Ambrose, Linda M. "Pentecostal Studies Face the #MeToo Movement Introduction." *Pneuma* 41 (2019) 1–7.

Anderson, Allan. *To the Ends of the Earth: Pentecostalism and the Transformation of World Christianity*. Oxford: Oxford University Press, 2013.

Ardayfio-Schandorf, Elizabeth. "Violence against Women: The Ghanaian Case." Paper presented at Expert Group Meeting organized by UN Division for the Advancement of Women, Geneva, Switzerland, April 11–14, 2005. https://www.un.org/womenwatch/daw/egm/vaw-stat-2005/docs/expert-papers/Ardayfio.pdf.

Asamoah-Gyadu, J. Kwabena. *African Charismatics: Current Developments within Independent Indigenous Pentecostalism in Ghana*. Leiden: Brill, 2005.

———. *Sighs and Signs of the Spirit: Ghanaian Perspectives on Pentecostalism and Renewal in Africa*. Oxford: Regnum, 2015.

———. "'You Shall Receive Power': Empowerment in Pentecostal/Charismatic Christianity." In *Pentecostal Mission and Global Christianity: An Edinburgh Centenary Reader*, edited by Wonsuk Ma et al., 45–66. Oxford: Regnum, 2014.

Barnes, Naomi. "Trace Publics as a Qualitative Critical Network Tool: Exploring the Dark Matter in the #MeToo Movement." *New Media & Society* 22 (2020) 1305–19.

Boakye, Kofi E. "Culture and Nondisclosure of Child Sexual Abuse in Ghana: A Theoretical and Empirical Exploration." *Law & Social Inquiry* 34 (2009) 951–79.

Boyd, Alicia, and Bree McEwan. "Viral Paradox: The Intersection of 'Me Too' and #MeToo." *New Media & Society* (2022) 1–18.

Duncan, Graham A. "Church Discipline: *Semper Reformanda* in Reformation Perspective." *HTS Theological Studies* 66 (2010) 1–6.

Emmanuel, Kojo. "Bolgatanga: Women Protest against Sexual Violence at Work." *Pulse*, September 10, 2021. https://www.pulse.com.gh/news/local/bolgatanga-stop-sex-for-jobs-as-women-protest-against-sexual-violence-at-work/fdw6fzh.

Ghana Broadcasting Cooperation. "Thousands March against Sexual Assault." March 15, 2021. https://www.gbcghanaonline.com/world/thousands-march-against-sexual-assault/2021/.

Grey, Jacqueline. "A Prophetic Call to Repentance." *Pneuma* 41 (2019) 9–25.

Jewkes, Rachel, et al. "Sexual Violence." In *World Report on Violence and Health*, edited by Etienne G. Krug et al., 147–81. Geneva: World Health Organization, 2002.

Kärkkäinen, Veli-Matti. "The Pentecostal Understanding of Mission." In *Pentecostal Mission and Global Christianity: An Edinburgh Centenary Reader*, edited by Wonsuk Ma et al., 26–44. Oxford: Regnum, 2014.

Knott, Stacey. "Women in Ghana March against Sexual Violence." *VoA Africa*, September 25, 2019. https://www.voanews.com/a/africa_women-ghana-march-against-sexual-violence/6176427.html.

Kosma, Marietta. "Sexual Rights and the #Metoo Movement in Ghana." *Right for Education*, November 25, 2021. https://rightforeducation.org/2021/11/25/sexual-rights-metoo-movement-2/.

Kpalam, Ebenezer T. "A Pastoral Response to Child Sexual Abuse in Ghana: An Interdisciplinary Study Informed by a Relational View of the Trinity." PhD diss., North-West University, South Africa, 2021.

Leung, Rebecca, and Robert Williams. "#MeToo and Intersectionality: An Examination of the #MeToo Movement through the R. Kelly Scandal." *Journal of Communication Inquiry* 43 (2019) 349–71.

Ma, Julie C., and Wonsuk Ma. *Mission in the Spirit: Towards a Pentecostal/Charismatic Missiology*. Oxford: Regnum, 2013.

McMahon, Christopher. "Theology and the Redemptive Mission of the Church: A Catholic Response to Milbank's Challenge." *Heythrop Journal* 51 (2010) 781–94.

Miazad, Amelia. "Sex, Power, and Corporate Governance." *UC Davis Law Review* 54 (2020) 1–88. https://ssrn.com/abstract=3675968.

Ministry of Gender, Children, and Social Protection. "16 Days of Activism against Gender-Based Violence Launched." November 25, 2021. https://www.mogcsp.gov.gh/16-days-of-activism-against-gender-based-violence-launched/.

Mordi, Kiki. "Sex for Grades: Undercover inside Nigerian and Ghanaian Universities—BBC Africa Eye Documentary." *YouTube*, October 7, 2019. https://www.youtube.com/watch?v=we-FoGioLqs.

Osei, Phinehas N. "#ChurchToo: A Conversation on Sexual Abuse in the Church." *GracedLife TV*, January 22, 2021. https://www.facebook.com/gracedlifeTV/videos/churchtoo-a-conversation-on-sexual-abuse-in-the-church/1399354653741476/.

Osei-Tutu, Ellen M., and Ernest Ampadu. "Domestic Violence against Women in Ghana: The Attitudes of Men toward Wife-Beating." *Journal of International Women's Studies* 18 (2017) 105–16.

Quarshie, Emmanuel N., et al. "Clergy-Perpetrated Sexual Abuse in Ghana: A Media Content Analysis of Survivors, Offenders, and Offence Characteristics." *Journal of Religion and Health* 61 (2022) 3028–54.

Quayesi-Amakye, Joseph. "Prophetism in Ghana's New Prophetic Churches." *Journal of the European Pentecostal Theological Association* 35 (2015) 162–73.

Rodino-Colocino, Michelle. "Me Too, #MeToo: Countering Cruelty with Empathy." *Communication and Critical/Cultural Studies* 15 (2018) 96–100.

Sossou, Marie-Antoinette, and Joseph A. Yogtiba. "Abuse, Neglect, and Violence against Elderly Women in Ghana: Implications for Social Justice and Human Rights." *Journal of Elder Abuse & Neglect* 27 (2015) 422–27.

Suk, Jiyoun, et al. "#MeToo, Networked Acknowledgment, and Connective Action: How 'Empowerment through Empathy' Launched a Social Movement." *Social Science Computer Review* 39 (2021) 276–94.

Takyi, Baffour K., and Enoch Lamptey. "Faith and Marital Violence in Sub-Saharan Africa: Exploring the Links between Religious Affiliation and Intimate Partner

Violence among Women in Ghana." *Journal of Interpersonal Violence* 35 (2020) 25–52.

Tenkorang, Eric Y., et al. "Factors Influencing Domestic and Marital Violence against Women in Ghana." *Gender Issues in Violence and Trauma* 28 (2013) 771–81.

Tsekpoe, Christian. "Navigating the Shades and Nexus of Ghanaian Pentecostalism(s): A Search for an Appropriate Metaphor." *Ghana Journal of Religion and Theology* 10 (2020) 27–46.

UNFPA Ghana. "Current Generation Marches against All Forms Sexual and Gender-Based Violence." January 13, 2020. https://ghana.unfpa.org/en/news/current-generation-marches-against-all-forms-sexual-and-gender-based-violence.

Webster University. "Webster Ghana Panel Discusses '#MeToo from an African Perspective.'" https://www.webster.edu.gh/news/2018/ghana-metoo-africa-perspective-panel.php.

Conversation 4

Models of Women's Power

— 10 —

Restoring the Heart of the Nation

Shari Russell

> Woman is the centre of the wheel of life.
> She is the heartbeat of the people.
> She is not just in the home, but she is the community,
> she is the Nation, one of our Grandmothers.
> The woman is the foundation on which Nations are built.
> She is the heart of her Nation.
> If that heart is weak, the people are weak.
> If her heart is strong and her mind is clear,
> then the Nation is strong and knows its purpose.
> The woman is the centre of everything.
>
> — Elder Art Solomon[1]

---

1. ONWA, "Eliminating Violence against Indigenous Women and Girls," para. 2.

BOOZHOO (*GREETINGS*).

Niin Anishinaabekwe onji Pagan Sagahiganiing. (I am an Anishinaabe woman from Yellow Quill First Nation.)

Nimaamaa onji Kipwapkikang. (My mother is from Kinistin First Nation.)

Niin Shari Russell nindizhinikaaz. (My name is Shari Russell.)

I am part of the 60s scoop.

I am the wife of Robert celebrating our thirtieth year.

I am the mother of three adult sons.

I am a leader in our denomination and the Associate Director for NAIITS: An Indigenous Learning Community.

It is customary as an Anishinaabe person to begin with an introduction which would include a greeting, where we come from, our relations, and our name. I have also included my occupation, which is not typical in our introductions but may be helpful for this conversation on power and leadership within Western institutions. It is from this perspective as an Indigenous woman (*Anishinaabekwe*), I posit that reclaiming Indigenous concepts such as "deep listening" (*Dadirri*), "all my relations" (*Indinawemaaganidog*), and communal identity contribute to the agency of all women through radical resurgence[2] thus enabling the flourishing and good life (*minobimaadiziwin*) of all.

As I have introduced myself, the impact of colonization is evident as I mention the 60s scoop. The 60s scoop refers to the practice in the 1960s–80s of removing Indigenous children from their families, often without parental consent, and placing them into the child welfare system. The purpose of this practice was to adopt us into non-Indigenous homes so we would assimilate into Canadian society.[3] The impact of colonization can be seen in my shift to speaking exclusively in English, not only because our language was taken from us, but because English is the language of the dominant culture/colonizer. Our language speaks not only to our identity but so much more; it embodies our worldview, our history, our kinships, our connection to land, and our spirituality. In an act of resistance and decolonization, I am now learning my language.

The impact of heteropatriarchy is evident when I state, "I am from Yellow Quill First Nation" rather than my mother's reserve, Kinistin. In

---

2. Leanne Betasamosake Simpson argues radical resurgence is more than cultural resurgence but also political, thereby unsettling settler identity and structures. She utilizes *Kwe* as a method, recentering gender as resistance and resurgence. For more information, see Simpson, *As We Have Always Done*, 47–54.

3. For more information on the 60s scoop, see Sinclair, "Indigenous Child Removal System in Canada."

Canada, Indigenous peoples were registered as Indians with the Canadian government under the paternal name, the result of the Indian Act's discriminating practice of privileging paternal descent. Consequently, I am registered at Yellow Quill. The Indian Act continues to govern our lives as Indigenous peoples in Canada and determines who is classified as Indian.[4] From my perspective as an Anishinaabe woman, the conversation about power and powerlessness cannot be bifurcated from the colonization, patriarchy, and racism we have experienced through the centuries. Furthermore, as a woman in leadership in my church and the academy, I am dismayed that there is little conversation around the subject of patriarchy despite the number of women it impacts. These are not abstract ideologies but continue to affect our daily lives as well as those of our families and communities.

The way I choose to introduce myself also expresses my ongoing resistance to the continuing patriarchy we experience. I intentionally seek to honour the legacy of my mother by identifying where she is from and acknowledging her role and significance in our family. As a mother of three boys, it is important for our boys to learn Anishinaabe traditional values, especially respect and honour for women. I seek to do things differently for my sons and the generations to follow by reclaiming these practices and protocols.

The resistance to patriarchy is also conveyed in the leadership roles I hold, both within my denomination as a Salvation Army Officer, and within the academy. My denomination has been a vanguard for ordaining women since its inception in 1887 and NAIITS: An Indigenous Learning Community has always sought to honor the role of women through intentional representation on our board of directors, faculty, and staff personnel.[5] This is an act of reclamation of our Indigenous epistemologies of leadership and governance. I posit that it is through this reclamation and revitalization of Indigenous identity, traditions, and ceremonies that Indigenous women and our communities are seeking to disrupt settler colonialism and heteropatriarchy. It is through participating in ceremony, the foundation of our personal and collective identity, that we will re-establish and restore *mino bimaadizin* to ourselves and other women. *Mino bimaadiziwin* is often translated as "the good life" but encompasses a more comprehensive understanding of health and well-being.[6] This is closely related to the Hebrew

---

4. Wilson and Hodgson, *Pulling Together*, s.v. "The Indian Act."

5. The founding board of NAIITS included two women: Cheryl Bear and Wendy Peterson. This legacy continues as our Board of Directors is comprised of a majority of women (67% women) with a female Chairperson, our faculty is 50% women, and our overall staff is 50%.

6. The concept of *mino bimaadiziwin* is expansive and includes balance of the physical, mental, emotional, and spiritual aspects but also seven principles:

concept of *Shalom* which Randy Woodley, Cherokee scholar, articulates as the *Harmony Way*.[7] As we grow stronger and recover the centre of communal life, our children, families, communities, and nations will also flourish and experience *mino bimaadizin* once again.

Recently I participated in a beautiful expression of this as I shared in a water ceremony at the conclusion of a weekend focused on Indigenous-Settler relations. As I pondered this ceremony, I reflected on three significant relationships being embodied. The obvious relationship is between Indigenous and Settler peoples as we participated together in learning from one another. The second relationship is that of humanity with creation expressed in the water. The third is the relationship between genders as no one was excluded or diminished but each had a different role to play.

In many Indigenous cultures, women are identified as water carriers and water protectors. This reflects the reciprocal relationship women have with *nibiish* (water) as "Water is a 'giver of life' and the first environment for new life is inside a woman's body."[8] As the women gathered in a circle to share in ceremony, the *Mindimooyenh*[9] asked the men in the group to form a circle on the outside of the women and to face outwards. The women were at the centre. As the men had their backs to us, their faces to the outside, the *Mindimooyenh* shared this was not only for privacy and respect, but the men were to be on the "lookout" so that we could participate in the ceremony without any external threat. As the water went from woman to woman around the circle, it was then extended to the men as we shared this gift with them. The men were recipients of this gift, not demanding or asserting their power but respecting our role and responsibility for the water and how women provide for the community. In a similar fashion to women's reciprocal relationship with water, there is also a reciprocal relationship between genders. Neither is in a position of dominance but both are in a posture of reciprocity, as we are interdependent and interconnected with one another and all creation.

---

anishinaabemowin (language/communication), *inaadiziwin* (behaviors, values, way of living), *inendamowin* (thinking, perceiving, beliefs, worldview), *gikendaasowin* (knowledge, ways of knowing), *izhichigewin* (ways of doing, living, quality of community), *inawendiwin* (interconnectedness, our relations and responsibilities), and *gidakiiminaan* (connection to land and all creation). For more information, see Earth Lodge, "Developing Anishinaabe Mino Bimaadiziwin Principles."

7. Woodley, *Shalom and the Community of Creation*, 73–74.

8. Dennis and Bell, "Indigenous Women," 278–86.

9. A reference to a female Elder, this term means "one who holds things together" economically, organizationally, and socially, reflecting woman's autonomy. The term "evokes the status, strength, wisdom, and authority of the older female in Ojibwe society," according to Child, *Holding Our World Together*, 63–64.

The reclamation of ceremonies is an act of resistance to the colonial enterprise. The reclamation of women's ceremonies is an act of resistance to heteropatriarchy through affirming our identity and personhood as women and the integral place we occupy for the flourishing of the whole community. Colonization has left an indelible mark on many Indigenous nations through the destruction it has inflicted on our communities and families, especially our women and children. Imposed policies and legislation by the colonial government have created obstacles to our autonomy and have stagnated representation in places of power or authority. One such obstacle pertains to our personhood and identity. In the Canadian context, the government developed criteria as to who would legally qualify as an Indian[10] and given status according to the Indian Act. The 1876 Indian Act defined an Indian as "Any male person of Indian blood reputed to belong to a particular band," "any child of such person," and "any woman who is or was lawfully married to such person."[11] Our personhood and identity as Indigenous women was devalued through the privileging of paternal lineage and discriminatory practices. Furthermore, a status Indian woman would lose any acknowledgement of her Indigenous identity, her rights, and her place in community if she married a non-status Indian or non-Indigenous person, effectively seeking the elimination of Indigenous women. This did not change until 1985.[12]

Indigenous women were also denied the right to possess any marital property until 1884 and only upon approval by the Indian Agent. Indigenous models of governance, some of which were inclusive of women, were supplanted with the federally imposed Band Council system. This new system of governance enacted in the Indian Act denied women power and agency in community governance as they were removed from their traditional leadership roles and not allowed to participate in the Band Council system until 1951. It also outlawed traditional ceremonies, such as the Potlatch and Sundance, even making it illegal to wear our traditional and ceremonial clothing unless given official permission for performative demonstrations.

---

10. Although legally still defined as Indian in the Indian Act, this may be considered a pejorative term. Many Indigenous peoples in Canada have reclaimed their endonyms such as Anishinaabe, Mi'kmaq, Haudenosaunee, etc. They may also choose to utilize First Nations or Indigenous.

11. Excerpt from the Indian Act, 1876 CHAP. 18. An Act to amend and consolidate the laws respecting Indians. (Assented to April 12, 1876.)

12. Although amended in 1985 in Bill C-31, this still is not satisfactory to many Indigenous communities as there is a second-generation limitation which in effect, continues to eliminate Indigenous peoples.

This elucidates why the reclamation of traditions and ceremonies is fundamental to our identity and well-being, individually and collectively.

In a series of legislative maneuvers to assimilate Indigenous peoples into the body politic and eliminate any fiduciary responsibilities for Indians, the Dominion of Canada introduced the Gradual Civilization Act of 1857, the Gradual Enfranchisement Act of 1869 and eventually incorporated aspects of both into the Indian Act of 1876. Enfranchisement meant First Nations people not only lost their Indian status and any associated rights but also their connection to family, community, and their whole sense of identity.[13] Enfranchisement was compulsory for First Nations people admitted to university for a degree or for those who sought to become a teacher, lawyer, doctor, veteran, or member of the clergy, thereby impeding Indigenous representation in baccalaureate education and church leadership. This remained in effect until 1961. Although the law had changed, when I entered seminary in 1992, not only were there very few women in general, but to my knowledge, I was the only Indigenous person attending that seminary at that point in time. It has been encouraging however to see more Indigenous people attending colleges and universities in the years to follow.

Some of these external obstacles have been removed which is reflective of the collaborative efforts of Indigenous people, especially women who have advocated for change. There are other obstacles however which are not always visible in public policy or practice which are often more difficult to overcome.

One such obstacle is how we have internalized the negative messages of colonization and patriarchy. My friend Richard Twiss has said that the final frontier of colonization is consciousness.[14] It is crucial, therefore, to address how colonization has reached our consciousness both personally and collectively. The external subjugation concomitant with colonization has somehow become embedded in our consciousness. All too often we have internalized oppressive messages that we are not good such as being called heathen Indians; we are expendable evidenced in the Missing and Murdered Indigenous women and girls; we are incompetent and will amount to "nothing"; we are unworthy and, henceforth, the recipients of the goodwill of others; we are irrational when we stand up for our rights, we are an inconvenience, we are "too much" and the list goes on. Lee Maracle says, "the result of being colonized is the internalization of the need to remain invisible. The colonizers erase you, not easily, but with shame and brutality.

---

13. Stevenson, "Colonialism and First Nations Women in Canada," 69–70.
14. Wiconi International, "Richard Twiss."

Eventually you want to stay that way."[15] This applies to all women, regardless of cultural background, in our fight against patriarchalism. Too often we have been directly and indirectly told that women are not qualified to be leaders; we are too emotional; we are an inconvenience because things need to be adapted or changed because of our presence; and that we are not worth the same recompense as men. After centuries of colonization and patriarchy, it will take more than awareness of these internal messages; it will require courage, intentionality, and embodied experience by all to eradicate these negative messages from society.

One way erasure continues is in the scarcity or absence of role models in places of leadership, especially for Indigenous women. Although there are some Indigenous women in academia, their presence is even more sparse within Christian academic settings. Even when there is representation, attacks are often encountered from both the oppressor/colonizer and their own families and communities. Macro and microaggressions are utilized to question credentials and capabilities. These questions may come from both their peers and those who hold leadership positions in the church and the academy. Women may also experience the rebuffs from their own families and communities who feel betrayed by the one who has seemingly joined the system of patriarchy and/or colonialism. In an attempt to gain respect and acceptance, Indigenous peoples and women may tend to acquiesce to the politics of recognition. The temptation to think "if only they knew us, they would accept us" lulls us into spending much of our time doing awareness training or being token representatives on various committees. While it is important to have this representation and it is necessary to facilitate cultural awareness and safety, these can divert the necessary attention and focus required for systemic change. This distraction of responding to the concerns of the patriarchy/oppressors may provide temporary relief for the dominant culture while allowing the systems to continue rather than dismantling them as we had hoped. The danger is to spend our time trying to convince the colonial/patriarchal society of our validity as human beings. Sadly, this attempt to convince them of our legitimacy exposes how we continue to be enslaved to their power.

Even within the Christian academic world, this dynamic is evident. At the 2004 NAIITS[16] symposium in Ranchos Palos Verdes, Tite Tietenou challenged us with the idea that Indigenous Christian scholars are often

---

15. Maracle, *I Am Woman*, 8.

16. NAIITS originally represented the North American Institute for Indigenous Studies. It is now a global community of learning and although the acronym remains it is now officially NAIITS: An Indigenous Learning Community.

viewed as "purveyors of exotic, raw intellectual material."[17] Despite our achievements, credentials, and reputations, our contributions are marginalized through the derived discourse of offering the "Indigenous perspective." Tietenou continues to note, "This is a case of inclusion by marginalization." The romanticization that occurs when we are "purveyors of exotic, raw intellectual material" continues to render our voice to the margins, albeit, some may be encouraged to at least be included, even if at the margins.

Likewise, within the feminist movement when we are invited to speak, it is often to speak about a particular topic connected to our Indigeneity. The contemporary usage of the hyphen is a powerful but obliterating tool. I am thankful we speak about intersectionality; the pitfall is it can fall back into the polarizing hyphen: Asian-American women; African-American women, Latinx-women, Indigenous-women, etc., breeding competition between us as "minority" groups. There is limited space for our voice and experience, so it is morphed into a common experience, or it becomes a point of division between us. When there is division, the peril of the hyphenated identity results in our experiences being eclipsed by the needs of the dominant group. The presumption is that we all have the same experience when, in fact, it differs vastly for each of us. Although we come from different cultural backgrounds seeking for justice and equity, we may find ourselves in competition, engaging in "oppression Olympics" due to the limited space for our voice and experience. Audre Lorde expresses this in her statement "we have been taught to either ignore our differences, or to view them as causes for separation and suspicion rather than as forces as change."[18] When we do this, our experience is minimized and subsumed into the uniform experience of the dominant culture. Rather than allowing this to occur, we must find space for our unique experiences and utilize the power of our collective voice to bring about necessary change for justice.

In the battle against colonization, our identity, roles, and relationships as Indigenous women have prompted a reassessment of the notion of power within our communities. The misuse of power and patriarchy that is visible in some Indigenous communities reflects the devastation of colonialism. The danger of power is that we want to acquire it and assert it over others as has been done to us. This is why the reclamation of our identity, traditions, and ceremonies is integral to holistic well-being or the "good life" of *mino bimaadizin*. It is the restoration of our personal and communal identity that brings health. Cindy Blackstock's dissertation "When Everything Matters" discloses the fact that Abraham Maslow based his hierarchy of needs on the

---

17. Tiénou, "Indigenous Theologizing," 14.
18. Lorde, *Master's Tools*, 18.

teachings of the Blackfoot Nation.[19] His model focused on the individual experience with self-actualization at the pinnacle rather than the Blackfoot model which places self-actualization as the foundation. Self-actualization is intimately linked with one's identity, hence the reclamation of identity is foundational for Indigenous peoples. It is when this identity is restored that community actualization flourishes and cultural perpetuity is realized. To paraphrase the words of wisdom from Elder Art Solomon, when Indigenous women are affirmed in their identity, the nation is strengthened and knows its *raison d'être*.

The acquisition of power for women is not the solution or antidote for patriarchy, at least not power as defined by Western epistemology. Dana Hickey speaks to this in her article when she compares Indigenous and Western notions about power as it pertains to the source of power and how it is bestowed; the goal of power and the outcomes achieved; and the focus of power and what values it seeks. Not surprisingly, the concept of power is different in the dominant Western context than it is within many traditional Indigenous cultures. Hickey asserts the source of power within the Western context is often accomplishment or positionality "by virtue, by right, or by legitimacy."[20] Since power is sought by an individual, this can result in the disproportionate accumulation of power by a select few as "it is considered either virtuous, righteous, or legitimate."[21] Within Indigenous communities, the source of power is the collective affirmation of the individual rather than their self-aggrandizement. It is based on the "sacred network of interconnectedness of all elements of the universe, swirling around in a dance of perpetual change and transformation—or the flux."[22]

The goal of power, according to Hickey's research, also differs between Western and Indigenous societies. The objective for Western societies focuses on productivity and the establishment and maintenance of order based on individual accomplishment, capitalism, and rivalry. For Indigenous societies, the assertion of one individual holding power over another person or aspect of Creation would result in imbalance and harm. For there to be health and well-being for people and communities, we need to seek and maintain balance and reciprocity in all our relations with Creation.

Hickey also points out the differentiation on the focus of power within Western and Indigenous epistemologies. She asserts that the focus of power for Western societies is on the qualification of superiority

---

19. Blackstock, "When Everything Matters," 35–36.
20. Hickey, "Indigenous Epistemologies," 21.
21. Hickey, "Indigenous Epistemologies," 21.
22. Hickey, "Indigenous Epistemologies," 21.

versus inferiority whereas Indigenous societies are not inclined to make value judgments or comparative analysis. Since many Indigenous epistemologies articulate that all creation is sacred, the principles of respect, reciprocity, and responsibility are valued in all relationships rather than superiority, accumulation, and power.

Utilizing Indigenous epistemologies is the primary means by which Indigenous women are overcoming barriers to our leadership roles whereby the whole community flourishes. One such concept is the process of Deep Listening (*Dadirri*), conveyed by Laura Brearley who learned this from Indigenous elders in Australia. She reiterates the words of Aunty Miriam Rose Ungunmerr-Baumann, a Ngangikurungkurr elder from northern Australia:

> In our Aboriginal way, we learn to listen from our earliest days. We could not live good and useful lives unless we listened. This was the normal way for us to learn—not by asking questions. We learnt by watching and listening, waiting and then acting. Our people have passed on this way of listening for over 40,000 years.[23]

Deep listening involves emptying our personal agendas and removing obstacles so that space can be created in which authentic interactions are encouraged. Intimately linked to Deep Listening is the concept of "presencing—a term that blends presence and sensing"[24] and reciprocity. As we engage in Deep Listening, core tenets of community leadership unfold to bring about holistic flourishing. Within the Australian context, Brearley articulates these core tenets in terms of respect, trust, learning, creativity, and care. Within other Indigenous communities, similar values exist such as the Seven Sacred Teachings of the Anishinaabeg people. Deep listening encompasses listening to community, to culture, and to our ancestors, and in humility, learning from them. As we engage in deep listening, the stranglehold of patriarchy begins to unravel as respect, reciprocity, and responsibility to one another galvanize and transform our relations.

In many Indigenous traditions another concept that has encouraged overcoming barriers is the reclamation of our identity through kinship. The phrase "all my relations" has rich expressions in many Indigenous languages such as *Nii'kinaaganaa* (Anishinaabemowin), *Mitakuye-Oyasin* (Lakota), *Msit No'kmaq* (Mi'kmaq), *Wahkohtawin* (Cree), and *Ohen':ton Karihwate'hkwen* (Mohawk). Patty Krawek in her book shares the morphology of the Anishinaabmowin word *Nii'kinaaganaa*, as taught to her by Josh Manitowabi. She shares: "*Nii*: 'I am' or 'my.' *Kinaa*: 'all of them.' *Ganaa*:

---

23. Brearley, "Deep Listening and Leadership," 95.
24. Brearley, "Deep Listening and Leadership," 94.

'relatives, my relatives.' The phrase could mean any of these things: I am my relatives, all of them. I am related to everything. All my relations."[25]

This concept encompasses more than the limited translation of English, it grounds us in our identity and reminds us of the kinship relations we have with all creation. It speaks of the interconnectedness between and among all of creation. Situating our humanity within the greater circle of life changes our understanding of power dynamics as we realize our dependence upon creation for life and sustenance. Humanity cannot survive without the gifts given by the rest of creation; their sacrifice provides sustenance (whether plant or animal), shelter, warmth, medicine, and refreshment. Even the laws that govern us are modelled for us within creation. We are reliant on the rest of creation for everything. This reverses the narrative that humanity is the most powerful when, in fact, we are the most dependent.

This concept of "all my relations" helps us overcome obstacles we may encounter in leadership as it reminds us that we are not alone. We are interconnected. The tendency is to isolate: to think that we must stand alone. The antidote is not individual achievement but collective strength. Rather than dividing and conquering, which colonialism is predicated on, the concept of "all my relations" seeks to "define and empower"[26] as Audre Lorde beckons. Our leadership is viewed through kinship perspectives of interrelatedness rather than adversarial. If we were to have this view of leadership in churches and academia, it would impact how we support and encourage one another. Rather than focusing on our individual accomplishments or competing with another for a position, we would see the assets each one brings and how, together, we bring health to the whole body. Closely linked to this is the concept of the seventh generation principle. The seventh generation principle reminds us that our decisions and actions should take into consideration the generations that have gone before us as we prepare and care for the future generations to come. When we take the time to do this, the focus is not on individual achievement but on how we, building upon the wisdom and experience of those who have gone before us, can collectively work together to create a future of possibilities and hope.

It is only through a community response that we can overcome the obstacles created by patriarchy, colonialism, and racism. This is a collective fight; not an individualistic one. When we encounter challenging words such as "I accomplished this on my own, why can't you?," this approach leads us to comparison and eventually abandonment of one another as we seek to make it on our own. Lee Maracle states: When we do this, "the end

---

25. Krawec, *Becoming Kin*, 1.
26. Lorde, *Master's Tools*, 19.

result is each of us digging our own way out of the hole, filling up the path with dirt as we go. . . . Until all of us are free, the few who think they are remain tainted with enslavement."[27]

As women, we need to support each other. All too often we are the most critical of one another as we are vying for a position or recognition. A few years ago, three other Indigenous women and I were asked to speak at a conference. Before we spoke, the eldest in our group brought us together for prayer and shared words of encouragement. She then cautioned us with this image of not becoming like "crabs in a bucket" trying to get out by climbing all over one another. All too often I have seen this competition between women as we battle against one another. When we use tactics and skills that are recognizable to the patriarchy, we become complicit in the erasure of ourselves as women. The patriarchal domain continues to dictate our thinking and behaviors as we strive for their acknowledgement.

Finally, a reclamation of ceremony is concomitant with a reconnection to land, especially the intimate relationship as women with our mother, the Earth. This reconnection to land is not only applicable for Indigenous peoples who have an inherent relationship with land but also those who have been taken from their land or have come as settlers searching for a connection to land. Mississauga Nishnaabeg Scholar Leanne Betasamosake Simpson reminds us: "A great deal of the colonizer's energy has gone into breaking the intimate connection of Nishnaabeg bodies (and minds and spirits) to each other and to the practices and associated knowledges that connect us to land, because this is the base of our power."[28] Hence the reclamation of land-based ceremonies is necessary for the healing and wellbeing (*mino bimaadizin*) of the whole nation and central to this are women's ceremonies as we carry the potential for new life within us. It is this connection to land that is the "base of our power," but it is not power as defined by Western definitions. Rather, power according to Indigenous perspectives is more accurately defined as:

> Power is honouring all of Creation. Power is connectedness to Mother Earth and respect for her life systems. Power is caring for the Ancestors and using the knowledge and ceremonies they passed down. Power is Indigenous women who bring balance, carry the water, and give life. Power is our languages, our voices, our stories, and our songs. Power is the collective cognitive experience known as Indigenous knowledge, which is based on experience, language, and shared beliefs. Power is

---

27. Maracle, *I Am Woman*, 13.
28. Simpson, *As We Have Always Done*, 41.

kinship, community, and good relationships. Power is remaining resilient, adapting to change, and ensuring that Indigenous knowledge survives the colonial assault.[29]

It is this power, based on respect, that honors the dignity and essence of all creation. It is this power, shared in reciprocity, that nourishes and brings health to all. It is this power, governed by humility, that produces *shalom* (harmony) in all our relations and ensures the flourishing of all within creation. It is not a power over another; it is not a power of individual accomplishment; it is not a power that breeds competition and rivalry. It is a transformational power fostering health and *mino bimaadiziwin* for the whole of creation. It is a generative power which nourishes our relationships, our families, our communities, and our world. As women in leadership, in academia, and in positions of authority, may we strive to ensure our hearts are strong so that our families, communities, and nations may flourish in the community of creation.

Bibliography

Blackstock, Cindy. "When Everything Matters: Comparing the Experiences of First Nations and Non-Aboriginal Children Removed from Their Families in Nova Scotia from 2003 to 2005." PhD diss., University of Toronto, 2009.

Brearley, Laura. "Deep Listening and Leadership: An Indigenous Model of Leadership and Community Development in Australia." In *Restorying Indigenous Leadership: Wise Practices in Community Development*, edited by Cora J. Voyageur et al., 91–127. Banff: Banff Centre Press, 2015.

Child, Brenda J. *Holding Our World Together: Ojibwe Women and the Survival of Community*. New York: Viking Penguin, 2012.

Dennis, Mary Kate, and Finn McLafferty Bell. "Indigenous Women, Water Protectors, and Reciprocal Responsibilities." *Social Work* 65 (2020) 378–86.

Earth Lodge. "Developing Anishinaabe Mino Bimaadiziwin Principles for the Lodge." http://lodge.fnt2t.com/wp-content/uploads/2021/04/Seven-Guiding-Principles-full.pdf.

Hickey, Dana. "Indigenous Epistemologies, Worldviews, and Theories of Power." *Turtle Island Journal of Indigenous Health* 1 (2020) 14–25.

Krawec, Patty. *Becoming Kin: An Indigenous Call to Unforgetting the Past and Reimagining Our Future*. Minneapolis: Broadleaf, 2022.

Lorde, Audre. *The Master's Tools Will Never Dismantle the Master's House*. London: Penguin, 2018.

Maracle, Lee. *I Am Woman: A Native Perspective on Sociology and Feminism*. Vancouver: Press Gang, 1996.

Ontario Native Women's Association. "Eliminating Violence against Indigenous Women and Girls Begins by Listening to Their Voices." November 25, 2020. https://

---

29. Hickey, "Indigenous Epistemologies," 105.

www.onwa.ca/post/eliminating-violence-against-indigenous-women-and-girls-begins-by-listening-to-their-voices.

Simpson, Leanne B. *As We Have Always Done: Indigenous Freedom through Radical Resistance*. Minneapolis: University of Minnesota Press, 2017.

Sinclair, Raven. "The Indigenous Child Removal System in Canada: An Examination of Legal Decision-Making and Racial Bias." *First Peoples Child & Family Review* 11 (2016) 8–18.

Stevenson, Winona. "Colonialism and First Nations Women in Canada." In *Scratching the Surface: Canadian Anti-racist Feminist Thought*, edited by Enakshi Dua and Angelia Robertson, 49–80. Toronto: Women's, 1999.

Tiénou, Tite. "Indigenous Theologizing: From the Margins to the Center." *NAIITS* 3 (2005) 5–17.

Wiconi International. "Richard Twiss: The Biggest Problem." *YouTube*, May 7, 2008. https://youtu.be/6JojNNniUso.

Wilson, Kory, and Colleen Hodgson. *Pulling Together: A Guide for Indigenization of Post-Secondary Institutions*. https://opentextbc.ca/indigenizationfoundations/.

Woodley, Randy S. *Shalom and the Community of Creation: An Indigenous Vision*. Grand Rapids: Eerdmans, 2012.

—11—

What to Do with Fragile Masculine Egos

Patrick B. Reyes

Child in the Wilderness

I SIT BETWEEN FIVE generations of Carmelitas. My great-great-grandmother, as far back as we have records, is Carmelita. My grandmother, to whom I have dedicated both my books, and who saved my life, was Carmelita. My daughter's name is Carmelita. And, in five generations there will be another Carmelita. This is how I always introduce myself. My people are matriarchal.

My daughter Carmelita is the most magical and electric human I know. She connects with wild animals. When we walk in the arroyo, the coyotes or roadrunners always come to say hello. She talks to the ancestors. She tells everyone and everything exactly what is on her mind, which is usually how much she loves their dog, their haircut, the clothing they chose to wear, or if they did something really cool.

Carmelita is neurodivergent. When we were receiving her diagnosis, the evaluator asked Carmelita if she had any questions. She told the evaluator, "I want to feel more electric!" My daughter is a joy. She is fierce. She is sensitive. She is wonder and awe.

Because of her magic, Carmelita was almost thrown out of her first preschool. Researchers at Yale found that children of color are more likely than their White classmates to be expelled from preschool.[1] She was called wild by a teacher. Her teacher told us the environment might not be right for her. In a conversation with a close friend, someone asked if Carmelita was going to be in her wedding. "I don't want her to ruin it." Why does my Carmelita's wildness keep her from school and family? It is heartbreaking, destructive, and hurtful to my wonderfully wild, sensitive little girl. The book, *Wild Things: The Art of Nurturing Boys (A Practical Guide to Christian Parenting)*—two boys fighting adorn the cover—reflects how to take that energy and make those wild boys into thriving men. Wild is their nature. Wild is acceptable. Wild is who they are. Boys will be boys. *This is a problem.*

It is not just a problem because of the inherent sexism, classism, and racism. That analysis would be far too limiting. What have we missed is the wilderness, where the wild things are. Affirmation and confirmation that her powers are gifts is exactly what Carmelita needs. She is wild. Why is it that we cannot claim her connection to the divine? How do we not create the space for her to be—to affirm her ontology as a powerfully intuitive, sensitive, intelligent, truthful, fun, and yes, wild girl? The answer is we have no sense of wilderness. And this wilderness is where many have come to find mission. In Scripture, the people of God are either leaving to, escaping to, or cast into the wilderness. The wilderness is where God speaks with Moses. It is where Miriam leads the community. It is where Hagar has a conversation with God. The wilderness is where Jesus goes to connect to the divine. In order to find our freedom, we sometimes have to recognize we are wild. As my people are born of the deserts of the southwestern United States and northern Mexico, we resonate deeply with the call in Scripture to the wilderness.

The wilderness is the ancestral leadership in my Carmelita lineage that knew how to survive migration, poverty, and yet always create a sense of abundance. My grandma Carmelita was wild. She was adored by friends and family alike, because the love she carried in the wilderness, in her survival, created conditions for the rest of us to thrive.

Recovering this love of the wild could not be more necessary for these times. Just like in dominant society, in the wilderness men rear their ugly, patriarchal heads. Hagar is given a little bit of water and cast out with her son, referred to only as a slave. Moses allows his sister, who saved his life, to be cast out of the community. And following this action, Moses and Aaron have the gall to try and assess whether or not they can conquer land when they have cast out their matriarch, to which, thank goodness, the

---

1. Peart, "Pre-K Students Expelled."

community neither moved without Miriam nor got behind the men's less than compassionate thinking.

It is in the wilderness that leaders go, and it is where our leaders meet the divine. My daughter is in the wild. The arroyo and the high desert are her home. How we create space for her gifts, gifts passed down from the ancestors despite the violence of patriarchy, is our leadership task. The question is what are we up against? The answer: fragile male egos.

Fragile Male Egos

> **Fragile**: easily broken or shattered.
> **Male**: the qualities associated with men.
> **Ego**: a person's sense of self.

The ultimate warrior, dominating, decision-making, confident, and emotionally distant—a man. Unfortunately, while not unique to Christianity, the less than positive traits attributed to male leadership takes their genesis in our Scriptures, traditions, and practices. Worse, we keep repeating and celebrating toxic male leaders. From stories of dismissal and abuse of women—Hagar and Miriam, in particular, who are matriarchs of our tradition—to laws that prohibit the movement of a woman's body, our Scriptures demean women and their bodies, and limits their role in the community as leaders. This is a fact. What is also a fact, we still live in a culture that values the hyper masculine leader (even women who embody this style of leadership), and demeans anything other than the dominant male. Violent patriarchy, and the fragile male egos it perpetuates, is baked into the tradition.

The late bell hooks wrote to challenge notions of traditional masculinity, opting for roots of love. *The Will to Change: Men, Masculinity, and Change* was a direct treatment of how masculine leadership—embodied by any gender or person—creates havoc in our communities. Her subject, however, was not where most treatment of the fragile ego begins: abuse of power, domination, strength, and so on. Her diagnosis is that we need to address an unmet desire for and expressions of love—for men and women both. The lack of connection with emotion, demonstrated that at the heart of a fragile masculine ego, is in not meeting, understanding, exploring, or respecting the need for love. Love above all things.

Love does not come easy. To lead with love as the divine loved humanity is leadership. It is a love that holds your community accountable. It is a love that listens to women, women in the wilderness. It is a love that gathers in the upper room. It is the love that defies culture and spreads Good News, despite it being countercultural.

In my world, that means love and lead like my Grandma Carmelita Reyes. Grandma held no titles, was bestowed no honorifics, and received no formal leadership roles for her work in the community. She did not lead a movement or write the treatise on leadership. But for anyone in the community, it was clear Grandma Carmelita was *our* leader.

Grandma Carmen was the embodiment of living the mission of God.

As Kat Armas has written in *Abuelita Faith*, our grandmothers have led our communities in ways often unrecognized in the literature and broader society. That is not to say there is no place for our grandfathers (or for any men reading this) or that *all* grandmothers showed up this way, but it is to say in the ways we gather, make decisions, think about the world, and pay attention to the energies around us, we need to love and lead like grandma.

To lead like our grandmas, abuelas, babas, oumas, lolas, mémés, abbas, cocos, mimis, or bubbes, we need to unpack our own insecurities of what it means to lead.

Here I am going to turn and speak directly to men. As a Chicano, I am constantly aware of the ways machismo makes and unmakes young men. It is defined as much by a warrior culture as it is by the stereotypes that are used to depict us as criminals, thugs, gang members, impoverished migrants, and manual workers. We have in our families and communities limited or devalued women. We do not get to a place in society where one in three women will be sexually abused in their lifetime by not having toxic views of women.[2] In the US, four out of five Indigenous women have experienced violence, and half have experienced sexual violence.[3] Violence against Black women and Latinas is at an all-time high. Violence and murder against trans and gender-nonconforming bodies continues to take place across the country at alarming rates.[4] One in four children are exposed to violence and abuse by the time they reach adulthood.[5] Until we, men, take responsibility for deconstructing and reimagining the roles men play in society—the way we lead, the way we speak, the way we love—the violence will continue.

How do we imagine a new space from hooks' call for love, from the love of my grandma, and undoing machismo, both in our culture and defying stereotypes? Acclaimed Chicano author and scholar, the late Rudolfo Anaya, offered an alternative to machismo:

2. World Health Organization, "Violence against Women."
3. Indian Law Resource Center, "Ending Violence against Native Women."
4. Human Rights Campaign, "Fatal Violence."
5. Child Trends, "Children's Exposure to Violence."

Nature dictates much. The chemicals, hormones, and elements in the blood and in the psyche are elements she needs for the job of the procreation of the species. But she also provides a fantastic interplay of forces within the essence of the human, within the soul. The soul exists as a motivating, energizing force within. We can transform ourselves, and in that transcendent encounter, or epiphany, we become more than the humans whose feet are bogged down in the mud.

To do that we need to pay full attention to the forces within. We are not all male at any given time, nor are we all female. We need to find balance and harmony in the deep currents of our nature. Macho need not be all male, puro hombre. Nothing is pure one thing or the other, especially when we speak of human nature. The old dictates of the fathers have to be transformed to create a new macho, and for that we need to listen to the feminine sensibility. To listen within.[6]

Anaya offers us a powerful opportunity to reimagine leadership. He offers a vision for how to reimagine the leader led by the internal wilderness, to connect with nature, to reimagine coming of age. In *Bless Me, Ultima*, his most famous work, Anaya tells the story of Antonio.[7] Antonio is seven years old. The entire book surrounds his grandma, Ultima, who is a *curandera*, healer, *bruja*, and matriarch of his family. She heals. She is accompanied by an owl. She is wild. Antonio is fascinated. As a young boy, he is transformed by his abuela's love, and comes to terms with the fact that he is also gifted like his grandma. It scares him, because although the community sees her power to heal, they also fear her. And because of that fear, they want to destroy her.

Without spoiling the ending of the story, I want us to notice that Ultima, as a spiritual leader in the community, occupies the wilderness. She comes with her power. In order for Antonio to be his most authentic self, he must return to the wisdom of his grandmother's love. It is not just a feel-good leadership metaphor. It is a requirement for learning to lead if we are going to make the world anew. What Antonio needs to learn is what we will call *feminist ancestral leadership*.

---

6. Anaya, *Essays*, 16.
7. The book celebrated fifty years in print in 2022.

Feminist Ancestral Leadership

The answer to obtaining grandma's love is not simply putting women in charge—though I do believe if one were to read Scripture closely and be a good student of where society is thriving, it would solve a lot of problems. Looking at Kate Raworth's research on how women are reshaping economies to be more equitable, it is clear economies based on well-being, equity, and regenerative science—that is energy and technology outputs that restore this planet—can be realized.[8] During the pandemic, researchers Jack Zenger and Joseph Folkman found that women are seen as better leaders and more effective in a crisis.[9] The solution to finding this love is to embrace feminist ancestral leadership. Anaya describes while it is inherently about the body, it is also about the spirit we have inside that body. Can we tap into a feminist ancestral spirit? For men, can we tap into what Anaya and hooks were pointing to? That is a serious question for men: can you?

Let me break down each of these terms and then put them back together to help answer that question.

Feminist. Why label this feminist and feminism? Patriarchy destroys and harms every-body. In particular, it does damage in our culture to anything that is not White, Christian, and male. Those most threatening to patriarchy are women, children, and bodies that resist or diverge from the norm. This includes people of color, gender non-conforming persons, those experiencing poverty, those in the disabled and differently-abled community, and people who are neurodivergent. For a biblical list of those who threaten patriarchy, one need look no further than the beatitudes: poor in spirit, meek, those who mourn, who hunger and thirst for righteousness, who are merciful, pure of heart, peacemakers, and the persecuted. Pharaoh and Herod go after children, innocent children because of what they represent in challenging their authority.

Feminism, today, seeks equality and equity. This general principle, I wholeheartedly stand behind.

There have been many waves of feminism. And the classist and racist assumptions made by first generation White feminists about women (and men) of color have done and continue to do real harm to communities of color. Women of color have reminded us though that the language does not belong to the first-generation feminism, and we should rightly interrogate and advance its claims. Chela Sandoval in her groundbreaking work *Methodology of the Oppressed* recovers a movement to acknowledge that we

---

8. Raworth, *Doughnut Economics*.
9. Zenger and Folkman, "Research."

are in a moment where women of color are celebrating their right to be, to breath, and to live. Feminism as it is defined by Sandoval from those most marginalized by society, centers equality and justice across all people. Mikki Kendall says it best in her book *Hood Feminism*, "Feminism in the hood is for everyone, because everyone needs it."[10] To define feminism, hooks again is helpful here. She writes, "Feminist struggle takes place anytime anywhere any female or male resists sexism, sexist exploitation, and oppression. Feminist movement happens when groups of people come together with an organized strategy to take action to eliminate patriarchy."[11]

This is every-body work. It is intersectional work. Hooks reminds the reader that feminism can never be about just sex or gender. It is at the intersection of race, class, and other social factors that the movement must be built in order to create real change. Men can still be in leadership, but they must lead with equity, freedom, and liberation at the heart of what they do, how they behave, and not just how they think.

Feminist theory, grounded in the women's liberation movement, is the cornerstone of how we imagine leadership. I track my own lineages in Chicana and Indigenous feminisms. Radical women like my grandma, who would never have called herself a feminist, found new ways to express leadership so that her children and grandchildren could have a better life. Her very survival was an act of undermining patriarchy. Feminism is for everybody and affirms the belief that we should be working for equity. Feminism is not afraid of the wild child. In *Latina Evangelicals*, Martel-Otero, Maldonado-Perez, and Conde-Frazier reflect on the *wild* as dancing with the Holy Spirit.[12] I cannot think of a more appropriate image for my daughter. She never ceases to dance.

In short, feminism advances the work of diversity, equality, equity, justice, inclusion, and belonging. In fact, I cannot imagine any of these terms without it. The only addition I would make, given more space, is to attend to womanist, *mujerista*, and indigenous feminist writing that reorients the survival, community, and connection to the planet.

Ancestral. Multi-generational. Talk about the failure of male kings here, where your leadership is only justified by how much time one lasts on the throne or how long one's legacy can impact a community. When I see the pyramids, I do not see beauty or a wonder. I see an enslaved peoples building over generations to venerate a man. We should not celebrate that

---

10. Kendall, *Hood Feminism*, xx.
11. hooks, *Feminist Theory*, xii.
12. Martell-Otero et al., *Latina Evangélicas*.

leadership, but teach that it is in this context that our tradition teaches us to find liberation.

One of my favorite misguided appropriations in how we tell our own stories is the displays of Ramesses II, or Ramesses the Great. His reign was more than sixty years, included many wars, and continues to be studied and explored by scholars today. And what angers scholars is that Ramesses II is who we often see Moses pitted against in the dramatizations of Exodus. There is very little evidence that this would be the case (at least from the Egyptian record), but what do the people want: a strong man taking on a strong Pharaoh. Miriam, who is central to the whole story, is basically erased from the record. My colleague, Matthew Wesley Williams calls this emphasis on male-dominated leadership "warrior leadership."[13] We want to see the two gladiators fight for who is in charge, whose God/gods are more righteous. Certainly, there is another way to lead that honors one's ancestors and descendants—and not just ourselves.

In my training, both in the community and the academy, I pull from many lineages, call the ancestors into the space, and imagine futures where our descendants are thriving. Every night when I put my children to bed, my daughter asks, "Can we go see the ancestors?" My family's bedtime routine reflects this profound sense of in-betweenness that we occupy on this physical plane. Meaning, this generation is not the chosen generation. We are simply the generation now.

In Forum for Theological Exploration's podcast, *The Sound of the Genuine*, we have listened to the stories of many of the religious leaders leading differently. Each leader can point to the elder (now ancestor) that took them seriously when they were younger. It is not that elders did not share stories or leadership gifts across the many cultures these leaders represented. They all also named elders telling stories and, in many ways, especially for many communities of color, respect of elders is well-documented. But what strikes me across the now seventy interviews is all of them have an elder who listened. The elder took their questions and imagination seriously. What differentiates my grandma as my ancestor from, say, an inspirational elder of mine is that, in my darkest hour, my grandma, who faced far more obstacles than I ever have and who was a woman of God living in poverty, fed me, walked with me in her garden, listened to my stories, connected my challenges with the stories of our people, healed me with the magic of our peoples practices, hugged me, kissed me, and prayed for me as I left her house to go out in the world. She put future generations first.[14] Ancestral

---

13. Lewis et al., *Another Way*, 129, 143–44.
14. Edelman, *Measure of Our Success*; Edelman, *Sea Is So Wide*.

leadership demonstrates that love. Building legacies and heirlooms in a person's heart is just as important as creating the books, institutions, and buildings we leave behind. Ancestors make space for the next generation and broaden the imagination of what is possible.

Leadership. For almost a decade, I have been involved in deep research on leadership: the habits, practices, and supports they need in order to affirm, support, and hone the next generations' gifts for ministry to carry out the *missio Dei*. For almost a decade, my work supporting the next generation of Christian leaders included looking at what gave them meaning and purpose in their lives, what inspired them, and what were their hopes for their own leadership. My team engaged in deep learning: reading thousands upon thousands of pages of reports, leadership texts, theological texts, and reflections on vocation. Two of my go-to texts are Susan Maros, who wrote a fantastic book on vocation, and the impact of one's social location has on how you might live your life's purpose.[15] The other is Michaela O'Donnell's *Make Work Matter*. O'Donnell explores the way we think about work and leadership, and redefines it for ways that restores and heals our relationships to ourselves, our communities, and our world. What both are clear is that there is both a leadership gap and a knowledge gap. We are missing leaders from marginalized groups and the wisdom they and their ancestors bring to the table. Most notably, we are missing the women.

Feminist Ancestral Leadership

What does feminist ancestral leadership look like? Feminist ancestral leadership at least as I explore it here have the following five qualities:

1. **Leadership is about love.** Love like my grandma. It is a love that accepts people as they are, makes space for them to transform their fears into the joys and that provides them a home that makes them feel welcomed, have psychological safety, and a community that supports them.
2. **Leadership is for everybody.** All bodies are of God, and therefore have a leadership responsibility for the community of God. This follows hooks' feminist leadership model that is rooted in love and accountability.
3. **Leadership is never a one generation task.** Leadership includes ancestors and descendants. This affirms ancestral leadership that

---

15. Maros, *Calling in Context*.

understands the task is to prepare a new generation of leaders to take up leadership in the community.

4. **Feminist ancestral leadership looks for leaders on the margins.** When the community refuses to move when Miriam is displaced and stricken ill by God in Num 12, that is a story that represents awful male dominated leadership. And the community is wise enough to know to support the one who helps babies survive, find a way to make music and dance her people across the sea while being chased by the military for certain death and destruction, who is only in this place because of her calling out her brothers to pay attention to the leadership lineages they need to develop and to recognize her role in the community's leadership thus far. The text claims the community waited for her. She was a leader on the margin and the people knew to follow.

5. **Feminist ancestral leadership is about recognizing how to address communal harm.** For men, this means undoing Patriarchal mechanisms of leadership. Even if you are given a title that defines you as a leader, we need to find new ways to lead where circle is expanded. How do you move to the margins? How do you interrupt cycles of male domination and abuse? How do you train and equip a new generation of boys to really undo the harm men have caused? How do you recognize that gendered violence is still happening in your institutions, churches, and places of work, and use what power you do have to find new ways to embody love?

So how do we lead like feminist ancestral leaders?

I am a practical theologian and storyteller by training, so I want to offer a brief narrative. I attended a congregation that was redesigning its programming for children and youth ministry. The meeting had an agenda and was led by the executive director of the congregation. We had coffee and snacks. We sat around the table and white boarded some potential programs. The group generally felt good about what we came up with because it was in-line with what the executive director had already decided was good for the congregation. I was angry about the process and the programs we had come up with. It was an administrative meeting about children and children were not allowed in the room! Nothing could be further from how we should have conducted business. All of us had children. But what we did that night was completely antithetical to how a child thinks, imagines, plays, and explores the world. I want to acknowledge criticism can only get you so far and to be able to diagnose without any sort of treatment plan is also a tragic flaw of male-dominated leadership. I told the group that after the next Sunday school classes, we should host a meeting during the bagel hour.

After service on Sunday, the children ran to the bagel bar as they always do, playing, eating, licking the cream cheese off one side, leaving half a bagel uneaten, dropping them, and of course I need you to imagine that one dad who insists on eating the leftover, half-eaten bagel. The parents who were part of the group earlier in the week, stood as awkwardly as they always do, attention split between their children and the group. They patiently waited for me to call a meeting (and probably nervous about what that would mean for how to watch their children). As soon as my son was done with his bagel, I motioned to some of the other parents that we were going out to play on the playground. I made a brief announcement at the door that we were going to have a "meeting at the top of the castle for any parents who want to come!" The castle is what the children affectionately called the play structure. About two thirds of the parents who were at the bagel hour were not able to or simply not invited to the meeting earlier in the week, but the invitation to the playground intrigued them to come.

They knew the meeting spot and they climbed the accessible play structure. Hands on the wheel at the top of the play structure, I began: "Friends, we have to get this castle to a place that matters. We only have X amount of money and I don't know where or how to navigate this! We need ideas, but we can't get out of this castle until we have a plan, because the ocean will swallow you (pointing at the ground below). One other rule is that our children are the only people who can swim, so if you need anything or need to get off the castle, you need to get help from your kids. We have fifteen minutes because some of us have soccer."

Parents immediately jumped into the strategic play. They took turns driving the castle. They asked their children to come up and test ideas. We had navigators on their phones looking up answers to questions we had about costs or ideas. At one point, the executive director of the congregation asked for permission to board the ship. I think we all relished a little too much in the redistribution of power and told him the only way he could join us if he could convince one of the children he had a good idea and could swim him across the water. And to make it even more hilarious, he had to ask several of our children before one caring soul decided he did not have any good ideas, but that we should not leave him out of the game.

I tell this story only to showcase how feminist ancestral leadership operates. In that boardroom, we were conditioned to affirm the male leader at the front of the room—the one who was doing his best to model strongman leadership. He had the best idea. He knew how to execute it. He just needed our agreement. What we came up with while playing with our children the way my grandma played with us, included more parents and allowed the conditions to shift from the executive director to the imagination of the entire congregation. We were no longer thinking as adults for children. We were strategizing, playing, and exploring possibilities as and with children, with children's voices in the center of the conversation. Do you think they were happy that a bunch of parents were occupying the castle? No! We lost many good parents to the deep that day, thrown overboard for not letting the children lead. That dad that I said ate all of his children's leftovers, well he was thrown overboard for stealing food from his son. And if you have not guessed it, I am that dad. I took notes from the shores of the game and was not even allowed to participate in this reimagined process aside from documenting decisions that were made.

Disrupting who, how, and where leadership takes place is how to do feminist ancestral leadership. When you place the people who have the highest stakes at the center, in this case children, and when they have agency and power, there is incredible buy-in to wherever the community is headed. For those of us in leadership roles, the research suggests that serving others is at the heart of what gives so many of us meaning and purpose. The roles we play have to shift. We have to move the meeting outside of the box. Once we are out there, we have to let go enough for others to play. We have to be committed to seeing that dream become a reality. How we move in the world is what matters.

It is the wild that I hoped for Carmelita.

What Is Our Next Step?

Many of our communities are led by and with men who have fractured senses of self. They demand authority without accountability. They lead from words, and not from their actions. They have visions, but no practical imagination. My interest in addressing the fragile male ego is because it gets in the way of feminist ancestral leadership. And perhaps more importantly, because fragile male egos are often rewarded, all people who aspire to have forms of power baked in domination, can also behave like this. As hooks was clear to remind us, there is but a thin veil between classism, racism, and patriarchy. Fragile male egos, problem. Feminist ancestral leadership, answer. Even this framing falls short of the complexities of the world, but it is a start.

For those in the pews or on boards, do not reward the ego. Reward the community. For those who have less power, pay attention to your intention. If your intention is to find new ways to be in the world where women can live into their full-potential and power, then give attention to this intention. Where and who is building spaces for women of color to thrive in their vocation? Celebrate those spaces and teams where leadership is shared. An image I use often and can be found in *The Purpose Gap* is to stop looking at that one shining star, but look for the constellations.[16]

Men who have fragile male egos, and I'd argue most of us do, we need to do the following:

1. Acknowledge what happens in your body when your ego is tested. Notice the way a challenge to your leadership, an idea, or even your being, is tested and find ways to constructively process those feelings.

2. Practice love. Find new spaces—where you have no authority or power—and be a good participant. Showing up to help the community succeed will provide new areas for you to practice shared leadership. I want to acknowledge that our religious training very rarely helps us to be better participants in shared life.

3. Seek shalom and repair. The world is a broken place because of men. We have destroyed the planet and made the future uncertain for our descendants. We need to seek new ways of being together, and repent for the damage we have done in the world.

Feminist ancestral leadership is available to everybody. We need all people to lead in and with community, lead like good ancestors, and lead for the thriving of those most vulnerable in our community. Returning to the beginning, let's rewild our leadership. Carmelita deserves a world where her wild self can thrive.

Bibliography

Anaya, Rudolfo. *Bless Me, Ultima*. New York: Penguin, 2022.
———. *The Essays*. Norman, OK: University of Oklahoma Press, 2009.
Armas, Kat. *Abuelita Faith: What Women on the Margins Teach Us about Wisdom, Persistence, and Strength*. Grand Rapids: Brazos, 2021.
Child Trends. "Children's Exposure to Violence." June 17, 2020. https://web.archive.org/web/20190502152822/https://www.childtrends.org/indicators/childrens-exposure-to-violence.
Edelman, Marian Wright. *The Measure of Our Success: A Letter to My Children and Yours*. New York: Harper Perennial, 1993.
———. *The Sea Is So Wide and My Boat Is So Small: Charting a Course for the Next Generation*. New York: Hyperion, 2008.

16. Reyes, *Purpose Gap*.

FTE Leaders. *Sound of the Genuine*. Apple Podcasts. https://podcasts.apple.com/us/podcast/sound-of-the-genuine/id1572223219.

hooks, bell. *Feminist Theory: From Margin to Center*. New York: Routledge, 2015.

———. *The Will to Change: Men, Masculinity, and Love*. New York: Simon & Schuster, 2004.

Human Rights Campaign. "Fatal Violence against the Transgender and Gender Nonconforming Community in 2022." https://www.hrc.org/resources/fatal-violence-against-the-transgender-and-gender-non-conforming-community-in-2022.

Indian Law Resource Center. "Ending Violence against Native Women." https://indianlaw.org/issue/ending-violence-against-native-women.

James, Stephen, and David Thomas. *Wild Things: The Art of Nurturing Boys*. Carol Stream, IL: Tyndale House, 2009.

Kendall, Mikki. *Hood Feminism: Notes from the Women That a Movement Forgot*. New York: Penguin, 2020.

Lewis, Stephen, et al. *Another Way: Living and Leading Change on Purpose*. St. Louis: Chalice, 2020.

Maros, Susan L. *Calling in Context: Social Location and Vocational Formation*. Downers Grove, IL: IVP Academic, 2022.

Martell-Otero, Loida I., et al. *Latina Evangélicas: A Theological Survey from the Margins*. Eugene, OR: Cascade, 2013.

O'Donnell, Michaela. *Make Work Matter: Your Guide to Meaningful Work in a Changing World*. Grand Rapids: Baker, 2021.

Peart, Karen N. "Pre-K Students Expelled at More Than Three Times the Rate of K–12 Students." *YaleNews*, May 17, 2005. https://news.yale.edu/2005/05/17/pre-k-students-expelled-more-three-times-rate-k-12-students.

Raworth, Kate. *Doughnut Economics: Seven Ways to Think like a 21st Century Economist*. White River Junction, VT: Green, 2017.

Reyes, Patrick B. *The Purpose Gap: Empowering Communities of Color to Find Meaning and Thrive*. Louisville: Westminster John Knox, 2021.

Sandoval, Chela. *Methodology of the Oppressed*. Theory Out of Bounds 18. Minneapolis: University of Minnesota Press, 2000.

World Health Organization. "Violence against Women." March 9, 2021. https://www.who.int/news-room/fact-sheets/detail/violence-against-women.

Zenger, Jack, and Joseph Folkman. "Research: Women Are Better Leaders during a Crisis." *Harvard Business Review*, December 30, 2020. https://hbr.org/2020/12/research-women-are-better-leaders-during-a-crisis.

— 12 —

Transforming Collectivity
Empowering Women Leaders through Gendered Spaces

EVELYN HIBBERT

Introduction

MY ENTRY INTO CHRISTIAN ministry as an adult was my first encounter with disempowerment. Throughout my childhood and youth, I did not consciously encounter gender bias. In leaving secular employment and choosing a mission organization, I trusted its written values of women's equality with men. However, the reality did not match the rhetoric. As a missionary, I saw a movement of thousands of Muslims to Christ, led by women, falter and stagnate when the women voluntarily handed over leadership to newly converted men.[1] In three decades of serving as a leader in multiple roles, my disempowerment increased despite success in ministry. On leaving that mission organization, I encountered even more disempowering Christian contexts. My crushing through these experiences was profound. The only relief came through employment under female leadership in a secular university.

With time, I met other women missions leaders and scholars and learned that my experience was the norm. We banded together to create a

---

1. Hibbert, "Gendered Approach to Church Planting."

research center, the Angelina Noble Centre (ANC), for mutual empowerment. We enjoyed the way this structure enabled us to lead in a way that honored the feelings and experiences of women (and men), as well as live out our more communal values. Sadly, despite our achievements, we experienced the ultimate disempowerment of total exclusion by being forced out of the academic institution we were part of at that time.

In many ways, this forced exile into fully female space was liberating. It enabled us to take control of what we do in ways that promote women's learning and leadership. It also provided a platform to support and mentor women to speak back into the public space that continues to exclude them.

This chapter arises out of my reflections on the experience of establishing the Angelina Noble Centre (ANC), much reading about women's leadership in Christian and Islamic contexts, and an autoethnographical exploration of the means of my disempowerment and its effects. It presents the locus of most women's leadership, which is out in everyday life rather than at the center of institutional Christianity. This essay forefronts women's emphasis on building community and recognizes the impact of our bodies on life and leadership. The nature of gendered (female) space and what women do in it is explained. I then outline how women leaders are rendered invisible and have their voices muted. Following this, the haven of gendered space for women leaders is described as a potent means to affirm and empower women to continue to lead in both gendered and public spaces. The chapter concludes with a plea for acknowledging the value of female space alongside recognizing what women have to bring to Christian leadership more generally.

Leading at the Margins of Institutions

If the majority of the world's Christians and missionaries are women,[2] logically, they should be the majority of Christian leaders. In fact, women *are* leading but often their leadership is not publicly recognized. Some women lead as equals of men. Some lead in contexts controlled by men where their leadership is usually relegated to "women's ministries" such as care for children, women, or the sick and needy. Others create gendered spaces where they can exercise their God-given gifts.

Male Christian leadership is inextricably bound up with institutions. Susan Smith documents in her work writing women back into mission history, how, as the church moved from households into larger, more organized

---

2. Robert, "Women's Movement"; Mwaura, "Gender and Power"; Lee, "Women in World Evangelization."

structures, women were relegated into private space.³ This resulted in the institution of the church being led almost exclusively by men. The institutions of the church came to assume male characteristics and thus became predominantly male spaces. As the church interacted in public society, it also adopted characteristics of public space, including anti-female bias.

Formal spiritual authority is conferred by men at the institutional center. But informal recognition of spiritual authority is given by those who directly benefit from that leadership. Today, formal recognition of spiritual leadership depends on gaining abstract knowledge through tertiary education study (that is, gaining degrees). This knowledge, along with male approval and control, translates into formally recognized spiritual authority. This is very different from the more intuitive and easily communicated knowledge found in informal religion.⁴ This knowledge is focused on applying Christian teachings to concrete daily problems. Often, even when women earn the same degrees as men, they still cannot achieve male approval for leading. As leaders who are rejected by the establishment, women are often vulnerable to baseless accusations of unorthodoxy. However, Belaynesh Abiyo believes that women can take courage and hope from Jesus as "the boundary breaker" who was in constant conflict with the religious institutional leaders of his time.⁵

In some instances, women have been allowed to lead in the institutionalized church but only as "fictive males" through taking on male characteristics.⁶ Silvia Rodgers uses the term "honorary men."⁷ Fictive males are not seen as women but conflated with the male role they represent. That is, they are essentially perceived as functioning as men. An extension of this dynamic is Leanne Dzubinski's "two-person career structure"⁸ and Cathy Ross's "mute appendages"⁹ where missionary wives' identity is subsumed in their husbands' roles. This denial of personal identity often crushes the women involved and may also result in the decline of their ministries. In such instances, the perspectives these women bring to Christian faith and leadership are lost to the church.

When women are excluded from leading in the institutional church, they very often move their ministry into a female-controlled space alongside

3. Smith, *Women in Mission*.
4. Whitehouse, "Toward a Comparative Anthropology of Religion."
5. Abiyo, "Women in Ethiopian Christianity," 148.
6. Ardener, *Women and Space*, 9.
7. Rodgers, "Women's Space," 53.
8. Dzubinski, "Portrayal vs. Practice," 80–81.
9. Ross, "Women's Absence," 84.

the church.[10] They lead on the growing edges of the church where it interfaces with everyday life. When faced with need in their communities and families, women lead to promote the flourishing of the people they are caring for. They do this within the contexts where those people are found. Female spaces may be small gatherings in homes, larger community-based groups addressing local needs, or national and international women's guilds formed to address wider issues. This gendered space allows women's ministry to prosper. Sometimes it provides a platform for a transformative voice back into public contexts, including the institutional church.[11]

One often-cited historical example of women's ministry outside male control is the twelfth- and the thirteenth-century movement in Western Europe called the Beguines. The Beguines set up flexible communities of diverse women who cared for the sick and the poor. They also provided Christian teaching for the laity. The ministry of the Beguines was a reflection of and a contributor to a revival movement in Europe in their time.[12]

As ultimately happened with the Beguines, women have historically been forced out of leadership of churches or ministries they have founded. Dana Robert documented the demise of the very successful women's mission societies in the early twentieth century when they were merged with denominational and other male-led boards.[13] Sometimes, the women themselves hand over leadership. Something similar happened in the Turkish-speaking movement I worked with. Although women led thousands to Christ and established churches across Bulgaria, as soon as men became Christians, the women handed over the leadership of the churches to them.[14] The new male leaders did not include the more experienced women leaders in church leadership.

A risk of developing structure, or institutionalization, is that it can pull leaders away from everyday life.[15] This is understandable as the requirements of maintaining the institution can become all-consuming. At the same time, an institution can become an insular world closed in on itself. Institutional

---

10. "Church" is used in this chapter in its broadest meaning including all its congregations and its various associated institutions such as missions organizations and educational institutions for theological training.

11. Public life is usually recognized as being a male space in contrast to the private, female space of the home. For this reason, the terms "institution," "public space," and "male space" are commonly conflated. They are used interchangeably in this chapter.

12. Bass, *People's History*, 141–44; Dzubinski and Stasson, *Women in the Mission*, 107–14.

13. Robert, *Gospel Bearers*.

14. Hibbert, "Gendered Approach to Church Planting."

15. Hibbert and Hibbert, "Nurturing Vitality."

rules, routines, rituals, and ways of thinking reinforce themselves if there is no open, critical engagement with outside perspectives. In contrast, a grassroots community orientation compels leaders to engage with the everyday struggles of ordinary people. Separation from everyday life can tend to encourage a more cognitive faith. Everyday community engagement forces practitioners to ground their faith in everyday experience.

In recent times, apart from women's overrepresentation in the caring professions (e.g., health and education), gender segregation has decreased in the secular West. This is largely because of the successful advocacy of feminists over the last century. However, decreased gender segregation has often been accompanied by a decrease in women's groups' membership, and loss of recognition of what such groups can achieve. In contrast, many Islamic societies still retain strong gendered space and activities. These gendered spaces enable women to flourish and transform their societies especially through the education and support of women, and mobilization of women to address community needs.[16] These female spaces are transformative for the women within them.

The church needs both female and male leaders. But, as Susan Smith explains, for much of Christian history women's leadership has been "systematically and ruthlessly expunged from the Christian communities."[17] Women's Christian leadership has usually arisen in gendered space either because of this exclusion or in spontaneous response to the needs women see around them. Out on the margins amid everyday life, institutional control is diminished. There, the real life needs of community members often supersede the priorities of upholding the institution. It is in this domain that women's leadership especially thrives. The next section outlines how women's leadership responds to its embeddedness in everyday life through its emphases on community and embodied experience.

Describing Women's Leadership

A number of scholars propose that women have a leadership style which is participatory and transformational.[18] This contrasts with the dominant model of leadership taught and recommended in academia, business and the church which is competitive and individualistic. This dominant model

---

16. For example, see Mahmood, *Politics of Piety*; Doorn-Harder, *Women Shaping Islam*.

17. Smith, *Women in Mission*, loc. 170.

18. de la Rey, "Gender, Women, and Leadership"; Ngunjiri, *Spiritual Leadership*; Hoyt, "Women and Leadership."

mirrors the leadership of middle class, White, and Western men.[19] Amanda Sinclair argues that most leadership research presents androcentric prescriptions for leadership as if these are gender neutral.[20] Along with other female scholars, such as Filomina Steady,[21] she suggests that androcentric leadership paradigms tend to focus on hierarchy and domination, assertiveness and aggression whereas women are more communal in orientation.[22] Black womanist writers emphasize the ordinariness of women's leadership in contrast to the image of the heroic, male leader. They suggest that women lead more from the background and among the grassroots.[23] For example, Marilyn Byrd states that African American women's leadership is a "more interactive and collaborative process of leadership, emphasizing empowerment through community building."[24]

Leadership always involves a community. Leaders and followers are in an interdependent relationship. This contrasts with much leadership scholarship which emphasizes the individual leader. It assumes "universal rules for leadership that can be distilled and applied regardless of context."[25] Toni King emphasizes the group in her description of a leader as someone who

> believes in the possibilities, strength, and wisdom of groups. A communal leader contributes to a group's development and wholeness by assisting the group in valuing and drawing upon the talents of all of its members to achieve an overarching vision that contributes to the group and to the larger society.[26]

Communities are built through interdependent relationships. Women's leadership values connections with friends, relatives, and even ancestors and descendants.[27] As they care for their families, one another, and community members' needs, women "co-create their own well-being" and "co-create a path together."[28] Studies of Muslim women leaders describe them proactively creating bonds between women,[29] and gathering women

19. Byrd, "Theorizing Leadership Experiences," 12.
20. Sinclair, *Leadership for the Disillusioned*.
21. Steady, *Women and Leadership*.
22. Sinclair, *Leadership for the Disillusioned*.
23. Diggs, "I Remember Mama"; Ngunjiri, *Spiritual Leadership*.
24. Byrd, "Theorizing Leadership Experiences," 11.
25. Sinclair, *Leadership for the Disillusioned*, 23.
26. King, "Don't Waste Your Breath," 87.
27. Lajimodiere, "Ogimah Ikwe."
28. Fuller Studio. "Panel."
29. Hafez, *Islam of Her Own*.

of diverse backgrounds.[30] Together, women develop a "communal exegesis" that reframes their perception of themselves and their community.[31]

Focusing on an individual leader inadvertently excludes the community that is interdependent with the leader. Miroslav Volf states that exclusion cuts "the bonds that connect, taking oneself out of the pattern of interdependence and placing oneself in a position of sovereign independence."[32] Stressing interdependence reminds leaders that all people are "socially embedded"[33] and dependent on relationships, including family relationships.[34]

Ultimately, all leadership is embodied, affective, and relational. It is not possible to separate leaders from their bodies. Leadership is not just a set of principles or decontextualized tasks. It occurs in a context full of people and what leaders do affects and is imitated by those around them.[35] Women cannot ignore the effects of the body[36] and emotion[37] in all human experience and relationships, including interactions in the church. This means that "bodies and body performances" are integral to leadership.[38] And the performance of leadership cannot be separated from bodily weakness and distress.

Traditionally, women have been strongly associated with the virtues of comforting, nurturing, and healing. They embrace the simile of leadership being like caring for and nurturing children.[39] They help each other for the benefit of their own and others' children and families.[40] They care about outcomes for the flourishing of future generations. For example, when Irene Cybulsky, a Canadian surgeon and leader, fought against discrimination in her workplace, her primary motivation was the creation of policies that would benefit the next generation of women.[41]

Women may see this caring style of leadership reflected in Scripture. Jesus and his disciples were cared for by women (e.g., Luke 8:3). Although Jesus commanded his disciples to care for one another (John 13:1–17,

30. Raudvere, "Knowledge in Trust."
31. Rouse, "Shopping with Sister," 249.
32. Volf, *Exclusion and Embrace*, 67.
33. Mahmood, *Politics of Piety*, 32.
34. Jansen, "Contested Identities."
35. Hibbert and Hibbert, *Multiplying Leaders*.
36. Dale, "Purity"; Adeney, *Women and Christian Mission*.
37. Shaw, "Divine Heartbeats."
38. Sinclair, *Leadership for the Disillusioned*; Kuepers, "Embodied Inter-practices."
39. Alidou, "Rethinking Marginality."
40. Gibson, "Braiding My Place."
41. Frangou, "Only Woman in the Room."

34–35), the Twelve were quick to outsource their practical care obligation to others (Acts 6:2–4). In contrast, Jesus made women's caring the standard for what care should look like through his elevating the example of foot washing.[42]

Women leaders are immersed in their communities and highly aware of the performances of bodies within those communities. They build communities through strengthening relationships. They accept emotions and physical weaknesses, nurturing the people around them for community growth. Mostly, this occurs in homes and communities where people share everyday life together. These flexible, non-institutional gathering places are often gendered spaces. In gendered space, free from male control, women leaders are more able to develop ministries in ways which support these tendencies. The concept of gendered space is explored in the next section.

Understanding Gendered Space

People create spaces around their bodies, assigning meaning both to these spaces and the boundaries that protect them.[43] Most people are aware of the strong delineation of space in Muslim cultures.[44] However, they are less aware of how it also occurs in Christian contexts.[45] Essentially, female space, like the home, is private and intimate, invisible to the public surrounding the home. Its intimacy is poignantly expressed in Alexandra Canales's reference to the "sacredness of the kitchen."[46] Commonly felt as the heart of the home, the kitchen is where mothers nurture their families. Bass describes how when female leadership moved from the convent to the home, it hallowed "the sphere of activity that most European women already occupied."[47]

The idea of male space is associated with control through law and order. This applies to wider society but also to the control of doctrine and order in the institutional church. Fatima Mernissi, a female Islamic scholar, explained the way in which women are seen as a risk of chaos to male order in Islam.[48] Moyra Dale identified the same views of women by men in Christian

---

42. Hibbert and Hibbert, *Multiplying Leaders*, 115.
43. For example, see Delaney, *Investigating Culture*.
44. Dale, "Windows into Islam."
45. See Brasher, *Godly Women*; Rodgers, "Women's Space"; Dale, "Purity"; Juster, *Disorderly Women*.
46. Fuller Studio. "Panel."
47. Bass, *People's History*, 190.
48. Mernissi, *Beyond the Veil*.

contexts.⁴⁹ The need to control the threat that women embody is an important, often subconscious, theme that affects how women are treated.

While there are problems with this view, quarantining women into female space does provide a safe, generative space for women. That is, separating women out can give them freedom to fulfill their created potential. As long as women are hidden away in invisible, private spaces, they are not seen as threats to male order. In these private, gendered spaces, they are free from "monitoring."⁵⁰ Without monitoring, women are able to develop what they do in ways that suit women. Women can be freer to explore spiritual experience that may not be acceptable to male-controlled orthodoxy.⁵¹

The dress and demeanor of women become a marker of public versus private space. That is, men's power over public space also extends to women's bodies. However, women can utilize this control for their own purposes. While this might be more strongly the case among Muslims,⁵² Christian women have also devised ways of using modest dress as a means for ministering in the public space. Muslim coverings and Christian modest dress or uniforms create a "portable 'sacred space.'"⁵³ This portable space protects women but also enables them to venture into the public sphere from which they are otherwise excluded. This extends the reach of women's style of ministry beyond the physical home.

Together, women develop the "power of being able" as they develop activities and structures that enable them "to participate in the matters that affect them directly."⁵⁴ They have proven themselves adept at educating children and other women in their private spaces.⁵⁵ In recent times, increased access to education, books, and recordings has resulted in religious knowledge becoming more accessible.⁵⁶ Women have exploited this to learn and teach it on to others. Many women leaders have studied extensively both through recognized institutions and personal study.⁵⁷ Although they are of-

---

49. Dale, "Purity."

50. Okely, "Gendered Lessons," 236.

51. Morris, *Religion and Anthropology*.

52. Mernissi, *Beyond the Veil* (2011); Göle, "Islam in Public"; Göle, "Contemporary Islamist Movements."

53. Guelke and Morin, "Missionary Women," 115.

54. Salazar, "Missionaries' Commitment," 309.

55. For example, see Duval, "New Veils"; Kamalkhani, "Reconstruction of Islamic Knowledge"; Alidou, "Rethinking Marginality"; Janson, "Guidelines"; Mack, "Muslim Women's Knowledge Production."

56. For example, see Göle, "Voluntary Adoption."

57. For example, see Raudvere, "Knowledge in Trust"; Doorn-Harder, *Women Shaping Islam*; Hafez, *Islam of Her Own*.

ten more qualified than men in formal positions, their authority (based on knowledge and ministry experience) is rarely recognized by those in power. But this does not prevent women from passing on their knowledge to other women in gendered spaces.

Although there is increasing participation of women in public space in the West, this is not mirrored in the institutional church. However, as institutional gaze tends to focus centrally, the unmonitored margins are fruitful places for women's ministry. The experience of many women leaders in the church's public spaces is introduced in the following section.

Women Leaders' Experience

To understand the value of female space, it is important to appreciate women leaders' experience in public space and their responses to what they encounter. This section outlines the common experience of women missions leaders in the Angelina Noble Centre (ANC).

The ANC was set up in response to women missiologists' exclusion from academic institutions in Australia.[58] The gendered space of the ANC has enabled women to recognize the normality of their experience in Christian higher education and cross-cultural mission contexts. Their common experience also affirmed that their disempowerment is because of bias against women rather than due to individual faults and inadequacies.

An autoethnographic exploration of my own experience in Christian leadership helped to unveil the ways women leaders are disempowered.[59] These include being made invisible and mute, being marginalized and excluded. When these actions are not called out by bystanders, it makes those who experience them vulnerable to a distorted perception of themselves. Yet, this research also revealed that women utilize gendered space to overcome disempowerment. Together, women leaders can redeem their marginalization through gendered space, reclaim their identity and voice, and correct their distorted self-perceptions. Thus, female space can be a safe haven for women leaders' healing and empowerment.

Even when women are physically present, they are frequently rendered invisible. Leanne Dzubinski described this phenomenon in relation to women executive leaders of mission organizations:

> The men disregard women almost to the point of bigotry; their actions in occasionally stopping to consider the "woman's

---

58. Hibbert, "Angelina Noble Centre."
59. Hibbert, "Mechanisms of Disempowerment."

perspective" indicate that they can choose whether or not to notice women. They live in the world of the privileged, where the less privileged are visible only when wanted, and fade into the background again as soon as they are no longer needed.[60]

Part of the violence against women is the constant repetition of discourses that perpetuate the nullity of women. Edwin Ardener described the subsuming of women in a null or indistinct background.[61] In missions, women are frequently allowed to lead, teach, and start churches "where there is no man" (from a dominant Christian culture). However, as soon as men appear, women are pushed into the background and made to disappear. Similarly, they may do these things out on the indistinct space of the "mission field" but not in the foreground of the institutional church "at home."

Because men have power to speak, act and lead in Christian contexts, it does not occur to them that women do not have the same power. People tend to assume that their own experience is common to others. When those without power raise the issue of non-voice, this then feels unfair to those with power and can result in anger, frustration and even attack. Robert Schreiter asserts that the "silencing of people's ability to speak" is "an act of power that is in itself violent, in as much as it does not respect the human dignity of those who are silenced."[62] As researchers, ANC members were constantly blocked from having a voice in institutional decisions relating to them. When this was raised as an issue, the ANC was forced out of the institution without discussion or recourse.

The constant non-acceptance of what women have to offer is like incessant clanging cymbals. The apostle Paul wrote, "If I could speak all the languages of earth and of angels, but didn't love others, I would only be a noisy gong or a clanging cymbal" (1 Cor 13:1).[63] Many women are overwhelmed by these clanging cymbals. They cannot think clearly about their experience, let alone speak out.

Women leaders frequently find themselves rendered invisible by being ignored or subsumed in men's identity. They are also forcibly muted in public space through being silenced and overwhelmed with non-acceptance. Gendered space offers a refuge where women can affirm one another's identity, find their voice, and together exert their agency to transform their communities.

---

60. Dzubinski, "Taking on Power," 291.
61. Ardener, "Belief and the Problem."
62. Schreiter, "Reconciling Presence," 103.
63. Biblical citations in this chapter are from the NLT.

Value of Gendered Space

Within the refuge of gendered space women leaders can envisage a different future. Grace Ji-Sun Kim, writing about Korean American women, talks about how their hybrid spaces can be a place for "reimagining home."[64] While she is referring to intercultural hybrid space, gendered space has the same potential as a non-mainstream, alternative space. In this alternative space, different possibilities can be imagined. From within this place of safety and refuge, women can, together, rebuild strength to step outside again.

A safe space is one in which diverse voices and ideas are welcome. Often, where a particular space is controlled by one group, the ideas of others are considered controversial. This is simply because they are different and may threaten existing systems.[65] In the ANC, it is safe to explore ideas that are seen as threatening in male-controlled spaces. These ideas may not be gender specific but often relate to issues that arise in relating faith to the messiness of everyday life.

As a gathering of women, gendered space counters the view that women do not exist and are not important. Within gendered space, women leaders feel validated. Many women leaders have been crushed through their experiences in Christian organizations. Validation enables healing through being given belonging in an affirming group of peers. Carolyn Ellis, Tony Adams, and Arthur Bochner observed that sharing stories helps those who feel isolated in their struggles to "validate the meaning of their pain."[66] Writing as autoethnographers, they described their role as witnesses who validate others' experience. Similarly, women in gendered spaces can share their stories with one another. They validate each other's experience. They can do this whether others' experience mirrors their own or is completely different. Together, they build their collective autonomy and give one another the strength to resist ways of speaking that foster oppression.[67]

Women redeem their exclusion zone (of gendered space) by proactively countering distorted perceptions of themselves. When their experiences are "dismissed as being unimportant, insignificant, or over-exaggerated,"[68] they, together, refute this evaluation, giving worth to one another. Women's stories are heard, affirmed, and valued rather than ignored and dismissed. Too often, in public spaces, women's stories are dislocated from their context

---

64. Kim, *Invisible*, 121.
65. Ardener, *Women and Space*; James, "Empowering Ambiguities."
66. Ellis et al., "Autoethnography," under subheading, "4.2 Writing as Therapeutic."
67. Salazar, "Missionaries' Commitment."
68. Byrd, "Theorizing Leadership Experiences," 11.

as if the issue is an individual problem rather than something caused by systemic prejudice. Within gendered space women's experience is normalized as common for women, denying narratives that blame the victim. Often, as individuals, it is hard to prove suspicions of prejudice. However, when individual experiences are compared with the repeating patterns of prejudice experienced by other women, suspicions are confirmed. Without this confirmation, it is easy to assume personal fault, distrust personal perceptions and, thus, become complicit in our own suppression and loss of self-respect.

Identity is also affirmed through collective belonging. Stevi Jackson discusses how each person's experience of being is constructed and reconstructed through social interaction.[69] In this way, although crushed in public space, by telling their stories in an affirming social context women are able to reframe them as they heal. Mirliana Ramírez-Pereira, Michelle Espinoza-Lobos, and Pamela Zapata-Sepúlveda confirm that, "Through our story, we are allowed to recognize ourselves in the heart of the others in a society determined to make us deaf, mute, and despicable."[70] In gendered space, women can use words to describe one another which are not applied to them in public spaces, such as "leader." Through this, they repair their "broken dignity."[71] Correcting distortions in a safe space gives confidence to speak their own narratives back into the space where they have been obstructed. They can do this even if their voice continues to be ignored. Doing this in a supportive group in gendered space reduces the feeling of individual vulnerability in public space.

In the ANC, we have countered our exclusion from institutional space by claiming our own independent worth and agency. We have been able to determine what happens in our own name and we are able to negotiate with other groups in our own right. We created our own identity when it was denied to us by others and have been able to protect it. The ANC has developed a thriving research community in gendered space despite lack of access to institutional power and resources.

Conclusion

We should not push for women's inclusion in the public space at the cost of their having to become fictive males or having to give up female space. There is often strong pressure to merge women's ministries with men's work. The cost of this is usually to assimilate women into men's space, on men's terms,

---

69. Jackson, "Self, Time, and Narrative."
70. Ramírez-Pereira et al., "Interpretive Autoethnography," 100.
71. Adichie, "Danger of a Single Story."

homogenizing women's experience with men's. This has partly arisen from feminist insistence in Western contexts on women's full incorporation into public space. Much progress has been achieved in valuing women through this advocacy. However, this has too often been accompanied by an inadvertent devaluing of women's distinct roles in the home and community.

At the same time, women who venture into male space should be given permission to be women within it. They should be allowed to embrace women's ways of leading rather than becoming fictive men. This means being free to build communities through strengthening interdependent relationships. It also means accepting the bodily expression of all human leadership in both its strengths and weaknesses.

It would be an ironic tragedy if women's empowerment in male space occurs at the cost of disempowering them through dismantling women's collectives. As long as the public sphere remains a predominantly male space, most women will need help to master the means and tools of men for successful engagement in it. This is especially so they can be successful without compromising their integrity as women. Gendered space provides a safe environment where women can help each other develop resilience and skills to succeed in public space. Experienced women leaders can act as mentors and role models for bridging from female space into the public sphere.

Female spaces should be protected. Gendered spaces offer safe places for engaging with different perspectives of the world. They also bring affirmation and belonging for women in a way that is often not possible in public space. They provide refuge for healing when women have been crushed and excluded in public spaces. If both gendered space and women's ways of leading are valued, there is hope of bringing enrichment to leadership in public space.

Bibliography

Abiyo, Belaynesh B. "Women in Ethiopian Christianity: An Appraisal of Their Impacts Past and Present." In *Putting Names with Faces*, edited by Christine Lienemann-Perrin et al., 147–67. Nashville: Abingdon, 2012.

Adeney, Frances S. *Women and Christian Mission: Ways of Knowing and Doing Theology*. Eugene, OR: Pickwick, 2015.

Adichie, Chimamanda N. "Danger of a Single Story." *TED*, July 2009. https://www.ted.com/talks/chimamanda_ngozi_adichie_the_danger_of_a_single_story/c.

Alidou, Ousseina D. "Rethinking Marginality and Agency in Postcolonial Niger: A Social Biography of a Sufi Woman Scholar." In *Gender and Islam in Africa*, edited by Margot Badaran, 41–68. Washington, DC: Woodrow Wilson Center, 2011.

Ardener, Edwin. "Belief and the Problem of Women: The 'Problem' Revisited." In *Perceiving Women*, edited by Shirley Ardener, 19–27. London: Malaby, 1975.
Ardener, Shirley, ed. *Women and Space: Ground Rules and Social Maps*. Rev. ed. Oxford: Berg, 1993.
Ask, Karin, and Marit Tjomsland, eds. *Women and Islamization: Contemporary Dimensions of Discourse on Gender Relations*. Oxford: Berg, 1998.
Badran, Margot, ed. *Gender and Islam in Africa: Rights, Sexuality, and Law*. Washington, DC: Woodrow Wilson Center, 2011.
Bass, Diana B. *A People's History of Christianity: The Other Side of the Story*. New York: HarperOne, 2009.
Brasher, Brenda E. *Godly Women: Fundamentalism and Female Power*. New Brunswick, NJ: Rutgers University Press, 1998.
Byrd, Marilyn. "Theorizing African American Women's Leadership Experiences: Socio-cultural Theoretical Alternatives." *Advancing Women in Leadership* 29 (2009) 1–19.
Dale, Moyra. "Purity: Guarding the Body Corporate." In *Grounded in the Body, in Time and Place, in Scripture*, edited by Jill Firth and Denise Cooper-Clarke, 60–76. Eugene, OR: Wipf & Stock, 2021.
———. "Windows into the House of Islam: Including Women's Spaces." *Missiology* 49 (2021) 132–48.
Delaney, Carol. *Investigating Culture: An Experiential Introduction to Anthropology*. Malden, MA: Blackwell, 2004.
de la Rey, Cheryl. "Gender, Women and Leadership." *Agenda* 65 (2005) 4–11.
Diggs, Rhunette C. "I Remember Mama: The Legacy of a *Drylongso* and *Ajabu* Leader." In *Black Womanist Leadership*, edited by Toni C. King and S. Alease Ferguson, 143–62. Albany: State University of New York Press, 2011.
Doorn-Harder, Pieternella van. *Women Shaping Islam: Indonesian Women Reading the Qur'an*. Urbana: University of Illinois Press, 2006.
Duval, Soraya. "New Veils and New Voices: Islamist Women's Groups in Egypt." In *Women and Islamization*, edited by Karin Askand and Marit Tjomsland, 45–72. Oxford: Berg, 1998.
Dzubinski, Leanne M. "Portrayal vs. Practice: Contemporary Women's Contributions to Christian Mission." *Missiology* 44 (2016) 78–94.
———. "Taking on Power: Women Leaders in Evangelical Mission Organizations." *Missiology* 44 (2016) 281–95.
Dzubinski, Leanne M., and Anneke H. Stasson. *Women in the Mission of the Church: Their Opportunities and Obstacles throughout Christian History*. Grand Rapids: Baker Academic, 2021.
Ellis, Carolyn, et al. "Autoethnography: An Overview." *Forum* 12 (2011) 273–90.
Frangou, Christina. "Only Woman in the Room." *Toronto Life*, December 20, 2021. https://torontolife.com/city/irene-cybulsky-surgeon-fired-for-being-female-hamilton-general-hospital/.
Fuller Studio. "Panel | Confronting Gender and Power Asymmetries in Organizational Leadership." *YouTube*, April 13, 2023. https://fullerstudio.fuller.edu/video/panel-confronting-gender-and-power-asymmetries-in-organizational-leadership/.
Gibson, Nancy. "Braiding My Place: Developing a Foundational Selfhood through Cross-Racial Mothering." In *Black Womanist Leadership*, edited by Toni C. King and S. Alease Ferguson, 57–69. Albany: State University of New York Press, 2011.

Göle, Nilüfer. "Contemporary Islamist Movements and New Sources for Religious Tolerance." *Journal of Human Rights* 2 (2010) 17–30.

———. "Islam in Public: New Visibilities and New Imaginaries." *Public Culture* 14 (2002) 173–90.

———. "The Voluntary Adoption of Islamic Stigma Symbols." *Social Research* 70 (2003) 809–28.

Guelke, Jeanne K., and Karen M. Morin. "Missionary Women in Early America: Prospects for a Feminist Geography." In *Women, Religion, and Space: Global Perspectives on Gender and Faith*, edited by Karen M. Morin and Jeanne K. Guelke, 105–26. Syracuse, NY: Syracuse University Press, 2007.

Hafez, Sherine. *An Islam of Her Own: Reconsidering Religion and Secularism in Women's Islamic Movements*. New York: New York University Press, 2011.

Hibbert, Evelyn. "The Angelina Noble Centre: Prising Open a Space for Women Missions Researchers." Presentation at the Gender and Mission Study Group, International Association of Mission Studies, Sydney, Australia, 2022.

———. "Considering a Gendered Approach to Church Planting in Muslim-Background Contexts." *Missiology* 43 (2015) 286–96.

———. "Mechanisms of Disempowerment and the Means to Overcome It." Presentation at the Association of the Professors of Mission, St. Mary's College, South Bend, Indiana, 2022.

Hibbert, Evelyn and Richard Y. Hibbert. *Multiplying Leaders in Intercultural Contexts: Recognizing and Developing Grassroots Potential*. Littleton, CO: Carey, 2023.

———. "Nurturing Vitality through Appropriate Structure: A Challenge for Church Planting Movements." *International Journal of Frontier Missions* 36 (2019) 119–27.

Hoyt, Crystal L. "Women and Leadership." In *Leadership: Theory and Practice*, edited by Peter G. Northouse, 349–82. 6th ed. Thousand Oaks, CA: SAGE, 2013.

Jackson, Stevi. "Self, Time, and Narrative: Re-thinking the Contribution of G. H. Mead." *Life Writing* 7 (2010) 123–36.

James, Wendy. "Empowering Ambiguities." In *The Anthropology of Power: Empowerment and Disempowerment in Changing Structures*, edited by Angela Cheater, 13–26. London: Routledge, 1999.

Jansen, Wilhelmina. "Contested Identities: Women and Religion in Algeria and Jordan." In *Women and Islamization*, edited by Karin Askand and Marit Tjomsland, 73–102. Oxford: Berg, 1998.

Janson, Marloes. "Guidelines for the Ideal Muslim Woman: Gender Ideology and Praxis in the Tabligh Jama'at in the Gambia." In *Gender and Islam in Africa*, edited by Margot Badaran, 147–72. Washington, DC: Woodrow Wilson Center, 2011.

Juster, Susan. *Disorderly Women: Sexual Politics & Evangelicalism in Revolutionary New England*. Ithaca, NY: Cornell University Press, 1994.

Kamalkhani, Zahra. "Reconstruction of Islamic Knowledge and Knowing: A Case of Islamic Practices among Women in Iran." In *Women and Islamization*, edited by Karin Askand and Marit Tjomsland, 177–93. Oxford: Berg, 1998.

Kim, Grace Ji-Sun. *Invisible: Theology and the Experience of Asian American Women*. Minneapolis: Fortress, 2021.

King, Toni C. "Don't Waste Your Breath: The Dialectics of Communal Leadership Development." In *Black Womanist Leadership*, edited by Toni C. King and S. Alease Ferguson, 87–107. Albany: State University of New York Press, 2011.

King, Toni C., and S. Alease Ferguson, eds. *Black Womanist Leadership: Tracing the Motherline*. Albany: State University of New York Press, 2011.

Kuepers, Wendelin. "Embodied Inter-practices of Leadership: Phenomenological Perspectives on Relational and Responsive Leading and Following." *Leadership* 9 (2013) 335–57.

Lajimodiere, Denise K. "Ogimah Ikwe: Native Women and Their Path to Leadership." *Wicazo Sa Review* 26 (2011) 57–82.

Lee, Sandra S. K. "Women in World Evangelization: More Study Needed." *Lausanne World Pulse Archives*, June 2007. https://lausanneworldpulse.com/lausannereports/740/06-2007.

Lienemann-Perrin, Christine et al., eds. *Putting Names with Faces: Women's Impact in Mission History*. Nashville: Abingdon, 2012.

Mack, Beverly B. "Muslim Women's Knowledge Production in the Greater Maghreb: The Example of Nana Asma'u of Northern Nigeria." In *Gender and Islam in Africa*, edited by Margot Badaran, 17–40. Washington, DC: Woodrow Wilson Center, 2011.

Mahmood, Saba. *Politics of Piety: The Islamic Revival and the Feminist Subject*. Princeton: Princeton University Press, 2005.

Mernissi, Fatima. *Beyond the Veil: Male-Female Dynamics in Modern Muslim Society*. Rev. ed. Bloomington: Indiana University Press, 1987.

———. *Beyond the Veil: Male-Female Dynamics in Muslim Society*. New ed. London: Saqi, 2011.

Morris, Brian. *Religion and Anthropology: A Critical Introduction*. Cambridge: Cambridge University Press, 2005.

Mwaura, Philomena N. "Gender and Power in African Christianity: African Instituted Churches and Pentecostal Churches." In *African Christianity: An African Story*, edited by Ogbu Kalu, 359–407. Trenton: Africa World, 2007.

Ngunjiri, Faith W. *Women's Spiritual Leadership in Africa: Tempered Radicals and Critical Servant Leaders*. Albany: State University of New York Press, 2010.

Okely, Judith. "Gendered Lessons in Ivory Towers." In *Identity and Networks: Fashioning Gender and Ethnicity across Cultures*, edited by Deborah F. Bryceson et al., 228–46. New York: Berghahn, 2007.

Ramírez-Pereira, Mirliana, et al. "Interpretive Autoethnography as a Way of Social Transformation in Academic Teaching and Learning Spaces in Chile." *Cultural Studies Critical Methodologies* 18 (2016) 99–106.

Raudvere, Catharina. "Knowledge in Trust: Sufi Women in Istanbul." *Social Compass* 50 (2003) 23–34.

Robert, Dana L. *Gospel Bearers, Gender Barriers: Missionary Women in the Twentieth Century*. Maryknoll, NY: Orbis, 2002.

———. "World Christianity as a Women's Movement." *International Bulletin of Missionary Research* 30 (2006) 180–88.

Rodgers, Silvia. "Women's Space in a Men's House: The British House of Commons." In *Women and Space*, edited by Shirley Ardener, 46–69. Oxford: Berg, 1993.

Ross, Cathay. "Women's Absence and Presence in the History and Records of Christian Mission: Historical Survey of Women in Mission." In *Putting Names with Faces*, edited by Christine Lienemann-Perrin et al., 84–86. Nashville: Abingdon, 2012.

Rouse, Carolyn. "Shopping with Sister Zubayda: African American Sunni Muslim Rituals of Consumption and Belonging." In *Women and Religion in the African Diaspora: Knowledge, Power, and Performance*, edited by R. Marie Griffith and Barbara Dianne Savage, 245–64. Baltimore: Johns Hopkins University Press, 2006.

Salazar, Marilu R. "Missionaries' Commitment in Mexico: Women's Education and Resistance to Violence." In *Putting Names with Faces*, edited by Christine Lienemann-Perrin et al., 297–315. Nashville: Abingdon, 2012.

Schreiter, Robert J. "Reconciling Presence and the Sounds of Silence." In *Engaging Our Diversity: Interculturality and Consecrated Life Today*, edited by Maria Cimperman and Roger P. Schroeder, 95–110. Maryknoll, NY: Orbis, 2020.

Shaw, Karen L. H. "Divine Heartbeats and Human Echoes: A Theology of Affectivity and Implications for Mission." *Evangelical Review of Theology* 37 (2013) 196–209.

Sinclair, Amanda. *Leadership for the Disillusioned: Moving beyond Myths and Heroes to Leading That Liberates*. Crows Nest: Allen & Unwin, 2007.

Smith, Susan E. *Women in Mission: From the New Testament to Today*. Maryknoll, NY: Orbis, 2007. Kindle.

Steady, Filomina C. *Women and Leadership in West Africa: Mothering the Nation and Humanizing the State*. New York: Palgrave Macmillan, 2011.

Volf, Miroslav. *Exclusion and Embrace: A Theological Exploration of Identity, Otherness, and Reconciliation*. Nashville: Abingdon, 1996.

Whitehouse, Harvey. "Toward a Comparative Anthropology of Religion." In *Ritual and Memory: Toward a Comparative Anthropology of Religion*, edited by Harvey Whitehouse and James Laidlaw, 187–205. Walnut Creek, CA: AltaMira, 2004.

Conversation 5

Women's Leadership

—13—

Agency and Mission
Rethinking the Approach of "Women in Mission"

KIRSTEEN KIM

Introduction

WORLD EVANGELIZATION IS TRADITIONALLY and popularly attributed to "missionaries" who are White Western males. One way in which this perception of mission and missionaries has been challenged is by attempts to recover "women in mission." This approach amounts to highlighting the contribution of Western women, and perhaps some women leaders from other backgrounds, in world mission history in order to encourage women today and discuss their role in mission. However, although such an approach may raise the systemic issues of patriarchy and colonialism that lead to women's exclusion or suppression in the historical narrative, it does not go far enough to challenge the prevailing conceptions of mission that so minimize the contribution of women to it. In order to draw out further the implications of the study of women in mission for mission itself, this chapter interrogates the concept of "agency" that is used to identify "women in mission" and also questions assumptions from a feminist perspective about the nature of mission.[1] Drawing on research for *A History of Korean Christianity*,[2] this chapter offers a case study of the role of women in the evangelization of Korea. It suggests that neglect of women's agency in mission history is not only due to systemic social and historiographical reasons but also because mission is defined too narrowly and in a way that does not allow for consideration of women's contributions to it.

Interrogating Agency and "Women in Mission"

In order to understand the contemporary approach of "women in mission," we need to appreciate the prevailing discourse of "agency," or the capacity to exert power or effect change. Discussion of agency came to the fore in the 1990s in cultural anthropology as the result of a number of factors: first, social history that questioned the usefulness of the idea of free will as something that is exercised by rare individuals who are unconstrained by social norms and began to focus instead on other actors; second, from studies of social movements in which agency tends to be equated with resistance; and third, from discussions of power that totalize it to the extent that there can be no other exercise of agency. Discussion of how social change comes about suggested a more integrated model in which agency is always exercised within an environment that shapes its effects, or, more satisfactorily, a dialogical process between agents and environment through which change comes about.[3]

The study of women's history was especially stimulated by this confluence of interest in the ordinary, in social movements, and in power. Against this background of discourse on agency, and in the context of what is often called "the second wave of feminism," Western historians of Christian mission and world Christianity drew attention to "women in mission" in the colonial period. From his study, the mission historian R. Pierce Beaver described the Women's Foreign Mission Movement in North America (1812 onwards) the first feminist movement in North America[4] although it is also more soberly seen as part of a wider range of evangelical women's social activism connected with the Second Great Awakening.[5] At its height in the

---

1. In this chapter, "feminist" and "feminism" are shorthands to refer to a perspective that takes account of scholarship by women (not necessarily White women) relating to the lower status accorded to them in society.
2. Kim and Kim, *History of Korean Christianity*.
3. Ahearn, "Language and Agency," 109–37.
4. Beaver, *American Protestant Women in World Mission*.
5. As described, for example, in Hardesty, *Women Called to Witness*.

early twentieth century, Western women in foreign mission fields outnumbered Western men by two to one.[6] By that numerical measure, it might be argued that the world missionary movement of the first half of the twentieth century was a women's movement. However, structurally, the movement was largely gender-separate, so women lacked authoritative roles in mission organizations in the male-led missionary societies, in which they went out to the mission field as appendages to their husbands. Furthermore, even the women-led associations for single women were constrained by social norms in the field, and also by the relations between missions and governments, to do only "women's work for women." So, although, as Dana Robert shows, women not only did mission but also strategized about it, their plans and priorities had a secondary place in the world missionary movement. Robert also shows that, like Western men, Western women missionaries were inclined to cultural imperialism, but on the whole, their understanding of mission was less about proclaiming the message and gate-keeping the church, and more to do with building a Christian home, with serving women and children rather than converting men, with reining in men's excesses and propensity to violence (through temperance, for example), with personal witness and friendship, with an ethical and holistic understanding of the kingdom, and with bodily healing, liberation, and empowerment rather than an otherworldly gospel.[7] The women's missionary movement was undone in the mid-twentieth century by the rise of male conservatism regarding women's roles and moves to subsume successful women's missions under male-led organizations.[8]

In the 1980s and 90s, studies of "women in mission" highlighted individual women leaders from the mission fields—mostly White foreign missionaries, but with a few indigenous women, whether dignified with the name missionary or not. Their stories were accompanied by the study of women in the Bible and the tradition as an argument for the recognition of women, whether married or single, in contemporary mission.[9] The recovery of women in mission history continues and so does the need for textbooks to inspire a new generation of theological students.[10] The desire to recover the role of women in mission may be fueled by a deep sense of

---

6. Robert, *Gospel Bearers*, 5.

7. Cf. Robert, *American Women in Mission*, 409–18.

8. Robert, *American Women in Mission*, 302–16.

9. A pioneering example of this approach is Tucker, *Guardians of the Great Commission*. This followed her earlier work with Liefeld, *Daughters of the Church*. Cf. in the UK context, Byrne, *Hidden Journey*.

10. Dzubinski and Stasson, *Women in the Mission of the Church*, is a recent example of the same genre that has the scope of both Tucker volumes.

injustice on the part of women who, in the secular world, are proclaimed to be equal to men and expect to be recognized as having agency but find that in the church and in mission history this is not the case. This righteous anger can be seen in the following quotation from Cathy Ross:

> It was the little "m" that got me going. When I discovered that the early Church Missionary Society (CMS) missionary wives to New Zealand were expressed as an anonymous little "m" [for "married"] next to their husband's names in the *CMS Register*.... These women accompanied their husbands to a distant land, learned the language of the local people, suffered real hardships and made their own contribution to the cause of the CMS mission and yet were unnamed and unacknowledged by the mission society that sent them.[11]

Over time, the textbooks on women in mission increased their level of gender analysis from a simple statement of fact that women are absent from the historical record and detailing women's achievements despite the obstacles and opportunities they overcame.[12] Now they may go further to consider some of the reasons for these obstacles and for women's absence from the mission history books, such as, belief in women's inferiority and cultural expectations that women would serve in the background.[13] However, they do not reflect on (1) the problematic nature of agency, or (2) the way in which mission has been rethought from a postcolonial and decolonial perspective, both of which will be examined next.

First, regarding the nature of agency, the anthropologist Webb Keane argues that Protestants, or at least Calvinists, who have greatly influenced modern culture, ascribe particularly high moral value to human agency.[14] As a result of a preoccupation with agency, Keane observes that ascribing agency has become such an ethical imperative that without it we cannot recognize another's humanity.[15] This becomes more problematic if agency is defined through a Western lens of individual fulfillment that may not be observable in another cultural context. It may also distort the understanding of history if we feel the need to find in it what today is understood as agency. From a feminist perspective, equally problematic is that the most agency is attributed to individual males. Given that women are socialized into roles of dependence, service, and embodied-ness, it is not realistic to expect many to

---

11. Ross, "More Than Wives," 277.
12. As in Tucker, *Guardians of the Great Commission*.
13. Dzubinski and Stasson, *Women in the Mission of the Church*, 11–14.
14. Keane, *Christian Moderns*, 52–53.
15. Keane, *Christian Moderns*, 3.

aspire to autonomy, independence, and free-thinking. Should their subservient role in families and hidden service to society be understood to mean that women do not exercise agency? Taking a cue from Keane, we could ask whether perhaps, in the case of women, agency is found in a different form. Arguably, women's orientation to relationships and caring is a higher value and a fuller expression of humanness, and therefore it could even be a more morally desirable way of exercising agency. This form of agency would be more a function of doing and acting for others than of thinking and aiming for self-actualization. It would be exercised collectively by the sisterhood, that is by movements and coalitions for the collective good, rather than being based on identity and autonomy.[16] The problematic way of defining agency limits the understanding of women's contributions to mission. If only individual human beings who are visibly exercising power or effecting change are identified as agents of mission, then agency in mission is limited to missionaries in the sense of leaders who stand out from the wider community—not their wives, not the local people, and not the women who care for families and bring up the next generation of Christians. If agency in mission is about activism, then if there is no public action, apparently mission is not taking place. In this case, the question of women in mission is not only about gender justice in mission history, but also raises broader questions of gender issues in mission, mission organizations, and mission theology.[17]

Second, regarding the nature of mission, the histories of women in mission so far mentioned refer only to women who joined the women's world missionary movement, and perhaps to some indigenous women mission leaders. In this respect they do not reflect current missiological thinking.[18] Since the early 1950s in the ecumenical movement, and more recently in evangelical mission circles, the post-colonial (although not post-imperial) context has led to significant changes in the understanding and practice of mission. For colonial mission leaders, the dawning world order in which formerly colonized peoples were forming new nations that were not necessarily open to Western missions caused a rethinking of the foundations for mission. The setbacks for world mission of the closure of China and the ending of missionary visas in India—the two largest mission fields in the mid-twentieth century—occasioned the development of a theological view that mission should be understood as an initiative of God in which churches are privileged to participate rather than as enterprises of Western churches

16. Cf. Bowden and Mummery, *Understanding Feminism*, 123–49.

17. Lienemann-Perrin et al., *Putting Names with Faces*, 18. See for example, the suggestions for mission organizations in Mayer and Schmidt-Hesse, *Mission und Gender*; Dietrich et al., *Diakonia in a Gender Perspective*.

18. As reflected, for example, in Kim et al., *Oxford Handbook of Mission Studies*.

in foreign countries. This new way of thinking became known as the theology of *missio Dei*, or the mission of God. In terms of salvation history, this expanded mission to include the development of the reign of God not through human kingdoms or the expansion of Christendom but through personal and social transformation wherever the gospel is witnessed to. The *missio Dei* was described in terms of trinitarian theology to be a reflection of the mutual love of Father, Son, and Spirit that overflows toward the whole creation. Consequently, responsibility for mission does not rest only with the so-called Christian countries of Europe but with God's people in every continent. Furthermore, mission was seen as not only as a matter for missionaries who are sent overseas but as the responsibility of all disciples or baptized Christians—including those in the formerly colonized world—in every time and place.[19] Such thinking was also spurred by the realization that adherents to the Christian faith and churches were multiplying rapidly outside the West, apparently without the help of Western missions. Christians in formerly colonized countries read the same Bible and believed themselves to have a mission to all nations, the ends of the earth, or the whole creation. Moreover, since their churches were growing rapidly while churches in the West were declining, it seemed obvious that Western missionaries needed the help of missionaries from Africa, Asia, Latin America and other regions in world evangelization. Moreover, since the Western churches had been so closely linked to the atrocities of colonialism, from the perspective of some Majority World church leaders, the churches and the people of the West had badly misunderstood the gospel and were the most in need of evangelization. In this context of "world Christianity," world mission became "from everywhere to everywhere."[20] Since mission was now also the responsibility of each church in its vicinity, it was increasingly thought that churches themselves should be "missional" in their structures and orientation, ready to witness to and serve their community and reach out to others—near as well as far, and even within.[21]

Taken together, this broadening of agency and mission to include all Christians everywhere and its affirmation of many forms of agency have shifted the potential scope of the discussion of women in mission from Western women missionaries evangelizing in foreign parts to include questions of the witness of women Christians both locally and globally.[22] With

---

19. For an account of the rethinking of mission in the second half of the twentieth century, see for example, Wrogemann, *Theologies of Mission*.

20. Nazir-Ali, *From Everywhere to Everywhere*. See also Escobar, *New Global Mission*; Yeh, *Polycentric Missiology*.

21. The classic expression of this view is Guder, *Missional Church*.

22. Some broadening of who is doing mission and what that entails is reflected in

this broader brief in mind, I will summarize some of our findings regarding the agency of Korean Christian women in previous research[23] in the following case study that identifies women in mission who would not be considered to have "agency" but whose work can nevertheless be seen as part of the *missio Dei*.

Women in the Evangelization of Korea

In Korea, as in most non-Western contexts in the colonial period, local leaders in mission were not dignified with the title "missionary," nevertheless, the actual work of evangelization was done by Korean people themselves. Although the foreign missionary connection was necessary at the beginning to link the local church with the universal body of Christ, Koreans were the main human agents or subjects in the impact of the Christian gospel in Korea. In particular, as I shall show in this section, the work of women—not only in the mission organizations and churches but also in the home—was essential, even foundational, to the establishment of Christianity in Korea. However, the contribution of these women to mission was not by the kind of agency attributed to Western male missionaries of being pioneering individual leaders. Rather, the agency of Korean women was as mothers and grandmothers, wives, faithful workers, courageous witnesses, and collective organizers.

Women in pre-modern Korea were socialized in ways derived from Korean traditional religion (including shamanism, animism, Daoism), Mahayana Buddhist teachings, and especially neo-Confucian thought, which became dominant after the year 1392. Female-male is a key polarity of yin-yang philosophy, which dates from before Confucianism, and is pervasive in East Asia. Female-male corresponds to shade and light, earth and heaven, weak and strong, and so on. These metaphors indicate where the power lies in gender relationships. Furthermore, although it can be understood as promoting harmony, in the Korean context at least, yin-yang is dualistic and so tends to divide male and female and justify the domination of the public sphere by men. According to Confucian custom, females were expected to follow their fathers, then their husbands, and then their sons. Women and men were socialized differently, and from childhood, the two genders lived

---

two edited volumes on women in mission: Robert, *Gospel Bearers*; Lienemann-Perrin, *Putting Names with Faces*. This present volume is even more inclusive in terms of its understanding of mission, and in that respect, it reflects the scope of the Missiology Lectures at Fuller Theological Seminary in October 2022 from which it arises.

23. Kim and Kim, *History of Korean Christianity*.

separate lives. In the family home, the men's and women's quarters were separate, and in respectable families, the wife was the "inside person" whose domestic role complemented that of the husband in wider society. What constituted women's work and men's work and the distinction between private life and public life were different in some respects than in traditional Western societies—for example, women had control over the household finances; nevertheless, men claimed they dealt in big and weighty matters while women concerned themselves with small affairs of little consequence. Girls were of little benefit to the household economy because a dowry was required for marriage, after which they moved to the groom's home, so educating them for anything other than a good marriage was a poor investment. The bride's main role, after childbearing, was the care of her parents-in-law. Only when they were old and free of domestic responsibilities, as grandmothers, especially widows, could women enjoy some measure of autonomy and behave as they wished to. There was no clear role for a single woman in society—at least not a respectable one.[24]

The first women who became Christians—both Catholic and Protestant[25]—testified that the faith gave them new freedoms. For example, in the first century of the Catholic Church (from 1777), women saints and religious modeled a Christian life without marriage. Privileged women with some education were attracted to an ascetic life of faith. They wrote some of the earliest Christian texts, including a manual for Christian women that denounced the subjugation of a woman to her husband on the grounds that both were created in God's image. Women exercised agency in new ways. For example, a divorced woman, Colomba Kang, not only looked after the women in the church but also, at the cost of her life, hid a Chinese priest who had been smuggled into the closed country. During times of persecution many women testified to their faith at trial and were martyred as well as men. In the church, unlike in the home and in public, women ate with men, and ritually they shared the same bread and wine.

Some of the first Protestant women were excited at their baptism to be given personal names whereas, until then, they had only been referred to by their relationship to someone else. Church groups gave women a reason to be out of the house and enabled them to gather with women not of their immediate household. The church women's group could also be a means

---

24. For further detail, see Deuchler, *Confucian Transformation of Korea*.

25. This history of Korean women's Christian witness is drawn from Kim and Kim, *History of Korean Christianity*. Other more specialized English-language sources used to compile the History include: An, *Korean Women and God*; Choi, *Gender and Mission Encounters in Korea*; Clark, "Mothers, Daughters, Biblewomen, and Sisters"; Lee, *One Hundred Years*.

of support against an abusive husband or in-laws. The Protestant foreign missionaries translated the Bible using a Korean script that could be easily learnt rather than using the complex Chinese script preferred by most Korean elites. In the churches ordinary women learned to read the Bible and some could also get an education in mission schools founded for girls. Their literacy enabled them to read newspapers and books as well and so to understand what was happening in society. Women campaigned publicly for literacy and also for temperance. In the March 1st independence movement in 1919 against the annexation of the country by Japan, protests were led by Christian schoolgirls, some of whom were cut down by Japanese swords. The images of women as protesters and patriots, and the model of the educated woman professional, which resulted from the movement of educated Christian women into the public sphere, changed social expectations of women for future generations.

Women not only brought up their children in the faith and witnessed to their husbands, they also evangelized and discipled other women. The church offered training and employment for a few, mainly widows without any family responsibilities, as "Bible women" or "helpers" to the Western missionaries. Bible women were involved in various tasks of evangelization, including distributing Bibles, teaching women to read them, and sharing the Christian gospel through proclamation, prayer, healing, and exorcism. Women like Dorcas Gang walked thousands of miles in mountainous terrain fulfilling these tasks while in personal danger and often subject to abuse. The foremost of the first generation of Korean church leaders, Gil Seon-ju preached the equality of women and men, promoted women's education, and encouraged the women's group meeting in his church to grow into a national network, even though women's ministry was suppressed by other indigenous church leaders. Although there was no route to ordination for Bible women, they often supported the male church leader through educational and community initiatives, and even led churches that were without a permanent pastor. From 1908, the women's group in Gil Seon-ju's church Pyongyang also sent Bible women abroad. In total, 164 such women cross-cultural missionaries were sent between then and 1945.

Women continued their work to extend the kingdom of God even after the missionary period. However, despite the proof of women's giftedness and ability, the number of Bible women declined by the 1920s as the number of male Protestant seminary graduates grew. From the 1930s, women petitioned their respective denominations for proper recognition of their church leadership and ordination. Although in the case of these older denominations, this was realized at least by the 1990s, the options for the employment of ordained women in the church still tend to be limited to education, music and youth work because few congregations will call a woman pastor and few men would be content to serve under one. Korean women nevertheless have other ways of exercising ministry. The Bible women were usually trained in hygiene and so they also worked both formally and informally for women's health. Many served like hospital chaplains and counselors, ministering to patients and their families and also following up discharged patients at home. Women found solidarity and were mobilized through the Korean YWCA, which was founded in 1922 by two Korean women, Kim Hwal-ran and Kim Pil-rye. The former went on to earn a PhD, became president of the mission-founded Ewha Women's University, and later served in government and as an ambassador. The YMCA not only catered to the aspirations of urban women but also worked in villages and factories. Educated Christian women were employed by the missions in professional capacities as nurses (and occasionally doctors), teachers, and secretaries. Korean Christian women founded women's journals and nationalistic girls' schools during the colonization by Japan. In the Catholic Church, in which women's ministries had been almost completely suppressed after the first generation, women also played indispensable roles in home, church, and community. Some of these ministries became recognized through the formation of women's religious communities from the 1930s. In the Protestant churches, some charismatic women also exercised parallel ministries to men's, which in some respects were functional substitutes for the traditional roles of female shamans and also suited the context of revivalism. In particular, some women—both Protestant and Catholic—became known as healers and exorcists. They operated through women's networks and in the mountains—the traditional places of prayer. Some were accused by church authorities of heresy for syncretizing Christianity with indigenous practices.

Restrictions on religions tightened during the 1930s as Japanese rule was militarized, and many church activities went underground. Then the mountains became the only places where people could gather for church services. During the instability of Communist suppression in northern Korea after 1945, during the displacement caused by the Korean War (1950–53), and during the privations afterwards, women were very often the leaders of small Christian groups meeting in homes. This cell-group pattern continued as part of the push for church growth during nation-building in South Korea that largely depended on the ministry of women evangelizing their neighbors and growing congregations. In the 1950s to the 1980s, this mission of hospitality also extended to practical support of other women and their families. Many women who joined churches were suffering from physical or mental illness or facing domestic violence. They found support in the church women's groups and through church ministries, kindergartens, and business networks that helped women move into the workplace. In the mainline denominations, the extent of women's contribution was hidden behind the decorous male-led public face of the church but it came to light in Korean Pentecostalism, which started in the 1930s through the work of single women missionaries from the West like Mary Rumsey. David Yonggi Cho, the founder in 1958 of the enormous Yoido Full Gospel Church, publicly acknowledged the ministry of his theologically-trained mother-in-law Choi Ja-sil, his wife Kim Seong-hye, and other women church workers, although the church still does not grant women equal status with the male pastors. In 1967, Lee Yeon-ok founded the Korea Church Women United, which was influenced by Minjung Theology, Korea's home-grown form of political or liberation theology. This ecumenical organization brought together various progressive groups to protest the treatment of women workers in sweatshops, support their families, and campaign for women's rights. Church Women United went on to protest against police brutality and sexual exploitation—including sex tourism and the historical case of the "comfort women" forced to serve Japanese soldiers sexually during the period of occupation. Progressive church women also worked for human rights, democratization (which came about in the 1990s), and reconciliation with the North.

Another key way in which Korean women have been essential to the Korean churches is through fundraising. In the late nineteenth century, Pastor Gil Seon-ju encouraged the women in his church to save a handful of rice daily as a Sunday offering. Women's control of the household finances enabled the strong women's groups to mobilize support for their churches and also for other causes, such as a campaign in 1907 to resist Japanese designs on the country by paying off the national debt. Catholic and Protestant women tried the same in 1998 during the Korean economic crisis. Women have influence in church affairs because their support is a significant factor in the church budget. The extent of the collective financial power of women in Korean churches is illustrated by two buildings close by each other in central Seoul built in the mid-1980s. The first is the headquarters of the Tonghap Presbyterian denomination, which is five storeys high, and the other is a twenty-two-story office and conference center belonging to the denomination's women's association. The women's building is staffed by women but even today few women hold office in the denominational building. Much of women's ability to support the churches in the twentieth century was because married women were expected to work only in the home. In Communist North Korea, in which women were immediately expected to work for the party outside the home, churches soon struggled to function. Similar pressures are one reason for the current decline of the Korean churches since around the turn of the century and show the extent to which women's voluntary work was taken for granted by male-led churches. Whether their agency was recognized by men in the church or not, women did the work that they considered was demanded of disciples of Christ in the way that seemed appropriate in their particular circumstances.

In 1898, the Presbyterian women's group at Gil's church sponsored Bible women to go and live in an area where there were no other Christians and to start a women's group. They would reach out to local women who, once they became Christians would be encouraged to convert their husbands until eventually there were enough men to legally establish a church and construct a building. The thinking of the women leaders, which was perhaps inspired by the story of Lydia in Acts 16, reveals how essential women were to Korean church growth. They not only brought their husbands to Christ but they could also be relied on to bring up children up in the faith. The evangelization of the home, the formation of the next generation of Christians, and therefore the biological growth of the church was largely in their hands. This domestic role in the kingdom of God was largely hidden from view, and was not rewarded with office or salary, but it was more significant statistically than conversion growth. In sum, whether in the family, in church, or in society, the work of Korean women was foundational to the evangelization of Korea.

Women Redefining Mission

Many of the same characteristics identified by Robert in US-American women in mission can also be said to be features of Korean women's roles in the Korean churches: working for women and children, a holistic approach, and practicing bodily healing, liberation and empowerment. To these could be added from the Korean side: love of nation, resistance to aggressions, and nation-building through a witness of suffering and hardship in solidarity with other Koreans and for the sake of the gospel. Particularly noticeable in both contexts was the importance of women's church groups and national organizations that facilitated collective action. Contemporary women may be able to just get on with what God called them to do without worrying about whether men permit it or consider it to be mission.[26] However, in their mission groups, both Korean and US women also formed their own ideas about the priorities of mission and exercised agency in ways that were

---

26. Lederleitner, *Women in God's Mission*, 203–5.

different from their male counterparts, not only because of their social constraints but also because they understood mission differently.

Rather than identifying women who fit within masculine definitions of agency or mission, this reasoning suggests that women should redefine mission from their perspective and in light of their circumstances.[27] Such redefinition has, in fact, been happening in the last half century. Some of the most fertile theology of mission has come from women in the Majority World who were not invested in the historic women's missionary movement but understood themselves to be involved in the wider mission of God both locally and globally.[28] Gemma Cruz identifies "six intersecting dimensions" that feminist scholars bring to mission studies: a belief in the full humanity of women (the anthropological dimension), sociocultural analysis of women's condition, ideological and political critique of patriarchy, scrutiny of gender inequities in the church, recovery of women's history, and criticism of interpretations that run against the clear biblical message of the equality of male and female.[29]

As a result of such feminist methodology, mission has been redefined by women in some distinctive ways. Stimulated by the seminal work of Indonesian novelist and theologian Marianne Katoppo in her 1979 book, *Compassionate and Free: An Asian Woman's Theology*, I will describe just three redefinitions by way of conclusion. First, a women's theology of mission has the flourishing of family and community at heart. Recognizing that, if women's gifts were developed through education, men, children, and the whole society benefit, Katoppo was one of the first to argue that "woman's liberation is also man's."[30] Such an understanding moved thinking about women in mission from a rights-based or identity approach, in which women are set against men, to women's participation in a holistic social transformation for the common good. This approach was more palatable and achievable in her context of Indonesia and other Asian nations but it had other advantages as well: on the one hand, it affirmed women's traditional domestic roles of bearing children and creating a Christian home as missional, and on the other hand, it recognized all women's call to share their God-given gifts also in the public sphere in response to the commission of Jesus. Katoppo argued that Mary, the mother of Jesus was "the first fully liberated human being" because she was a virgin in the positive sense

27. Adeney, *Women and Christian Mission*, provides some case studies of contemporary women doing mission theology.

28. For a discussion of the differences between theologies in the West and the Majority World, see Kim, "Gender Issues." See also Kim, *Holy Spirit in the World*.

29. Cruz, "Women in Mission."

30. Katoppo, *Compassionate and Free*, 9.

of being free to give life, to create.[31] From this perspective, Mary, although fulfilling a traditional role, is the ultimate example of women's agency in mission as she freely embraces God's call to serve the world by bringing forth the Savior. Mary's submission to God is only meaningful if it was free and not forced like submission to men. Mary carried Jesus. She taught her theology of liberation—the Magnificat—to her son at her knee and he carried forward this manifesto at Nazareth (compare Luke 1:46–55 with Luke 4:18–19). In addition, she worked behind the scenes to support Jesus' mission (e.g., at Cana: John 2:3–5). As the most faithful of all the disciples, Mary is the archetype of the new human being in Christ and the preeminent witness to the gospel.

Second, the act of giving birth and bringing new life can be especially resonant as a theological motif for women and it is also a biblical metaphor for mission. When the disciples asked what would happen after Jesus had gone to the Father and before they would see him again, he told them about this period of mission using the metaphor of childbirth:

> When a woman is in labor, she has pain because her hour has come. But when her child is born, she no longer remembers the anguish because of the joy of having brought a human being into the world. So you have pain now, but I will see you again, and your hearts will rejoice, and no one will take your joy from you. (John 16:21–22)[32]

Although Jesus' words are addressed to people who will not bear children literally, for women who do bear children, it is meaningful in that it affirms that childbirth is an actual form of mission. For women whose lives are largely confined to home and family, this verse validates this as an important way of fulfilling God's purposes. Again, Mary is the archetypal mother. Her womb is the source of life, even the life of the world. The birth of a child is a sign of hope and rejoicing not only for the immediate family but, in traditional societies at least, for the whole community. A child is a symbol of hope for the future, a sign of health and well-being for the whole family, and a foretaste of the new life of the kingdom (Matt 18:3). A second birth is the process that we must all go through to enter the kingdom (John 3:3). Women who know childbirth are potential midwives to the re-birthing process as well. The barrier to their participation in mission is a false one because the one birth leads to the other. Women's mission is unbounded. Women's role in bringing up children in the faith is interconnected with

---

31. Katoppo, *Compassionate and Free*, 16.
32. Biblical citations in this chapter are from the NRSVue.

evangelizing society and birthing churches. The groaning of women in labor does not stop at family, church, and society but is also part of the "groaning" of creation as it waits for "the freedom of the glory of the children of God" (Rom 8:21–23). Women who do not have the freedom to literally follow nevertheless, like the disciples of Jesus, participate in the processes of new life that join creation and recreation that we call God's mission.

Third, perhaps ministries of caring and healing are characteristic of women in mission historically not just because women are restricted from participation in other forms of mission but because they choose to do mission in a compassionate and holistic way, as Jesus did. The Hebrew word for compassion, as attributed to God, for example in Exod 34:6, is derived from the word for womb. Divine compassion is like the feeling a mother has for her child, the fruit of her womb (Matt 23:37). Feminist theology characteristically rejects dualisms of spirit and body, divine and material. So women's theology of mission is not confined to care of souls. In this life, and in the world beyond, souls are embodied and their well-being is dependent on food and other forms of nourishment within a healthy environment. Recognizing the integral nature of life, women in mission also address poverty, which affects women to a greater extent than men, and environmental degradation, which hinders women trying to feed, house and clothe families. The bulk of Katoppo's theological book is about the sociopolitical realities under which Asian women suffer as they are cowed by abuse, burdened by carrying children, exhausted from working in the fields, and overwhelmed by the cares of life. She compares them to the woman in Luke 13 who "was bent over and was quite unable to stand up straight" (v. 11). Jesus saw her, called her over, spoke to her, laid his hands on her, and "immediately she stood up straight and began praising God" (v. 13). Mission is about enabling bent-over women to stand up straight, and freeing them to raise their heads in praise to God. The leader of the synagogue (a man presumably) was indignant because Jesus broke the law to do this, but for Jesus this liberating act was exactly what should be done on the sabbath, and what was due to this woman, a daughter of Abraham. He declared, "ought not this woman, . . . whom Satan bound for eighteen long years, be set free from this bondage?" (v. 16). This story encourages all women to know their worth, raise their heads, and know their part in God's mission.

Nurturing human flourishing, giving birth and bringing new life, and caring and healing are all features of the mission of Jesus of Nazareth who "came that they may have life and have it abundantly" (John 10:10). If mission is defined in this way,[33] then the question of who is doing mission yields

---

33. As it is defined in the WCC's statement, "Together towards Life: Mission and

different answers from the traditional association with male missionaries. In this case, women are not on the periphery, as mission history might suggest, but rather at the center of what God is doing in the world.

Bibliography

Adeney, Frances S. *Women and Christian Mission: Ways of Knowing and Doing Theology.* Eugene, OR: Pickwick, 2015.

Ahearn, Laura M. "Language and Agency." *Annual Review of Anthropology* 30 (2001) 109–37.

An, Choi Hee. *Korean Women and God: Experiencing God in a Multi-religious Colonial Context.* Maryknoll, NY: Orbis, 2005.

Beaver, R. Pierce. *American Protestant Women in World Mission: A History of the First Feminist Movement in North America.* Rev. ed. Grand Rapids: Eerdmans, 1980.

Bowden, Peta, and Jane Mummery. *Understanding Feminism.* London: Routledge, 2014.

Byrne, Lavinia. *The Hidden Journey: Missionary Heroines in Many Lands.* London: SPCK, 1993.

Choi, Hyaeweol. *Gender and Mission Encounters in Korea: New Women, Old Ways.* Berkeley: University of California Press, 2009.

Clark, Donald N. "Mothers, Daughters, Biblewomen, and Sisters: An Account of 'Women's Work' in the Korea Mission Field." In *Christianity in Korea*, edited by Robert E. Buswell Jr. and Timothy S. Lee, 167–92. Honolulu: University of Hawaii, 2006.

Cruz, Gemma Tulud. "Women in Mission." In *The Oxford Handbook of Mission Studies*, edited by Kirsteen Kim et al., 652–69. Oxford: Oxford University Press, 2022.

Deuchler, Martina. *The Confucian Transformation of Korea: A Study of Society and Ideology.* Cambridge: Harvard University Press, 1992.

Dietrich, Stephanie, et al., eds. *Diakonia in a Gender Perspective.* Oxford: Regnum, 2016.

Dzubinski, Leanne M., and Anneke H. Stasson. *Women in the Mission of the Church: Their Opportunities and Obstacles throughout Christian History.* Grand Rapids: Baker Academic, 2021.

Escobar, Samuel. *The New Global Mission: The Gospel from Everywhere to Everyone.* Downers Grove, IL: IVP Academic, 2003.

Guder, Darrell L., ed. *Missional Church: A Vision for the Sending of the Church in North America.* Grand Rapids: Eerdmans, 1998.

Hardesty, Nancy A. *Women Called to Witness: Evangelical Feminism in the Nineteenth Century.* Nashville: Abingdon, 1984.

Katoppo, Marianne. *Compassionate and Free: An Asian Woman's Theology.* Geneva: WCC, 1979.

Keane, Webb. *Christian Moderns: Freedom and Fetish in the Mission Encounter.* Berkeley: University of California Press, 2007.

Kim, Kirsteen. "Gender Issues in Intercultural Theological Perspective." In *Intercultural Theology: Approaches and Themes*, edited by Mark J. Cartledge and David Cheetham, 75–92. London: SCM, 2011.

Evangelism in Changing Landscapes."

———. *The Holy Spirit in the World: A Global Conversation*. Maryknoll, NY: Orbis, 2007.

Kim, Kirsteen, et al., eds. *The Oxford Handbook of Mission Studies*. Oxford: Oxford University Press, 2022.

Kim, Sebastian C. H., and Kirsteen Kim. *A History of Korean Christianity*. Cambridge: Cambridge University Press, 2015.

Lederleitner, Mary T. *Women in God's Mission: Accepting the Invitation to Serve and Lead*. Downers Grove, IL: InterVarsity, 2018.

Lee, Yeon-ok. *One Hundred Years of the National Organization of the Korean Presbyterian Women*. Translated by Myung-woo Park and Ji-yeon Hong. Seoul: Presbyterian Church of Korea, 2011.

Lienemann-Perrin, Christine, et al., eds. *Putting Names with Faces: Women's Impact in Mission History*. Nashville: Abingdon, 2012.

Mayer, Gabriele, and Ulrike Schmidt-Hesse, eds. *Mission und Gender: Einblicke in die Praxis*. Stuttgart: EMS, 2011.

Nazir-Ali, Michael. *From Everywhere to Everywhere: A World View of Christian Witness*. London: Flame, 1991.

Robert, Dana L. *American Women in Mission: A Social History of Their Thought and Practice*. Macon, GA: Mercer University Press, 1997.

———, ed. *Gospel Bearers, Gender Barriers: Missionary Women in the Twentieth Century*. Maryknoll, NY: Orbis, 2002.

Ross, Cathy. "More Than Wives: Rediscovering the Little 'm' in Our Mission History." In *Putting Names with Faces*, edited by Lienemann-Perrin et al., 277–95. Nashville: Abingdon, 2012.

Tucker, Ruth A. *Guardians of the Great Commission: The Story of Women in Modern Missions*. Grand Rapids: Zondervan, 1988.

Tucker, Ruth A., and Walter L. Liefeld. *Daughters of the Church: Women in Ministry from the New Testament to the Present*. Grand Rapids: Baker Academic, 1987.

World Council of Churches. "Together towards Life: Mission and Evangelism in Changing Landscapes." https://www.oikoumene.org/resources/documents/together-towards-life-mission-and-evangelism-in-changing-landscapes.

Wrogemann, Henning. *Intercultural Theology*. Vol. 2, *Theologies of Mission*. Translated by Karl E. Böhmer. Downers Grove, IL: IVP Academic, 2018.

Yeh, Allen L. *Polycentric Missiology: Twenty-First Century Mission from Everyone to Everywhere*. Downers Grove, IL: IVP Academic, 2016.

— 14 —

The Expansion of Female Leadership Influence through Seven Developmental Domains

Anna Morgan

Women church leaders in the United States are gaining slow but steady progress in theologically egalitarian denominations, representing a growing minority of senior pastors. Despite progress in numbers of female senior pastors, they are nowhere near pastoring 50% of egalitarian churches. Not only are they a minority, but these women typically pastor smaller churches than their male colleagues. The National Congregations Study found in 2019, women pastored 16.7% of Pentecostal churches, but they pastored only 5.9% of the total number of Pentecostal congregants represented in the study.[1] This means that women pastors' churches were on average, smaller than their male colleagues' churches. Here's how this breaks down inside an egalitarian denomination. In 2019, 9% of Nazarene Churches were pastored by women, and the median number of congregants in a church pastored by a woman was thirty people. The median church size of the male-pastor-led Nazarene churches was fifty-two people.[2] After they have been trained for

---

1. National Congregations Study, "Denominational Affiliation."
2. Kubichek, "Pastoral Leadership."

ministry, ordained, and given leadership opportunities, women face new challenges in expanding the reach of their institutional authority.

The Nazarene study found that while male pastors' churches had shrunk on average by 22% over twenty years, women pastors' churches remained stable.[3] This means that in an era of declining church involvement, women pastors make a significant contribution in strengthening the church. Men and women alike are all called to make new disciples, which means together we steward the growth of the church, advancing the kingdom of God. Developing women for ministry leadership means we must consider more than just whether women are leading in churches, but the depth and breadth of their authority within their churches and movements. Women pastors who are gifted and called to leadership should experience the expansion of their kingdom influence. This expanded leadership in early stages of development might look like a woman growing from a church support role to a leadership role. An emerging female leader might steward the growth of a small church to a mid-size church or be appointed as pastor of a larger church. An advanced female pastor might assume a denominational leadership role, gain a significant social media following, preach at conferences, or publish. To support this kind of growth of female leader influence, we must not only understand how Christian women leaders are formed, but how they form influence.

The most significant leadership not only influences decisions an organization makes but sits in the decision-making role. This is the difference between influence and authority. A leader can have deep impact on a single life she mentors, cultivating transformation. But a leader can also have broad impact on many lives. The most fruitful leaders don't strive for one or the other, but for both/and. They build interlocking layers of leadership, investing in other leaders so they have width to their impact, and also cultivating deep life change. This creates multiplication of disciples. Even though we don't hear of many women with this kind of significant apostolic leadership, God is forming women pastors, and many have the potential for this kind of impact.

I am a practitioner-scholar. I write this chapter not as an academic observing a phenomenon, or a spectator searching for patterns, but as one located within my field of study. I am a woman co-pastoring an Assemblies of God church with my husband, and so have experienced my field of study for my entire adult life. I began my leadership journey as a teenager in a ministry internship. I entered full-time ministry at age twenty-one when I was licensed for pastoral ministry and became a youth pastor for two years

---

3. Kubichek, "Pastoral Leadership."

before spending twelve years as a megachurch worship pastor. I spent three years in itinerant ministry, training pastors and leadership teams around the world. For six years, I was executive pastor of ministries for City Church Chicago, a large downtown church, before moving to metropolitan DC to answer the call to pastor Word of Life Church. God develops leaders slowly, over time. As the Lord shaped me, my authority expanded. My interest in female ministry leadership flows from who I am, the experiences that shaped me, and the calling of Christ that compels me.

The challenges I've encountered led me to doctoral research into female leadership development in local churches. I wanted to understand how women leaders are formed for church ministry, how their leadership is created, and how women grow in their influence. For this study, I selected egalitarian churches already producing highly influential women leaders, where women lead at every level of the organization. This points to a pipeline of female leader development. Women leaders don't typically start their ministry development as senior pastors but are formed through a sequence of increasingly challenging leadership opportunities. I wanted to understand how highly influential women pastors were formed, and what environmental factors contributed to their flourishing. Even more importantly, I wanted to understand how these women became powerful leaders and expanded their leadership. Using a qualitative, mixed-methods approach, I gathered data from seventy-eight female and male leaders, mostly pastors, from seventy-one churches in the United States, Australia, and Canada. This study included women pastors from White, middle-class churches, intercultural churches, Latinx churches, and Black churches. Women in this study had no theological limits on the kinds of roles they can carry. Most churches in this study were Pentecostal or charismatic and all were evangelical. I used grounded theory to analyze that data, producing a new model for understanding the development of female ministry leadership, called the seven processes of female leadership development. The study identified seven major domains of leadership development that God uses to shape female ministry leaders. This chapter introduces the seven domains of female leadership development.[4]

Seven Domains of Female Leadership Development

Within each of these seven domains, a Sovereignly designed and Holy Spirit guided process of formation shapes a woman leader and her leadership. How she responds to shaping determines the contours of her leadership.

---

4. Morgan, "Female Leaders," 197.

J. Robert Clinton described leadership development as a lifelong process that involves sovereignly guided "process items," which are experiences God uses to shape a leader's character and values.[5] Clinton observed these as repeating patterns of shaping in Christian leaders' lives, where similar experiences produced similar results. "Response patterns" are ways leaders respond to these God-given experiences, ultimately forming a leader and his or her leadership capacity.[6] My study of women leaders found they experience seven major categories of "process items" in their formation, over the life of their entire ministry.[7]

These seven domains include aspects of her inner life: her spiritual, emotional, and cognitive development. They also include aspects of her environment: her home life and ministry context. These domains shape who she is as a leader. Her leadership is formed through two more domains: leadership relationships, and leadership communication. Leadership is an interactive process that occurs in the exchanges between leaders and followers.[8] Each of these seven domains contains essential processing. If a woman does not experience the right kinds of environmental supports or is not able to fully process and respond to an aspect of her inner life shaping, her leadership will be stunted. She must engage each of the seven domains in every season of her leadership to continue to grow in authority.

Inward Shaping

The nuts and bolts of leadership skills development begins with a leadership opportunity, but the inner work required for a woman to say yes to that leadership opportunity begins much earlier. Leadership development begins with inward formation. The Holy Spirit initiates this work, setting in motion three aspects of interwoven shaping: spiritual formation, forming patterns of leadership thinking, and developing emotional intelligence.

Spiritual Formation

God sovereignly guides a woman's early spiritual foundations and presents her with invitations and tests as she surrenders to God's shaping. Most of the time, a woman doesn't consider vocational ministry until God invites

---

5. Clinton, *Leadership Emergence Theory*, 81.
6. Clinton, *Leadership Emergence Theory*, 341.
7. Morgan, "Female Leaders," 197.
8. Northouse, *Leadership*, 16.

her, often through someone else inviting her into a ministry opportunity. When she accepts that invitation, she begins a journey of discovering her leadership calling. The mental maps a woman learned from childhood associating leadership with masculinity may impede her recognition of her ministry as a call to spiritual leadership.[9] Identifying this changes the trajectory of a woman's life. Her certainty that accepting ministry leadership is obedience to God gives her endurance through the resistance and difficulty she will certainly face.[10] Ministry as a career path has many challenges and obstacles, particularly for women, and so if a woman does not believe that accepting ministry leadership is required for obedience to God's call, the cost is far higher than the reward. It's just not worth the pain.

When a woman hears God's call to ministry leadership, she must process the theological implications of this path. Culture in the United States is polarized and so tends to bifurcate churches into easy categories of complementarian (men and women are equal in value but not in function) versus egalitarian (men and women are equal in value and in function, with no limits placed on female leadership).[11] As with most things, this is an oversimplification of something far more nuanced. These theological ideas fall on a spectrum, with many different practical interpretations of these theological positions. Budding women leaders must process all this complexity, untangling the practice and culture she has been exposed to into cohesive ideas that allow her to be obedient to what she is sensing God ask of her. She must reconcile herself with the leadership gifts God gave her.

This theological processing tends to be easier for women who grew up in theologically egalitarian churches. However, as these women's influence grows and they encounter resistance outside the environment where they were nurtured, they must be able to articulate their own theology of female leadership. Women who did not grow up in theologically egalitarian churches wrestle with Bible passages that seem to limit female leadership in an important developmental process.[12] To fully develop, these women must emerge from this study convinced that their leadership is validated by God, so that they are not inwardly shaken when their leadership encounters someone who challenges its validity. Without this inward certainty, women question their own ideas and decisions and hold back from speaking and leading.

Women leaders grow spiritually and in their awareness of Spirit-validation of their ministry leadership. God allows women leaders to experience

---

9. Maros, *Calling in Context*, 23.
10. Morgan, "Female Leaders," 101–2.
11. Warren, "Come out of Your Gender-Role Foxholes."
12. Morgan, "Female Leaders," 103–4.

painful tests of their submission, leading to deep processing that increases their dependency on God through prayer. As a woman leader grows spiritually, she becomes more like Jesus, leading with humble servant leadership. She learns to discern and participate in the work of the Holy Spirit. This produces spiritual authority, which gives a leader the weight of God's power behind her preaching and teaching, her ministry, and her leadership decisions (Luke 10:19; Jas 4:7). This spiritual formation shapes a woman leader's thinking.

Thinking Formation

When I was twenty-two years old, my ministry role was to support my youth pastor husband by handling anything administrative and leading the youth band. My senior pastors noticed, and when the worship pastor moved on, they asked me to consider leading our church's adult worship ministry. Our megachurch had mass choirs, large-scale productions, and five weekly services. To say I was intimidated by the invitation would be an understatement. I told my pastors I felt called primarily to support my husband's ministry, but if they needed help, I would give it six months until they found someone else. Twelve years later, I was still the worship pastor!

About six months into this new responsibility, I was treading water trying to maintain this large ministry. Nearly every team member was significantly older than me, and many had (quite reasonable) doubts about my abilities to lead this group. Most of our church's musicians were highly skilled, middle-aged Black men—professional Gospel music players. I was a young White woman with a classical music education, learning to play new music styles, trying to run this ministry, and making lots of mistakes. One night at rehearsal, one of these men became so impatient with my leadership that he packed up his instrument, complaining loudly, and left in the middle of rehearsal. I was humiliated and did my best to hold back the tears. I went home deeply discouraged. I never wanted to see the man again, but my leaders intervened and instructed me to confront this man about his behavior. I was terrified, but the next day I called the man. I expected to be berated again, but instead, to my relieved surprise, he thanked me for calling and apologized for his behavior. We settled on a compromise, and he returned to the team, serving faithfully and cheerfully for several years.

Despite my lack of confidence in my own leadership, and the intimidating nature of leading older women and men vastly more experienced and skilled than me, I had to lead. God had trusted me with this team, and managing the emotional climate of rehearsals was an important part of this responsibility. If I had not successfully engaged this challenge, I would not have learned confidence in leading older men. Without this confidence development, I would likely not be a pastor today.

Some women leaders grow up in homes that cheer them on in their leadership gifts and dominant personalities. But many girls never consider the possibility of leading. Women are not socialized to aspire to leadership. In fact, they are typically encouraged away from it.[13] Even fewer women dream about ministry leadership. They are socialized to value home and children above a career and advancement. Girls receive messages about what it means to be female from dolls, toy kitchens, and dress-up kits. As they grow, their ideas of womanhood are formed by media portrayals of women, their parents' relationship, and the way they see women participating in their churches.[14] All these cultural messages about what it means to be female shape a woman's identity from adolescence. To become a leader, a woman must begin by internalizing a new identity that is contrary to all these cultural messages. She must conceive of herself as a leader.[15] This identity work begins with a woman recognizing her own influence in the lives around her, and then assuming responsibility for the effects of that influence. This identity work continues throughout leadership development. To expand her leadership, a woman leading a small church must first be able to conceive of herself as a woman who can lead a large church.

A woman typically comes into leadership with a confidence deficit, which appears to originate in her brain structure and chemistry, and then is socially reinforced. Compared to men, women are less likely to view themselves as ready for an opportunity. When an opportunity to lead arises, they dismiss themselves as unqualified. Women experience negative emotion more easily than men, and so fear can hold them back from even the attempt.[16] This creates a self-defeating cycle, because the corrective to low confidence is establishing patterns of self-acknowledged successes. If a woman never attempts a challenge, she will never gain the confidence in herself she needs. In the church world, a lack of confidence can be mislabeled as humility and even encouraged.[17] In order to step into an opportunity for leadership, a woman must learn to view the challenge ahead not as an insurmountable obstacle, but as an opportunity to grow and learn new skills.[18]

---

13. Howell, *Buried Talents*, 2.
14. Howell, *Buried Talents*, 31.
15. Ely et al., "Taking Gender into Account," 475.
16. Mohr, *Playing Big*; Kay and Shipman, "Confidence Gap."
17. Beach, *Gifted to Lead*, 39.
18. Scott, "Study."

Even when a woman says yes to an incredible leadership opportunity, she often struggles with "imposter syndrome," making her feel undeserving.[19] This first leap into a leadership opportunity is a type of risk-taking. Men are more inclined than women to take big risks in life.[20] In order to grow her influence and authority, a woman leader must get increasingly comfortable with making decisions to move her organization forward, even when a risk of failure exists. A woman leader might be willing to assume risks to herself, but she is typically more concerned about the well-being of others around her than herself.[21] While leadership empathy is an excellent skill for creating a cohesive team, it makes it harder for a woman to make leadership decisions that might create risk for others, which is an essential component of high-stakes, powerful leadership.

A woman must be willing to say yes to intimidating leadership opportunities and engage the scary conversations for her confidence and trust in her own leadership ability to grow. This is essential to the growth of authority. A woman leader is continually learning patterns of thinking that run against the grain of ways she has been socialized to behave. As she does this, she also develops emotional intelligence.

Emotional Intelligence Formation

Successful women leaders learn to process their own emotions. Travis Bradberry and Jean Greaves identified four components of emotional intelligence: self-awareness, self-management, social awareness (or empathy), and relationship management.[22] Women leaders grow in each of these ways.

Self-awareness is an essential component of female leader development. The confidence problem means that women often compare themselves to other successful leaders with different giftedness and devalue their own. Or a woman may try to pattern her leadership on someone she respects but fails because she has different giftedness. As a woman becomes self-aware of her own God-given unique design, she develops fruitfulness.

---

19. Sandberg, *Lean In*, 29.

20. Byrnes, Miller, and Schafer found women are more risk-averse than men in, "Gender Differences," 379. This study examined gendered engagement in two high-risk behaviors, gambling and fast-driving as a result of several factors, including confidence, future-orientation, and socialization. Many men and women would consider these particular behaviors to be risks not worth taking, but other high-risk decisions are necessary to leadership.

21. Cadsby and Maynes, "Gender, Risk Aversion"; Schmitt, "Truth about Sex Differences."

22. Bradberry and Greaves, *Emotional Intelligence*, 24, 32, 38, 43.

This produces confidence. She knows what she is good at and what she is not good at. As she grows in her leadership, becoming comfortable with herself and authentic in her leadership expression, she learns to lead from who she is.

Hearing difficult feedback is one of the hardest things for a developing leader to process but it is essential to her growth.[23] A leader must learn to manage her own emotions, differentiating them from the praise and criticism she receives. If she responds emotionally to feedback, her leaders might perceive that she is too emotionally fragile to hear constructive criticism and hold back from giving her growth opportunities.[24] If she does not learn emotion management, she is likely to stagnate. Women leaders often have higher emotional intelligence than their male counterparts.[25] Likely this is because without it, they are not promoted. Women can work on this emotional regulation by using self-talk that externalizes criticism, focusing her self-corrections on the work itself rather than receiving it as personal to her. If she chooses not to hear criticism as personal rejection, it becomes easier to bear.

A women leader also develops the essential skill of empathy. Empathy helps a woman leader accurately perceive the mental and emotional state of those around her and adapt her communication appropriately.[26] A woman leader can encourage, challenge, or persuade someone on her team as needed.

External Shaping

A female leader's home and leadership environment provide both supports and hindrances that she must continually process in her thoughts and emotions, then respond and adapt to. How she responds to the external forces around her shapes who she is and how she leads.

Home Life

A woman's home environment impacts her leadership more significantly than a man's, particularly for a married woman. A married woman's husband's support of her leadership has a perfect correlation to her ability to

---

23. Hopkins et al., "Women's Leadership," 353.
24. Mohr, *Playing Big*, 94.
25. Eagly and Carli, *Through the Labyrinth*, loc. 892.
26. McConnell, *Cultural Insights*, loc. 2628.

lead. Without a husband's support, a married woman simply cannot lead.[27] The reason for this is both practical and emotional. Women still carry a heavier burden for domestic chores. A 2008 study found just having a husband creates an extra seven hours of housework a week for a woman.[28] For a woman leader to thrive and become powerful, her husband must recognize and value her leadership so much that he is willing to take on more responsibilities at home to see his wife's leadership flourish. He must also view her leadership not as a threat but as something to celebrate. A couple learns to navigate their relationship inside her leadership context. They might lead alongside each other in church, leading to overlap between ministry and home. Her husband might not lead at all in church, leading to a sometimes awkward dynamic if she leads the team he volunteers for. Influential female leaders and their husbands have defined how their marriage will function inside and outside their ministry leadership context.[29]

Leaders who are mothers need practical support to manage their children. Feminism has changed the culture of the West, in what has been described as three distinct waves. The first wave focused on women's suffrage, and the second wave focused on women's liberation, moving women into the workforce in the 1960s. Third-wave feminism, beginning in the US in the 1990s, has focused on reclaiming femininity, the impact of intersectionality on women, and diversity.[30] The social change brought by feminism has impacted church leadership teams in the West, and as a result, women in ministry today are less likely to abandon leadership roles during motherhood than previous generations. To do this, however, they need real support for child rearing, which can come from a variety of sources. Mother leaders may also need support with home responsibilities, like house cleaning. Women feel a social obligation to be able to keep their homes clean and their children well-organized, so many feel a sense of shame about needing this help. This becomes much more difficult if the father is not equally sharing the responsibilities at home. The ideal source of support comes from a father who wants to be a full partner in caring for his children.[31] Influential women make peace with needing support at home.

While a single female may not have the same kind of family obligations, she still must manage her home responsibilities and the expectations

27. Morgan, "Female Leaders," 150.
28. University of Michigan Institute for Social Research, "Exactly How Much Housework Does a Husband Create?"; Milkie et al., "Taking on the Second Shift."
29. Morgan, "Female Leaders," 151.
30. Evans, "What Makes a (Third) Wave?," 411, 414.
31. Eagly and Carli, *Through the Labyrinth*, loc. 972.

of extended family, without any help from a husband. Single women leaders often struggle with working too much in ministry and neglecting their domestic life.[32] These women need a team of people around them to help them fill those gaps, including a financial advisor, cleaner, or a landscaper.

Without these supports, a woman will not become more influential, because the pressures of home life responsibilities will overwhelm her ministry involvement. Women place a high priority on well-functioning home and family life.

Leadership Environment

A women leader is shaped by her ministry environment. Her church may be theologically egalitarian, but to thrive, a female church staff member needs more support. A church's culture of leadership has an enormous impact on a woman leader. In the worst environments, women must prove themselves to be capable before they are handed the opportunity to lead. They must have demonstrable influence before they are handed authority. Women in these environments may need to self-promote to be noticed, something Christian women are often deeply uncomfortable with. In the most supportive environments, women are invited to lead based on their potential, not because they have a proven track record of success.[33] To create a pipeline of female leadership, a church will need to intentionally recruit women to lead at every level. In denominations with centralized authority structures, this recruitment can become even more strategic. If a church does not have women ready to step into executive leadership roles, lead teams can prepare women to lead in lower stakes opportunities before promoting them.

In Western ministry contexts, a woman that says yes to a full-time ministry leadership opportunity will also need office policies that support her home life, granting flexible work hours and remote work.[34] Women value these freedoms so highly that they will accept lower pay to have the flexibly to better care for their families. Accommodations like on-site childcare make it easier for women to care for their families. When a woman's family life is running well, her capacity for leadership expands. Without these environmental supports, a woman's leadership will encounter a ceiling.

---

32. Jackson, "Why We Need Single Women Leaders."
33. Sandberg, *Lean In*, 8.
34. Ely et al., "Taking Gender into Account," 483.

Forming Leadership

As these environmental forces shape female leaders, the output is the formation of leadership. For women without a formal leadership role, leadership is influence. Others respect her expertise or skills and defer to her despite her lack of positional leadership. In a theologically egalitarian environment, however, a church validates a woman's leadership by handing her a formal leadership role, giving her authority. Authority comes from an organization, or society, and gives a leader power to make decisions and command.[35] With or without a leadership position, only women with significant influence become truly powerful. While power can seem like a dirty word to women, power itself is not good or bad. It is neutral. Power is a gift from God that unites us to accomplish his purposes together.[36] Influence, which creates power, is formed in two ways—through developing leader relationships and through leadership communication.

Leadership Relationships

About five years ago, I received a direct message on Instagram from someone I had never met. Melissa was a youth pastor in a mid-sized church who had recently bumped into my husband at a youth conference. Melissa wrote, "He told me I should reach out," so we set up a time to talk. Melissa had recently accepted her pastor's invitation to leave her middle school teaching position to become their church's youth pastor. Melissa needed advice from experienced youth pastors, but she did not know any woman in pastoral ministry and felt awkward networking with male youth pastors. That conversation initiated a friendship between me and Melissa. She called every few months to talk through leadership issues. After a few years, her pastor promoted her to be the church's executive pastor, and we kept talking. Melissa needed a mentor and a network of friendships, and so she went out of her way to build one. Successful female leaders find mentors and peers.

Influence is created through the connection of relationships, but a woman needs specific types of relationships to grow in influence. Early on, a female leader needs role models to inspire her that may turn into mentors. Mentors might be spiritual guides, or leadership coaches. These mentors help her recognize and cultivate her giftedness. Sponsors open vital doors of

---

35. McConnell, *Cultural Insights*, loc. 2650–59.
36. Villacorta, *Tug of War*, 10–11.

opportunity for women leaders. These leaders might be women or men who believe in her calling and encourage her in it.[37]

As women develop their leadership, they need professional peers. Peers provide best practices, new technologies and strategies for their area of ministry focus. They become friends with emotional support. Women find male-dominated professional networks difficult to break into, and ministry networks are often even harder. Both the so-called Billy Graham Rule (a man can never be alone with another woman), and the Me-Too movement cultivated fear-based male avoidance of women.[38] This is a real problem for women developing leadership, because peer networks broaden the reach of a female leader's influence. By establishing clear male/female relational boundaries, or by accessing male ministry networks through their husbands, women leaders might elbow into male networks, but powerful women leaders build their own networks. These networks are vital to accessing new, more challenging leadership opportunities, and for spreading ideas into new ministry contexts.

Women leaders need peer relationships with other leaders to rise. While women need male pastors to sponsor them into their networks of relationships, they also need relationships with other women leaders. Churches and denominations can invest into emerging female leaders by providing access to female church leader learning cohorts, which are increasingly more available. Inside these groups, women learn key skills and share experience and support. When a woman no longer feels alone, her confidence grows. When she doesn't know what to do, she has a tribe of experienced women leaders who can advise her.

Powerful women multiply their influence by investing into other emerging female leaders. Supporting the leadership development of another person is a significant way that women leaders grow their authority. Without continuously working on developing these kinds of relationships that expand a woman's influence, a woman's leadership settles within comfortable limits.

Leadership Communication

Leadership relationships are created through leadership interactions. A powerful female leader utilizes two types of communication, public and

---

37. Adeney, *Women and Christian Mission*, 23; Hopkins et al., "Women's Leadership," 355.

38. Wingard, "#MeToo"; Influence Magazine, "Healthy Workplace Boundaries in a #MeToo Era"; Trotter, "Problem with the 'Billy Graham Rule.'"

private. A female leader learns how to navigate the challenges of interpersonal communication. She must be both dominant and tough enough to command respect, as well as soft and kind enough to be liked.[39] This tightrope double-bind is only successfully traversed through excellent emotional intelligence that adapts its approach to each individual and the circumstances.[40] A powerful female leader will speak her perspectives and experiences with strength and grace around a conference table.

A woman's skillful public communication earns respect through her preaching, teaching, social media, or writing. As a woman presents ideas and develops her voice, she establishes herself as an authority. This authority opens listeners to the Word of God to be formed by it. Women's preaching has been shut down or minimized in many Christian circles, and this stifles women's leadership. Women pastors need regular opportunities to preach to develop their latent gifts. While not every woman leader has a preaching or teaching gift, they are vital components of pastoral leadership. Women are called to be more than high-level administrators and managers of churches—they are called to pastor. Pastors are developed through the practice of preaching. Church reformers Calvin, Luther, and Zwingli all stressed that the most important assignment of a pastor is preaching.[41] When a woman is not empowered to preach and teach regularly while she is developing, her influence is diminished, and her calling to pastor impeded.

Conclusion

Women leaders are shaped uniquely by their social expectations, and experiences. God uses all these elements to shape the women he has gifted for leadership and cultivate their influence. Clinton viewed process items as events. But often similar events repeat in new ways, and women must continually process the same kinds of issues. Rather than thinking about leadership development as a series of unique inputs and responses, a better way to conceive of female leadership development is as a continual flow of inputs and responses, all working together in the seven domains. As this process happens, a woman's leadership emerges over a lifetime.

Women leaders are shaped within each of the seven domains at the same time. A woman's leadership environment and home life shape her through experiences she must process and respond to. This inner work forms her spiritually, shapes her leadership identity and thinking, and her

---

39. Catalyst, "Double-Bind Dilemma for Women in Leadership."
40. Morgan, "Female Leaders," 184.
41. Willimon, *Pastor*, 171.

emotional intelligence. What emerges as she practices this new identity is the influence she develops through relationships and communication. As she steps into increasingly ranked leadership roles, her church gives her more authority.

God shapes women to lead in extraordinary ways, but he does not fast-track entrusting leaders with power. Slowly and carefully, he forms women and as they say yes and faithfully steward the opportunities he gives, he gives them more. Those leading in theologically egalitarian contexts will see kingdom expansion as women leading churches become more powerful. When female leaders bring their God-forged influence to bear on building local churches, remarkable things happen. As the church, we steward their authority through the culture and opportunities we provide. When female church leaders flourish, the church flourishes.

Women leaders need training that is specific to their needs, that helps them understand their own development. When women realize that they are not alone or crazy or flawed by their struggles, they feel relieved and encouraged. Confidence grows as the path before them comes into focus. Feminists and egalitarians have historically minimized the differences between men and women, because differences have been weaponized in the past as proof that women are unsuitable for leadership. Minimizing differences between male and female leaders creates an assumption that men and women have the same training needs, and so women leaders have received identical training to men. And yet, these male-focused developmental pathways have not resulted in equal outcomes for men and women.[42] Christian leadership training has been historically designed for men (by men). It stands to reason that the unique experiences of women and the social pressures that shaped them create a need for female-specific leadership training. This kind of female-informed leadership training recognizes that women most often come to ministry through an atypical career path. They usually didn't set out to be in ministry, and so are often under-trained in Bible, theology, preaching, public speaking, and practical ministry. They are probably already doing ministry, so they need learning structures that accommodate their busy ministry schedules and family life.

More than anything, women need to be invited into significant, risky leadership opportunities, where they can tinker with new ideas and learn by doing. Women need to be encouraged to speak up where they can lend strength to their brothers, speaking to relational fracturing, fidelity, sexual brokenness—places where the church has been weak because women have been silenced. Men carry responsibility for opening these doors for women

---

42. Tannen, *You Just Don't Understand*, 16–17.

because they hold the keys of power. Opening a door of leadership for a woman is more than the polite thing to do, it opens the way to mutual flourishing.

Bibliography

Adeney, Frances S. *Women and Christian Mission: Ways of Knowing and Doing Theology.* Eugene, OR: Pickwick, 2015.

Beach, Nancy. *Gifted to Lead: The Art of Leading as a Woman in the Church.* Grand Rapids: Zondervan, 2008.

Bradberry, Travis, and Jean Greaves. *Emotional Intelligence 2.0.* San Diego: TalentSmart, 2009.

Byrnes, James P., et al. "Gender Differences in Risk Taking: A Meta-Analysis." *Psychological Bulletin* 125 (1999) 367–83.

Cadsby, C. Bram, and Elizabeth Maynes. "Gender, Risk Aversion, and the Drawing Power of Equilibrium in an Experimental Corporate Takeover Game." *Journal of Economic Behavior & Organization* 56 (2005) 39–59.

Catalyst. "Double-Bind Dilemma for Women in Leadership: Damned If You Do, Doomed If You Don't (Report)." July 15, 2007. https://www.catalyst.org/research/the-double-bind-dilemma-for-women-in-leadership-damned-if-you-do-doomed-if-you-dont/.

Clinton, J. Robert. *Leadership Emergence Theory: A Self-Study Manual for Analyzing the Development of a Christian Leader.* Altadena, CA: Barnabas Resources, 1989.

Eagly, Alice H., and Linda L. Carli. *Through the Labyrinth: The Truth about How Women Become Leaders.* Boston: Harvard Business School Press, 2007.

Ely, Robin J., et al. "Taking Gender into Account: Theory and Design for Women's Leadership Development Programs." *Academy of Management Learning & Education* 10 (2011) 474–93.

Evans, Elizabeth. "What Makes a (Third) Wave? How and Why the Third-Wave Narrative Works for Contemporary Feminists." *International Feminist Journal of Politics* 18 (2016) 409–28.

Hopkins, Margaret M., et al. "Women's Leadership Development Strategic Practices for Women and Organizations." *Consulting Psychology Journal: Practice and Research* 60 (2008) 348–65.

Howell, Susan H. *Buried Talents: Overcoming Gendered Socialization to Answer God's Call.* Downers Grove, IL: InterVarsity, 2022.

Influence Magazine. "Healthy Workplace Boundaries in a #MeToo Era." August 15, 2018. https://influencemagazine.com/Practice/Healthy-Workplace-Boundaries-in-a--MeToo-Era.

Jackson, Amy. "Why We Need Single Women Leaders." *Christianity Today*, September 21, 2017. https://www.christianitytoday.com/women-leaders/2017/september/why-we-need-single-women-leaders.html.

Kay, Katty, and Claire Shipman. "Confidence Gap." *Atlantic*, May 2014. https://www.theatlantic.com/magazine/archive/2014/05/the-confidence-gap/359815/.

Kubichek, Amy. "Pastoral Leadership in the Church of Nazarene, 2000–2019: A Preliminary Report." *Religious Workforce Project*, May 5, 2021. https://religiousworkforce.com/nazarene-demo-v-1.

Maros, Susan L. *Calling in Context: Social Location and Vocational Formation.* Downers Grove, IL: IVP Academic, 2022.

McConnell, Douglas. *Cultural Insights for Christian Leaders: New Directions for Organizations Serving God's Mission.* Grand Rapid: Baker Academic, 2018. Kindle.

Milkie, Melissa A., et al. "Taking on the Second Shift: Time Allocations and Time Pressures of U.S. Parents with Preschoolers." *Social Forces* 88 (2009) 487–517.

Mohr, Tara S. *Playing Big: Practical Wisdom for Women Who Want to Speak Up, Create, and Lead.* New York: Penguin, 2014.

Morgan, Anna. "Female Leaders in Egalitarian Churches: A Model for Female Ministry Leadership Development." PhD diss., Fuller Theological Seminary, 2022.

National Congregations Study. "Denominational Affiliation (Collapsed) by Gender of Head or Senior Clergyperson." https://www.thearda.com/ncs/ncs2018/dencode3_clergsex.asp.

Northouse, Peter G. *Leadership: Theory and Practice.* 7th ed. Los Angeles: SAGE, 2016.

Sandberg, Sheryl. *Lean In: Women, Work, and the Will to Lead.* New York: Knopf, 2013.

Schmitt, David P. "Truth about Sex Differences." *Psychology Today*, November 7, 2017. https://www.psychologytoday.com/intl/articles/201711/the-truth-about-sex-differences.

Scott, Halee G. "Study: Female Pastors Are on the Rise" *Christianity Today*, February 26, 2017. https://www.christianitytoday.com/ct/2017/february-web-only/study-female-pastors-are-on-rise.html.

Tannen, Deborah. *You Just Don't Understand: Women and Men in Conversation.* New York: HarperCollins, 2007.

Trotter, Jonathan. "Problem with the 'Billy Graham Rule.'" *Relevant*, January 26, 2018. https://relevantmagazine.com/culture/problem-billy-graham-rule/.

University of Michigan Institute for Social Research. "Exactly How Much Housework Does a Husband Create?" *EurekAlert!*, April 4, 2008. https://www.eurekalert.org/news-releases/476236.

Villacorta, Wilmer G. *Tug of War: The Downward Ascent of Power.* Eugene, OR: Wipf & Stock, 2017.

Warren, Tish H. "Come out of Your Gender-Role Foxholes." *Christianity Today*, July 1, 2016. https://www.christianitytoday.com/ct/2016/july-web-only/come-out-of-your-gender-role-foxholes.html.

Willimon, William H. *Pastor: The Theology and Practice of Ordained Ministry.* Nashville: Abingdon, 2016.

Wingard, Jason. "#MeToo, Fear, and the Future of Women's Leadership." *Forbes*, March 11, 2019. https://www.forbes.com/sites/jasonwingard/2019/03/11/metoo-fear-and-the-future-of-womens-leadership.

—15—

Pushing Through Relational Awkwardness

The Importance of Communication in Flourishing Mixed-Gender Ministry Partnerships

Rob Dixon

Introduction

VAL AND JACOB WERE co-workers at a large Christian non-profit involved in development work in southeast Asia. Val had a long history in the organization, having served in various capacities for more than fifteen years. Due to her consistently effective ministry work, she had steadily risen through the ranks to a place on the organization's senior leadership team. Jacob was newer to the organization, having made a lateral move from a similar non-profit six months prior. Because their responsibilities overlapped, Jacob and Val had entered into a fairly robust ministry partnership. Thankfully, their early experiences were good. Over her time in the organization, Val had faced her share of gender-related challenges, but in the beginning she experienced Jacob as a good partner. In particular, he seemed happy to be working together and open to her ideas and input.

That positive start came to an abrupt stop during one particular high-level planning meeting. The mood in the meeting room that day was tense and Val was right in the middle of it. At one point, after Val had vigorously responded to some unhelpful comments delivered by a third colleague, Jacob spoke up, saying, "Val, maybe you should calm down a bit. I think you're being too emotional." An intense silence followed Jacob's comment. And, in a frantic effort to alleviate the evident tension, the meeting's facilitator immediately switched the topic and continued on with the agenda.

For Val, Jacob's comment had broken trust. Where she had previously felt largely safe with Jacob as a ministry partner, now she felt threatened. And, deep down, she knew that she would need to debrief her experience with Jacob's comment if she was going to be able to partner effectively with him going forward. After processing her experience with her leadership coach, Val reached out to Jacob and they met at a coffee shop near the office. From the outset, it was clear to Val that Jacob was uncomfortable. He was fidgety, kept breaking eye contact, and he repeatedly tried to steer the conversation to innocuous topics such as the weather, the latest movies, or the new restaurant that had recently opened down the street.

After steeling herself internally, Val initiated the debrief conversation. She reminded Jacob of the comment he had made in the group setting, and then she tried to articulate how his comment made her feel, both about herself and their partnership. Finally, she invited his response. In reply, Jacob mumbled what felt to Val like a half-hearted apology and said he would try to never do something like that again. Val was largely unsatisfied. Further, Val's attempts to create a learning conversation[1] were met with a lack of interest, and Jacob ended the meeting shortly thereafter, after saying something about needing to get back to work.

The following week, Val's leadership coach asked her how the debrief meeting had gone, and she said: "I just wish Jacob had been able to overcome the awkwardness he felt so that we could have had a fruitful conversation."[2]

---

1. In their book *Difficult Conversations*, the writers define a "learning conversation" as a conversation where people "come to appreciate the complexity of the perceptions and intentions involved, the reality of joint contribution to the problem, the central role feelings have to play, and what the issues mean to each person's self-esteem and identity . . . in fact, [they] may find that [they] no longer have a message to deliver, but rather some information to share, and some questions to ask." Stone et al., *Difficult Conversations*, 16.

2. Names and some details have been changed in this vignette. In addition, this story was chosen because it is unfortunately typical in too many mixed-gender ministry contexts. That said, there are other stories that could be used to illustrate an awkward interaction, including stories where men are the ones being marginalized in some way.

Defining a Term

If only the above experience was an aberration. Too often in Christian ministry contexts, the work that women and men do together is hampered by awkwardness in the arena of mixed-gender communication. The inability to overcome an awkward feeling can limit our ability to communicate well, and it can lessen our ministry effectiveness.

This chapter is concerned with the notion of "relational awkwardness" in the context of mixed-gender ministry partnerships. Relational awkwardness can be present in just about any interpersonal context, but I am particularly concerned with the US-American church context, a venue where there is plenty of room for growth. Indeed, as Bronwyn Lea puts it, "We live in a world where things can be clumsy and confusing between Christian men and women, and we can quickly feel lost in Awkwardville when it comes to how we relate to one another."[3]

This relational awkwardness can stem from a variety of sources. Sometimes, the subject matter engenders awkwardness. Other times, interpersonal dynamics make the interactions awkward. And then there are times, as with the story above, when one person's inability to fully engage in a conversation generates awkwardness. Whatever the cause, the baseline experience of relational awkwardness is the feeling that something is not quite right interpersonally, and it often results in paralysis or withdrawal.

Pushing through relational awkwardness is a key skill that mixed-gender ministry partners must cultivate as they work alongside one another in ministry.[4] I begin this chapter with an examination of how Jesus and the woman at the well dealt with the awkwardness embedded in their interaction. Next, I explore the possible origins of awkwardness that women and men can experience in communication, before the tangible consequences of giving in to the awkwardness and failing to communicate are considered. Finally, I present nine strategies for pushing through relational awkwardness in the context of mixed-gender ministry partnerships.

---

3. Lea, *Beyond Awkward Side Hugs*, xviii.

4. This notion of pushing through relational awkwardness in mixed-gender communication first found expression in the "Abundant Communication" chapter in my book on mixed-gender ministry partnerships. Dixon, *Together in Ministry*, 113–24.

An Awkward First-Century Conversation

The text in John 4:5–42 recounts the longest interaction between Jesus and a woman recorded in the Bible.[5] In the passage, Jesus is on a journey from Jerusalem to Galilee, and he opts to stop for water at a Samaritan well. As many commentators have noted, Jesus had made an intentional choice to travel through Samaria, which would not normally have been a stop on the route from Jerusalem to Galilee. "There is no geographical necessity for going through Samaria. The necessity is due to God's plan . . . the Father was sending [Jesus] there to look for those who would worship him in spirit and truth."[6]

After sending the disciples into town to buy food, Jesus is joined at the well by a woman who has come to draw water. Once Jesus and this woman are in place around the well, Jesus initiates a conversation that covers a range of topics including the woman's marital history and the very nature of worship. Eventually, the disciples return from a nearby errand and they express their wonder that Jesus is talking with this woman, before the interaction ends with the woman going back to her town with this testimony: "Come and see a man who told me everything I have ever done! He cannot be the Messiah, can he?" (John 4:29).[7]

One feature of this conversation by the well is that Jesus and the woman manage to push through whatever awkwardness they feel in order to communicate well. Specifically, four dynamics surrounding their conversation would very likely have been awkward in context.

First, it would have been highly irregular for a Jewish person to interact with a Samaritan. The passage speaks to this reality in verse 9. First, the woman asks Jesus, "how is it that you, a Jew, ask a drink of me, a woman of Samaria?" She can see, and likely feel, the awkwardness right at the beginning of the conversation. Next, as the narrator, John confirms the awkwardness of this cross-cultural interaction in the parenthetical that follows the woman's question, noting that "Jews do not share things in common with Samaritans." Indeed, in the first century context Jews and Samaritans "despised one another's places of worship and had remained hostile toward one another for centuries."[8]

---

5. Not only is Jesus' interaction with the woman at the well the longest interaction between Jesus and a woman, it is also the longest interaction with anyone recorded in the Gospels.

6. Whitacre, *John*, 101.

7. Biblical citations in this chapter are from the NRSVue.

8. Keener, *IVP Bible Background Commentary*, 272. This chapter is singularly focused on mixed-gender communication, but, as noted in the John 4 story, cultural differences were and continue to be an issue that can create an awkward dynamic between

Second, this conversation would likewise be awkward for Jesus and the woman when viewed through the lens of gender dynamics, given that "a Jewish man did not engage in conversation with a woman to whom he was not related, a non-Jewish woman, anyone of disrepute or any Samaritan."[9] In addition to being awkward from a cultural perspective, this mixed-gender interaction would be highly irregular.[10]

Third, the conversation's subject matter fairly quickly pivots to the woman's marital history. For instance, at one point Jesus says, "You are right in saying, 'I have no husband,' for you have had five husbands, and the one you have now is not your husband. What you have said is true!" (John 4:17–18). A Jewish man openly talking to a Samaritan woman would be awkward enough; add to that the reality that they are talking about the woman's marital history, and the scene becomes even more bizarre.

Finally, their conversation moves into a profoundly spiritual direction, and, in the end, Jesus reveals his Messianic identity to this woman. "Jesus identifies himself as the awaited Messiah of the Samaritans, but he does so in language that hints he is God's own presence, the Jewish God who brings the living water of salvation, who indeed is 'the spring of living water' (Jer 2:13)."[11] Throughout the Gospels, Jesus is extremely selective in revealing his divinity.[12] His choice to do so here compounds an interaction that would already be unusual, given the previously-mentioned racial tensions, gender dynamics, and subject matter.

Given these four dynamics present in their interaction, Jesus and the woman at the well could be excused from persevering in their conversation. After all, there were four good reasons to give into the awkwardness and end the conversation before it started. But thank God they didn't, because what flows from their conversation by the well is truly miraculous. As the text tells us in verse 39, "Many Samaritans from that city believed in [Jesus] because of the woman's testimony, 'He told me everything I have ever done.'"

---

ministry partners. When culture and gender (as well as other social dimensions) intersect, there can be even greater awkwardness, thus requiring more energy and effort to push through.

9. Blessing, "John," 597.

10. There remain places in the world today where women and men are systematically prohibited from communicating, often, as is true in this text, due to the strictures of culture.

11. Whitacre, *John*, 107.

12. Jesus doesn't do this often in the Gospels, especially early on in his ministry. Later on, he also reveals his identity to Mary Magdalene in the garden, which provides an interesting parallel to this text in John.

Causes of Awkwardness in Mixed-Gender Communication

To begin, it is worth examining exactly why present-day mixed-gender communication can so often be labeled "awkward." There are at least seven reasons to consider.

For one thing, when it comes to effective mixed-gender communication, we tend to have little experience. In too many church and organizational settings, communication between women and men is in short supply. In fact, often women and men are prohibited from robust communication because the genders tend to be relegated to separate ministry spheres. If, for instance, women aren't allowed in the decision-making processes of the church at a leadership level, how will women and men learn how to communicate effectively in making leadership decisions?

Further, this lack of practice often starts early, as in many cases girls and boys are separated in church programming. As plenty of developmental psychologists have pointed out, childhood is a crucial time in a person's development. For instance, Balswick, King, and Reimer note that "the school years are a critical period for the reciprocating self, a kind of peer-oriented proving ground that can validate or inhibit social development."[13] When we systematically separate girls and boys in childhood, we potentially inhibit their development and ability to interact in healthy ways with the opposite gender later on. To be sure, there are times when gender exclusive spaces are appropriate, but if girls and boys, or women and men, are consistently and systematically separated, it normalizes the lack of mixed-gender communication, and it increases the potential that any communication that does happen will be awkward.

Second, many churches tend to have bent toward silence around a litany of topics that are relevant to the issue of women and men in ministry partnership, including things like sex, gender dynamics, gender theology, interpersonal boundaries, social power, and more. The thinking seems to be that if we don't talk about these things, then they won't become problems in our congregations. We imagine that we will dodge awkwardness if we avoid talking about these matters in the first place.

Ironically, the opposite is often true. Not talking about these topics can actually increase the awkwardness we feel around them, as opposed to lessening it. In my coaching and consulting, I find that plenty of people really do want to talk about our gendered experience, including each of the topics named above. The church's unwillingness to talk about the dynamics

---

13. Balswick et al., *Reciprocating Self*, 164–65.

of women and men serving alongside one another will drive people elsewhere, to places that will talk about these issues. Sometimes I will caution groups of leaders that if they fail to create thoughtful, well-led spaces to talk about mixed-gender interpersonal dynamics, they will find their people being discipled—by videos on tik-tok.

Two colleagues of mine provide a useful example of pushing through whatever awkwardness is present to discuss topics that often are considered taboo in mixed-gender settings. Several years ago, my colleague Juana began supervising Mark, a younger male leader in our ministry. As Juana got to know Mark, both as a minister and as a person, she realized that one area of persistent challenge for Mark was his dating life. He was eager to date, but struggled to know how to date well, and he asked for Juana's help and counsel. At first, talking about this subject matter was awkward for both Juana and Mark. Juana felt self-conscious asking about this part of Mark's life, and Juana could tell that Mark had never talked about his dating experiences with a woman before. Thankfully, both Juana and Mark were willing to push through the awkwardness they felt. Juana kept asking thoughtful questions, and Mark kept sharing that part of his life. Over time, they both agreed that Mark's dating life could indeed become a regular topic of discussion during their supervision meetings, and Juana became Mark's "dating coach." Their interactions around this topic deepened their relationship and built trust that then benefited their ministry partnership.

Third, faith communities are too often held hostage by an unhelpful narrative that posits that if women and men communicate well, or often, they might end up transgressing sexual boundaries. This way of thinking is common for many who hold to a complementarian reading of the Bible.[14] For instance, Cort Gatliff, writing in the wake of a series of public moral failures involving prominent male pastors wrote,

> Like healthy gardens, marriages also need fences. The fence protects the garden from things that would destroy it. Billy Graham famously said he would not meet, eat, or travel with a woman alone. Not only was he protecting himself from temptation, but he was also protecting his marriage and ministry from

14. When it comes to the question of the Bible's vision for women in leadership and women and men in partnership, there are two primary theological positions. Complementarians believe that women and men are equal, but that God has set aside leadership roles for men with women in more supportive roles, both in the church and in the home. By contrast, egalitarians believe that women men are equal, and that there are no gender-specific roles. Egalitarians believe that God assigns leadership responsibilities by gifting and calling, not by gender. For more on the complementarian perspective, see Piper and Grudem, *Biblical Manhood & Womanhood*. For more on the egalitarian perspective, see Pierce et al., *Discovering Biblical Equality*.

any potentially damaging allegations. . . . If there's one thing we can learn from older men and women who have struggled with these particular temptations, it's that we all need to implement safeguards to help protect us from making bad decisions.[15]

In other words, the concern is that robust mixed-gender communication may end up opening the door to some sort of illicit romantic relationship. The presence of this narrative can accelerate the awkwardness people feel in mixed-gender communication, by injecting fear into the relational equation. As one example, living under this narrative can cause mixed-gender ministry partners to question whether a friendly conversation is actually flirting.

Without a doubt, communities of faith need to be on guard for sexual sin, and there are too many stories that illustrate the reality that this concern is warranted. Yet we should not be held captive to this narrative. The truth is that Christian history is also full of stories of women and men who communicated well and did not lapse into sin. The John 4 story illustrates this, but consider the many women who Paul partnered with in ministry, including a collection of women named in Romans 16: Phoebe, Prisca, Mary, and Junia among others. These women partnered closely with Paul, and they presumably communicated closely with him, and there is no evidence of sexual sin involving Paul and his female co-laborers in the biblical texts. It need not be awkward to relate as sisters and brothers in Christ, and freedom from this toxic and fear-based narrative will help make that happen.[16]

Fourth, many Christians have been discipled to believe that mixed-gender communication is impossible, or at least very difficult. This narrative is one advanced by John Gray in his popular book *Men Are from Mars, Women Are from Venus*, a book that suggests the notion that there are immutable differences in how women and men communicate. In its more than thirty years in print, *Men Are from Mars, Women Are from Venus* has sold more than fifteen million copies.[17] With that kind of reach, we should expect that its perspective has influenced how we communicate (or not) in the church. Indeed, one reason mixed-gender communication can be awkward is that we've been told, by Gray and others, that it will be.

This unhelpful narrative functions as an awkward straight-jacket for women and men. In his book, Gray asserts that women are intrinsically emotional and men are more logical. But what happens if someone violates

---

15. Gatliff, "3 Wise Safeguards."

16. For more on the concept of sacred siblingship, see Lea, *Beyond Awkward Side Hugs*; Edwards et al., *Mixed Ministry*.

17. HarperCollins, "About the Book."

these gendered norms? A rigid system of gendered communication can leave no room for women or men to function outside of the prescribed box. So, if a woman is from Mars in how she communicates, she is out of luck. Same with men from Venus. And that can create an awkward environment.

Fifth, sometimes conversations are particularly awkward for women because of pre-existing trauma. It can be risky for women to be vulnerable, especially if they have been hurt before. Imagine being a woman who has experienced abuse in the church context being asked to engage in conversations about that very topic. The potential for this woman to feel awkward is high, and it would be wise for a faith community to give her the freedom to not engage if the situation feels unsafe or unhealthy for her.

Sixth, if women and men don't have alignment in how they think conceptually about mixed-gender ministry partnerships, it can create an awkward situation. This is particularly true in the area of theology. If mixed-gender ministry partners do not share a theological perspective about what the Bible says about women and men serving together in ministry, their experience of partnership will almost certainly be challenging.

Finally, it may be that individuals are simply not in a place where they are able to communicate effectively, for any number of reasons. It could be that people have unresolved pain that keeps them from engaging effectively with someone of the opposite gender. Or unexplored biases might hinder people from connecting. Or people can simply struggle to deal with conflict. In the opening vignette, something prohibited Jacob from engaging with Val in the coffee shop, and the conversation was awkward because of it.

These seven reasons can fuel the awkwardness faith communities can experience in mixed-gender communication. Now, we must consider the costs if we do not push through the awkwardness in the context of women and men in ministry partnerships. If we give in to the awkwardness, what do we lose?

What We Lose If We Don't Push Through the Awkwardness

In my research, I discovered that flourishing ministry partnerships between women and men are marked by two key metrics. First, there is a high degree of personal satisfaction. That is, women and men enjoy working together, and, more often than not, the ministry partnership is a life-giving context for each of the ministry partners. Second, healthy partnerships are also missionally effective, as the ministry bottom line benefits from the partnership's existence. In other words, a flourishing mixed-gender ministry partnership is more than just two contented partners; the ministry thrives specifically because the partnership is in existence.[18]

In my book, *Together in Ministry*, I presented these two dimensions of flourishing mixed-gender ministry partnerships using the following 2x2 matrix:[19]

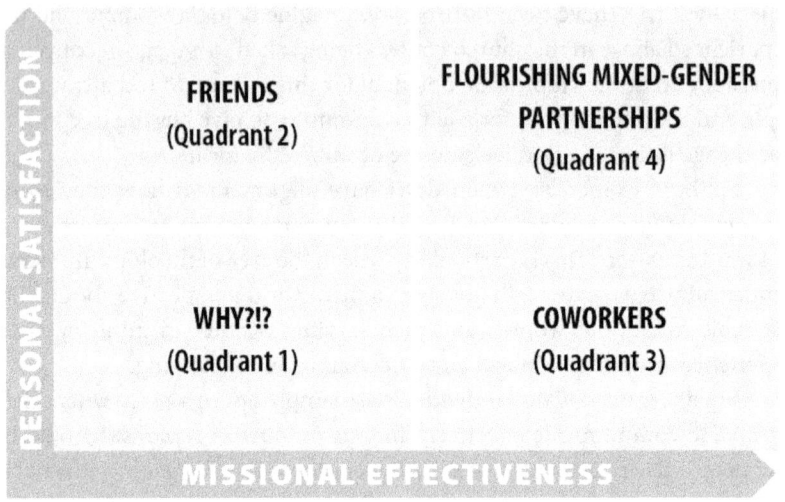

As seen in the above graphic, personal satisfaction is on the y-axis and missional effectiveness is on the x-axis. When both metrics are low, as in quadrant 1, one wonders why the partnership exists at all. After all, who wants to be a part of a mixed-gender ministry partnership marked by low personal satisfaction and low missional effectiveness?

Quadrant 2, where personal satisfaction is high but missional effectiveness is low, is better than nothing. After all, the church could use more healthy mixed-gender friendships. And yet the partnership would still not be fully flourishing, because the partnership does not advance the mission in tangible ways.

It is a similar situation for quadrant 3, where missional effectiveness is high but personal satisfaction is low. Mixed-gender ministry partnerships that advance our mission are no small thing. Still, a quadrant 3 partnership

---

18. Carol Becker first articulated these two dimensions of flourishing mixed-gender ministry partnerships, writing "mixed-gender teams in which all the members say that their work is effective and mutually satisfying are the exception rather than the norm." Becker, *Becoming Colleagues*, 9.

19. Taken from Dixon, *Together in Ministry*, 18. Used by permission of InterVarsity Press.

will fall short of full flourishing, since the partnership is not a life-giving, joyful scenario for the ministry partners.

The goal for mixed-gender ministry partnerships is quadrant 4, where both personal satisfaction and missional effectiveness are high. This is the place of flourishing, where ministry partnerships between women and men are operating at their very best.[20] In such a partnership, partners enjoy the working environment, and they see ministry fruit from their work together.

Unfortunately, when women and men fail to push through whatever awkwardness is present in their communication, both of the dimensions named above can suffer. Consider the personal satisfaction metric. When women and men are unable, or unwilling, to communicate well due to any of the seven reasons mentioned above, it can stunt their relational development. Pushing through that relational awkwardness can open the door to deeper relational connection and thus greater personal satisfaction.

In the story that opened this chapter, we can assume that Jacob's inability to push through the awkwardness he felt as Val confronted him about his comment from the meeting decreased the personal satisfaction level for both he and Val. For instance, it's not hard to imagine that Jacob would do almost anything to avoid Val around the office for the next stretch of time, and he certainly wouldn't be speaking up in meetings anytime soon. Likewise, we can surmise that Val's sense of personal satisfaction will have decreased as well. Her rueful comment to her leadership coach demonstrates the fact that their conversation was anything but personally satisfying for her. As a result, Val might also look to avoid Jacob around the office, and she'll certainly be guarded when they do interact. Imagine the awkwardness that could well be present in Val and Jacob's next interaction.

Next, consider the missional effectiveness metric. When women and men struggle to overcome awkwardness in communication, it can have a negative impact on the bottom line and therefore the mission can suffer. We see this in two places in the story that opened this chapter. On one hand, the meeting facilitator failed to push through the awkwardness provoked by Jacob's comment about Val. Their choice to soldier on with the agenda instead of responding to the moment likely undermined the rest of the ministry agenda. It's difficult to imagine that meeting producing anything fruitful given the palpable unresolved interpersonal dynamics in the room.

On the other hand, where does the interaction leave Val and Jacob? Will they be able to effectively do their work as colleagues? One would think not, and it's very likely that the organization's work in southeast Asia would

---

20. This 2x2 matrix can be useful for diagnosing how a mixed-gender ministry partnership is doing. Individuals can locate the partnerships they are in on the graph and then discern tangible ways to move them into quadrant 4.

suffer from their inability to overcome the relational awkwardness that marked their once healthy partnership.

Years ago, a female colleague was experiencing marginalization on her team. In particular, she felt like her male supervisor consistently favored her male co-workers. As a result, she was not even considered for most of the critical assignments. After receiving support and counsel from outside her team, she summoned the courage to bring up these negative power dynamics with her supervisor.

Sadly, the conversation didn't go well. The supervisor wasn't able to see her point of view, and this woman left the conversation feeling gaslighted and demoralized. Unsurprisingly, she left the ministry not long after. In this case, her supervisor's inability or unwillingness to push through the relational awkwardness that he felt having this woman on his team resulted in the ministry losing a gifted leader. The ministry's capacity for influence was weakened by the loss of this woman on the team.

Relational awkwardness exists in too many mixed-gender ministry partnerships, and there are identifiable interpersonal and organizational costs to pay if women and men do not push through in order to communicate effectively with one another. The stakes are high in this area, as both personal satisfaction and missional effectiveness can suffer when mixed-gender communication is stunted.

Strategies for Pushing Through the Awkwardness

How might women and men go about pushing through the relational awkwardness that can mark mixed-gender ministry partnerships? There are at least nine strategies women and men can consider in this area.[21] To start, as a general rule, a conversation is going to be less awkward if there is a high degree of relational trust. In the story of Val and Jacob, their initial experiences in partnership were positive. We can presume that trust was being built. Unfortunately, in the wake of Jacob's comment, whatever relational trust they had in reserve was insufficient to overcome the awkwardness that his unfortunate comment generated. Investing in trust-building, then, is a critical move for mixed-gender ministry partners.[22] While there are plenty

---

21. To be sure, these strategies would be useful for pushing through awkwardness caused by just about any interpersonal dynamic. In fact, they represent useful strategies for communication in general.

22. Trust is likewise crucial in organizational settings. "[Leaders] often do not realize that rust and healthy relationships among people, or relational capital, is just as important an asset for their organization to develop. Relationship capital is an organization's resources located within the relationships among employees, clients, constituents,

of ways to build relational trust, one practical step is to cultivate and exhibit a learner's posture. When women and men are able to develop a capacity to listen to one another's experiences and perspectives, they begin to understand one another and trust is built. Practically speaking, mixed-gender ministry partners can be intentional about asking questions designed to understand the other person's world. During my research, one respondent described the goal of a learner's posture as "the ability of both men and women to be able to describe the person's reality."[23] We can arrive at that point by asking thoughtful questions. When women and men do the work over time to cultivate a mixed-gender ministry partnership marked by trust, that partnership is more likely to either weather awkward interactions or avoid them altogether.

Second, as individuals start to perceive there is awkwardness present, they should take a moment for some introspection.[24] With the goal of understanding what is happening underneath the awkwardness they are feeling, individuals can spend time reflecting on the following questions:

- What specifically is awkward for me about this conversation? Is it the subject matter? Are there interpersonal issues? Perhaps some combination of the reasons articulated earlier in this chapter is in play.
- What is at stake for me here? On a scale of 1–10, with 10 being high, how awkward do I feel? Why?
- As I imagine a conversation where my partner and I try to push through this awkwardness, what will I need in order to successfully have this conversation? What will I need from myself? From my partner? From my community? From the Lord?
- What are my concrete and tangible next steps as I look ahead to pending conversations that feel awkward?

This introspective step is crucial, because often awkwardness produces dissonance. Understanding what is happening internally is one way to dial down the dissonance we can feel during awkward conversations.

---

providers, congregants, and other relevant people." Burns et al., *Politics of Ministry*, 23.

23. Dixon, "Together in Mission," 83.

24. The literature is in agreement that this introspective step is crucial on the front end of a conversation that may be charged in some way. For instance, the authors of *Difficult Conversations* note that the first step in resolving conflict is discerning when to raise something and when not to. Likewise, the authors of *Thanks for the Feedback* point to the importance of "getting aligned" before engaging in a feedback conversation. Stone and Heen, *Thanks for the Feedback*.

Third, before ministry partners have an awkward conversation like the one Val and Jacob attempted, they might benefit from a conversation that precedes the upcoming awkward conversation. In the opening story, Val opted to jump directly into the debrief, without giving Jacob a heads up about what was on her mind. Jacob's poor response might have been helped if there was a bit more time for him to prepare for the discussion. For instance, when she asked him to meet up, Val could have mentioned that she specifically wanted to debrief her experience in that meeting. The challenge with a pre-conversation is stopping short of the actual conversation and a pre-conversation may not work in every case. Particularly in conflict situations, though, a pre-conversation might be a useful step in a larger process.

Fourth, people might be served by scripting the conversation ahead of time. Especially since mixed-gender communication tends to be anemic in our faith communities, thinking through the potential contours of a conversation beforehand could be useful. At one point in my ministry career, I was mentoring a female leader in our faith community. In my view, she was in a dating relationship that wasn't healthy for her, and I knew I wanted to confront her about it. Because we had yet to talk about that aspect of her life, and because of the subject matter, I felt awkward, and I was certain she did as well. Before our meeting, I carefully scripted out the message I wanted to deliver. Ultimately, I was able to discern exactly what I wanted to say and, crucially, how I wanted to say it. In addition, spending time prepping the conversation helped me to imagine other things I wanted to feature as a part of the conversation, such as examining relevant Bible texts and concluding the time in prayer.

Fifth, it's often a good idea to pursue community support. On one hand, particularly if the conversation will involve some sort of conflict, it can be wise to have others praying around the encounter. The community can pray for things like peace, courage, and clarity in communication. On the other hand, sometimes we need people to help us prepare for what could be an awkward conversation. Val's ministry coach served this function, by helping Val process her experience. That discussion presumably galvanized Val's convictions for the awkward conversation to come.

To go one step further, there can be times when a third party mediator could be a useful agent in helping mixed-gender ministry partners push through their relational awkwardness. "The mediation process contains within it a unique potential for transforming people . . . by helping them wrestle with difficult circumstances and bridge human differences, in the very midst of conflict."[25] Bringing in a mediator could well be a beneficial

---

25. Bush and Folger, *Promise of Mediation*, 2.

next step for Val and Jacob, following their unsatisfying initial conversation. Involving others can be a helpful strategy in pushing through the awkwardness in mixed-gender communication, but it is important to be judicious about who those people are. Individuals who can keep sensitive things in confidence, who can be objective, and who have some degree of familiarity with the dynamics of women and men in partnership could be good candidates for a process helper type of role. And if mediation is involved, both partners would need to sign on to the mediator's participation.

Sixth, individuals can start a conversation by owning their awkward feelings. Sometimes, naming the awkwardness can begin or accelerate the process of disempowering it, and one way to do that is to explain why the conversation is personally awkward. This is particularly true when there is conflict. In their book on communication in the workplace, Kagan and Lahey talk about shifting from the language of blame to the language of personal responsibility. They write,

> Leaders who take an interest in fostering the language of personal responsibility are likely to find themselves in far more productive conversations with their employees and are likely to foster far more productive conversations among their employees. But just as important . . . the practice of this language form increases the possibility that we can engage in much more productive conversations with ourselves.[26]

One way to take personal responsibility is to, in effect, own the awkwardness. In the opening story, Val did this well, when she opened the conversation by reminding Jacob of what he said combined with a description of how it made her feel. Likewise, Jacob was unwilling or unable to own the awkwardness he felt in response. What gets said in an awkward conversation can either lessen the awkwardness or it can ratchet it up. Owning the awkwardness can be one way to lower the temperature in this area.

Seventh, individuals should aspire to listen actively. Active listening is a crucial tool in pushing through relational awkwardness, because it opens the door to mutual understanding. The authors of the book *Together* differentiate between hearing and listening. They write, "listening starts with hearing and then goes well beyond it . . . when you listen, you interpret the sounds you hear."[27] It is that interpretation step that is crucial in pushing through relational awkwardness.

Active listening involves a large collection of tools, both verbal and non-verbal. Some of the verbal skills include indicating understanding

26. Kegan and Lahey, *How the Way We Talk*, 38.
27. Stewart and D'Angelo, *Together*, 205.

with short, verbal affirmations, asking thoughtful follow-up questions, and paraphrasing to confirm understanding. Some of the non-verbal active listening skills include solid eye contact, nodding to indicate understanding and agreement, and facing the person to communicate connection, among others. As a leader in a large organization, I routinely hire and develop young leaders. When I started, I used to assume that the people I was hiring would know how to communicate effectively, but I don't assume that any longer. Instead, I have learned the importance of training younger leaders in the basic building blocks of communication, including the tools referenced above.[28]

Eighth, in the same way that personal reflection is beneficial before an awkward interaction, it is likewise useful following the interaction. After the engagement but before going into a debrief conversation with a ministry partner, individuals can reflect using the following questions:

- How am I feeling coming out of our interaction? Do I feel more awkward, less awkward, or about the same?
- If there has been change, why did it change? What specifically increased or lowered my personal awkwardness level?
- What have I been learning about myself in this process of pushing through (or trying to push through) the relational awkwardness?
- As I think about the road ahead, what do I think will need to happen to defuse any remaining awkwardness so that I am able to partner effectively?

Finally, mixed-gender ministry partners should be rigorous about debrief. Pushing through relational awkwardness should get easier over time, but only if we make space to learn from our experiences. Here are some questions that women and men could consider using as they debrief mixed-gender interactions:

- How did the conversation go? What did we do well? What could we do differently the next time we have to push through some awkwardness?
- What did each of us learn about ourselves? Did the experience of having the conversation clarify the reasons for the awkwardness?

---

28. As one example, many podcasters provide good examples of effective verbal active listening, and it could be beneficial to listen to a podcast interview with that in mind. In particular, Michael Barbaro on *The Daily* podcast from the New York Times is an excellent active listener.

- What did we learn from this experience of pushing through relational awkwardness that can benefit us going forward? What will we do next time we are experiencing awkwardness?

Pushing through relational awkwardness in the context of mixed-gender ministry partnerships is not an easy task. But, again, nothing short of personal satisfaction and missional effectiveness is at stake, so women and men should commit to do the hard work in this area. These nine strategies serve as tools in the relational toolkit. May we learn to use them well!

A Case Study Revisited

Let's return one more time to the case study that started this chapter. With these nine strategies in mind, how might Val and Jacob's interaction have gone differently? We will pick up the story after the introductory comments.

Thankfully, Val and Jacob's early experiences of partnership were good. Over her time in the organization, Val had faced her share of gender-related challenges, but in the beginning she experienced Jacob as a good partner. In particular, he seemed happy to be working together and open to her ideas and input. While this initial start was encouraging, Val knew that further investment would be beneficial, so she pitched the idea of a weekly lunch together. Jacob quickly agreed, and they began their new routine. Both Val and Jacob enjoyed the time to get to know one another more deeply, and they started to see fruit in their work together. In particular, it was fun to head into a meeting already clear about the agenda, following their conversations over lunch.

Unfortunately, their budding partnership hit a speed bump during one particular high-level planning meeting. The mood in the meeting room that day was tense and Val was right in the middle of it. At one point, after Val had vigorously responded to some unhelpful comments delivered by a third colleague, Jacob spoke up, saying, "Val, maybe you should calm down a bit. I think you're being too emotional." An intense silence followed Jacob's comment. And, in a frantic effort to alleviate the evident tension, the meeting's facilitator immediately switched the topic and continued on with the agenda.

For Val, Jacob's comment was seriously off-putting. She was offended. And yet Jacob's comment also felt incongruent, given everything she had experienced so far in their working partnership. Upon further reflection, Val decided she would need to debrief the interaction, as a way to discern if Jacob's comment was an aberration or if she had misread something fundamental about Jacob's character.

Before approaching Jacob, Val decided to have her leadership coach help her devise a plan for a resolution process. The first step, they decided, was for Val to use their next regularly-scheduled lunch meeting to let Jacob know she wanted to process his comment during the following week's lunch. When they sat down, Val brought up the comment and asked Jacob if he would be open to debriefing it the following week at their lunch. From his initial reaction, Val could tell he was carrying a good deal of shame about the whole situation. She proceeded to outline her plan for next week's conversation, and Jacob agreed to her plan. They both agreed that their interactions in between meetings might well be awkward, but they committed together to operate in business as usual, as much as possible.

Following the meeting, Jacob had a lot to think about. He was certainly ashamed that his outburst had hurt Val, and he decided he would spend time trying to understand what had prompted his comment. The next day, Jacob met with a long-time mentor, who helped him consider that he might have internal biases about women, including the view that women are too emotional by nature.

The following week, Val and Jacob met again. In line with their agreed-upon plan, Val began by sharing her carefully-rehearsed explanation of how Jacob's comment had made her feel, and he responded with what felt like legitimate remorse. When it was his turn to speak, he apologized and then explained how he was starting to interrogate his internal biases. After Val responded to his explanation, they spent the remainder of their time together making plans for their continued partnership. As one example, they agreed together to call out any relational awkwardness as soon as possible.

That one meeting didn't solve all of the problems for Val and Jacob. Jacob's unprocessed biases about women were deeply embedded in his worldview. Still, this conversation got them moving in the right direction, and they both began to feel trust become restored in their working partnership. Several weeks later, Val's leadership coach asked her how the debrief meeting had gone, and she said: "We're a work in progress, but I'm so glad we're progressing."

Final Comments

Until the church arrives in a place where mixed-gender communication is normative, there will always be awkwardness. As noted above, that awkwardness can come from a variety of places, including the subject matter, relational circumstances, the reality that we tend to be out of practice in this area, and more.

The question for everyone who would aspire to communicate effectively as women and men is whether or not they will be willing and able to push through whatever relational awkwardness is present. Indeed, the only way to eliminate relational awkwardness is to push through it. It's always going to be awkward right up until it's not. May we as a church push through our relational awkwardness with courage, and may we see the thing that Val saw in Jacob in the story's retelling: Progress.

Process Questions

- Think of a time when you experienced relational awkwardness in your ministry partnership with someone of the opposite gender. What did that feel like? How did you respond to how you felt?

- Of the seven causes of relational awkwardness referenced in the chapter, which ones resonate for you as especially relevant? Why?

- As you think about pushing through relational awkwardness with someone from the opposite gender that you work alongside, which of the nine strategies will be most useful for you? How might you use them to push through the awkwardness? What are your faithful next steps?

- How might someone in your community pray for you as you seek to push through the relational awkwardness in your mixed-gender ministry partnerships?

Bibliography

Balswick, Jack O., et al. *The Reciprocating Self: Human Development in Theological Perspective*. 2nd ed. Downers Grove, IL: IVP Academic, 2016.
Becker, Carol. *Becoming Colleagues: Women and Men Serving Together in Faith*. San Francisco: Jossey-Bass, 2000.
Blessing, Kamila A. "John." In *The IVP Women's Bible Commentary*, edited by Catherine Clark Kroeger et al., 584–605. Downers Grove, IL: InterVarsity, 2002.
Burns, Bob, et al. *The Politics of Ministry: Navigating Power Dynamics and Negotiating Interests*. Downers Grove, IL: InterVarsity, 2019.
Bush, Robert A. Baruch, and Joseph P. Folger. *The Promise of Mediation: Responding to Conflict through Empowerment and Recognition*. San Francisco: Jossey-Bass, 1994.
Dixon, Rob. *Together in Ministry: Women and Men in Flourishing Partnerships*. Downers Grove, IL: IVP Academic, 2021.
———. "Together in Mission: A Model for Flourishing Male/Female Ministry Partnerships in InterVarsity Christian Fellowship/USA." DIS diss., Fuller Theological Seminary, 2018.

Edwards, Sue, et al. *Mixed Ministry: Working Together as Brothers and Sisters in an Oversexed Society*. Grand Rapids: Kregel, 2008.

Gatliff, Cort. "3 Wise Safeguards in the Wake of Ashley Madison." *Gospel Coalition*, September 4, 2015. https://www.thegospelcoalition.org/article/3-wise-safeguards-in-the-wake-of-ashley-madison/.

Gray, John. *Men Are from Mars, Women Are from Venus: A Practical Guide for Improving Communication and Getting What You Want in Your Relationships*. New York: HarperCollins, 1992.

HarperCollins. "About the Book." https://www.harpercollins.com.au/9780007152599/.

Keener, Craig S. *The IVP Bible Background Commentary: New Testament*. Downers Grove, IL: IVP Academic, 1993.

Kegan, Robert, and Lisa Laskow Lahey. *How the Way We Talk Can Change the Way We Work: Seven Languages for Transformation*. San Francisco: Jossey-Bass, 2001.

Lea, Bronwyn. *Beyond Awkward Side Hugs: Living as Christian Brothers and Sisters in a Sex-Crazed World*. Nashville: Nelson, 2000.

Pierce, Ronald W., and Cynthia Long Westfall, eds. *Discovering Biblical Equality: Biblical, Theological, Cultural & Practice Perspectives*. 3rd ed. Downers Grove, IL: IVP Academic, 2021.

Piper, John, and Wayne Grudem, eds. *Recovering Biblical Manhood & Womanhood: A Response to Evangelical Feminism*. Wheaton, IL: Crossway, 2006.

Stewart, John Robert, and Gary D'Angelo. *Together: Communicating Interpersonally*. 3rd ed. New York: Random House, 1988.

Stone, Douglas, et al. *Difficult Conversations: How to Discuss What Matters Most*. New York: Penguin, 1999.

Stone, Douglas, and Sheila Heen. *Thanks for the Feedback: The Science and Art of Receiving Feedback Well*. New York: Penguin, 2014.

Whitacre, Rodney A. *John*. The IVP New Testament Commentary Series. Downers Grove, IL: InterVarsity, 1999.

Subject Index

Abraham, 83
abuse, 126, 129, 141–42
    emotional, 126
    physical, 76
    of power, 173
    sexual, 121–22, 143–44, 147
    spiritual, 99
    spousal, 148, 213
accountability, 121, 179, 182
Adam, 40, 83–84
affirmation, 172, 198
    collective, 165
African Christianity, 22, 26, 30, 38
agency, 30, 54, 90, 205, 208, 211
    collective, 4, 8–9, 12, 105
    cultural dynamics, 87, 89, 161, 182, 211
    definition, 5, 53, 55, 98, 206, 217
Asia, 17
authority, 6, 18, 232, 235
    challenge to, 34, 43, 176
    definition, 233
    development of, 229
    institutional, 223, 233
    organizational, 4

Bathsheba, 83, 147
Bible women, 213–14
Billy Graham rule, 234, 245

calling, 61, 114, 135, 224
change, 18, 53, 114, 162
change agent, 55, 59

church, 9, 24, 30, 49, 87, 149–51
    definition, 188
    institutional, 187–88, 192, 194–95
colonialism, 50, 58, 88, 159, 164, 205, 210
colonization, 159, 161–62
community, 92, 160, 183, 189–90
complementarian, definition, 226, 245

David, 83, 103, 108, 147–48
Deborah, 92–93
dignity, 78, 113, 123
Dorcas, 82, 94

earth, 50–51, 61, 85, 168
egalitarian, 93, 125, 222, 232–33, 236
    definition, 226, 245
Egypt, 31, 34
Eli, 102–7, 109–11
Elkanah, 99–102
emotional intelligence, 229
emotions, 173, 192, 229
empowerment, 44, 113, 151, 216
Ethiopia, 38–39, 41–42
Eve, 43, 67, 82–84

father, 33, 83, 89, 211, 231
female space, 192–94, 197–98
    definition, 188
feminism, 19–20, 176–77, 206, 231
    definition, 177
    first wave, 19–20, 78, 176
    second wave, 19–20, 206

flourishing, 95, 158, 169, 188, 217, 248–49

gender, 76, 89, 145, 177, 244
gender-based violence, 126, 132
gender norms, 18, 73, 89, 141–42, 211
Ghana, 47, 140–41

Hagar, 82–83, 92, 100, 172
Hannah, 97–115
healing, 140, 168, 194, 196, 219
health, 68, 159
Holy Spirit, 93, 123–24, 137, 210
home, 47, 50
husband, 83, 89, 207, 211

identity, 75, 165, 194, 197
   missionary wives, 187
   negotiated, 90
   social construction of, 8
image, God's (imago Dei), 48, 58, 94, 125, 134, 212
intersectionality, 20, 89, 164, 177, 231
Isaac, 83

Jairus, 59–60
Jephthah's Daughter, 130
Jesus, 58–60, 92–93, 148, 191, 219, 242–43

kinship, 83, 166
Korea, 211, 214, 216

Latin America, 17, 22
leaders, 27, 113, 178, 180, 191
   definition, 190
   impact, 223
leadership, 3, 179–80, 190–91, 228
   definition, 225
   indigenous, 159, 167
   institutional, 186
   women's, 186, 189, 192, 223
leadership development, 224–25, 228, 233–35

Mary, 82, 217–18
Mary Magdalene, 82, 92–93
ministry partnership, 241, 247

Miriam, 93, 180
mission, 5, 13, 51, 195, 205, 208–10
   agency in, 209
   definition, 9, 13, 50, 60, 217
mission of God (missio Dei), 8, 50, 58–60, 95, 210
Moses, 172
mothers, xiv, 46, 76, 159, 211, 231

oppression, 20, 50, 68, 87, 113
   structures of, 54, 59
organizational contexts, 4, 87
organizations, 6, 8
   definition, 6

patriarchy, 88, 94, 159, 165, 176
Paul, 195, 246
pentecostalism, xiii, 151, 222, 224
   Black, 124
   Ghanaian, 140
   sexual abuse in, 143, 145
Perpetua, 33–34, 45
Petros, Walatta, 41–44
pneumatology, 122–24, 135
poverty, 176, 219
power, 55, 87, 90, 112, 151, 159, 206
   collective, 8, 182
   definition, 5, 168–69, 233
   gendered, 84, 195, 211
   individual, 5, 165, 236
   organizational, 6
   social, 6, 19, 55, 98, 244
power imbalances, 18, 68, 147, 151
powerlessness, 53, 101, 109, 148, 159
prejudice, 197
   definition, 68
   systemic, 197
purpose, 179
   God's, 50, 60, 114, 218, 233

resistance, 55, 90, 216, 226
resources, 9, 69, 72, 197
restoration, 51, 112, 140, 164
role models, 94, 163, 198, 233

Śämra, Krestos, 39–42
Samuel, 103, 105–11
Sarah, 35, 62, 79, 83, 98

self-actualization, 122, 124, 165, 209
sexism, 68, 75, 89, 172
    ambivalent, 68, 72
    benevolent, 11, 69–70, 73, 77
    definition, 68
    hostile, 69–70, 73, 75
    structural, 72
silence, 54–55, 143, 147–48, 244
    culture of, 127, 141, 146
socialization, 211, 228–29, 231
social norms, 18–19, 26, 207
solidarity, 50, 57, 141, 214
spiritual authority, 109, 187, 227
suffering, 94, 135, 216

theological perspectives, 3, 48, 50, 58, 83, 124, 130, 226, 245, 247
traditions, 26, 73, 173

United States, 17, 26, 132–33, 222

violence against women, 126, 129, 139–40, 149, 174, 195

wife, 94, 212
women's role, xv, 20
women's roles, xv, 2–4, 19, 26–27, 48, 198, 205, 213, 223, 231
    academia, 48, 163
    church, 21, 41, 47, 187–88, 235
    community, 190
    family, 191, 212, 231
    mission, 4, 185, 207
    society, 89, 160–61, 176
World Christianity, 17, 20–21, 27, 210

Author Index

Abiyo, Belaynesh, 187
Adeney, Frances S., 191, 217, 234
Adichie, Chimamanda Ngozi, 54, 197
Ahearn, Laura M., 206
Aikman, David, 26
Alexander, Estrelda, xiv, xvi
Alidou, Ousseina D., 191, 193
Allison, Emily Joy, 121, 134, 142
Ambrose, Linda M., 142–43
Ampadu, Ernest, 140
An, Chi Hee, 212
Anaya, Rudolfo, 175–76
Anderson, Allan, 141
Anderson, Vincent, 124, 141, 152
Ardayfio-Schandorf, Elizabeth, 144
Ardener, Edwin, 195, 199
Ardener, Shirley, 187, 195–96
Armas, Kat, 174
Armour, Ellen T, 90
Arnold, Bill T., 105, 107, 109
Asamoah-Gyadu, J. Kwabena, 141, 151
Auld, A. Graeme, 102, 104
Avishai, Orit, 54

Baker-Fletcher, Karen, 123
Balswick, Jack O., 244
Bam, Brigalia, 49, 55–57
Barnes, Naomi, 141
Barreto, Manuela, 71, 77
Bass, Diana B., 188, 192
Bastardoz, Nicolas, 5
Beach, Nancy, 228

Beauvoir, Simone de, 87–88
Beaver, R. Pierce, 206
Becker, Carol, 248
Becker, Julia C., 71, 77, 248
Belcher, Wendy Laura, 40
Bell, Finn McLafferty, 160
Berman, Sidney K., 50, 52
Biale, David, 92
Blackstock, Cindy, 164–65
Blessing, Kamila A., 243
Boakye, Kofi E., 147, 152
Bongie, Elizabeth Bryson, 35
Bosch, David J., 9
Bosch, Rozelle R., 52
Bowden, Peta, 209
Boyd, Alicia, 141
Bradberry, Travis, 229
Brah, Avatar, 47
Brakke, David, 31
Branch, Robin Gallaher, 103
Brasher, Brenda E., 192
Braude, Anne, 17
Brearley, Laura, 166
Brooten, Bernadette, 21
Browne, Gerald M., 38
Bruce, Steve, 17
Brueggemann, Walter, 103–5, 108, 111
Buchanan, Ian, 53
Budge, E.A. Wallis, 38
Burdette, Amy, 74
Burn, Shawn M., 73
Burns, Bob, 251

Bush, Robert A., 252
Busso, Julia, 73
Byrd, Aimee, 112
Byrd, Marilyn, 190, 196
Byrne, James P., 229
Byrne, Lavinia, 207

Cadsby, C. Bram, 229
Calogero, Rachel M., 71
Campbell, Colin, 98
Carli, Linda L., 230–31, 237
Casad, Bettina J., 72
Cerulli, Enrico, 39–40
Cheah, Joseph, 89
Child, Brenda J., 160
Childers, Joseph, 53
Chirongoma, Sophia, 52
Chisale, Sinenhlanhla S., 52
Cho, Han Sang, 25
Choi, Hyaeweol, 212
Cixous, Hélène, 85–87, 91–92, 96
Clark, Donald N., 212
Clinton, J. Robert, 225, 235
Clouse, Bonnidell, 3
Clouse, Robert G., 3
Cole, Kadi, 114
Congar, Yves, 123
Connor, Rachel A., 69
Covington, Richard, 94
Crawley, Ashon T., 124–25, 137
Crenshaw, Kimberlé, 76
Crislip, Andrew, 31
Cruz, Gemma Tulud, 217
Czopp, Alexander M., 77

Dah, Ini Dorcas, 25
Dale, Moyra, 191–93
Daly, Mary, 84, 87
D'Angelo, Gary, 253
Dardenne, Benoit, 71
De Andrado, Paba Nidhani, 99–100, 102, 106–7, 110
DeHart, Tracy, 70
Delaney, Carol, 192
Delgado, Dara Coleby, 121
Denke, Robyn, 75
Dennis, Mary Kate, 160
Deomampo, Daisy, 98

Deuchler, Martina, 212
Dietrich, Stephanie, 209
Diggs, Rhunette C., 190
Dipboye, Robert L., 8
Dixon, Rob, 241, 248, 251
Doorn-Harder, Pieternella van, 189, 193
Doull, Marion, 98
Doyle, Dennis M., 123
Drury, Benjamin J., 77
Dube, Musa W., 49–51, 54–55, 57–58, 60
Dumont, Muriel, 71
Duncan, Graham A., 150
Durán, Mercedes, 70
Duval, Soroya, 193
Dzubinski, Leanne M., 4, 187–88, 194–95, 207–8

Eagly, Alice H., 230–31
Earth Lodge, 160
Edelman, Marian Wright, 178
Edwards, Sue, 246
El-Guzuuli, El-Shafie, 36
Ellis, Carolyn, 196
Ely, Robin J., 228, 232
Emerson, Michael O., 6
Emmanuel, Kojo,' 146
Escobar, Samuel, 3, 210
Esler, Phillip F., 98, 100, 109
Evans, Mary J., 104–6, 108

Fedi, Angela, 71
Fell, Margaret, 78
Fiske, Susan T., 68–69
Folger, Joseph P., 252
Folkman, Joseph, 176
Forbes, Gordon B., 70
Frangou, Christina, 191
Frymer-Kensky, Tikva, 108

Gabra, Gawdat, 32
Galawdewos, 41–44
Gallagher, Sally K., 73
Gammage, Sarah, 53–54
Gao, Xiongya, 85, 89
Gatliff, Cort, 246
Gerdes, Zachary T., 75
Gerhardt, Elizabeth L., 126, 130–32, 134–35

Author Index

Gervais, Sarah J., 71
Gerven Oei, Vincent W.J. van, 36, 38
Gibson, Nancy, 191
Gittens, Antony J., 7
Glick, Peter, 68–69, 72–73, 75
Göle, Nilüfer, 193, 200
Gonzalez, Justo, 123
Gray, John, 246
Greaves, Jean, 229
Grenz, Stanley J., 3
Grey, Jacqueline N., 147
Grudem, Wayne, 245
Guder, Darrell L., 210
Gudhlanga, Enna S., 52
Guelke, Jeanne K., 193

Habel, Norman C., 50
Hafez, Sherine, 190, 193
Haggard, Megan C., 74
Hall, M. Elizabeth Lewis, 74
Hamilton, Hannah R., 70
Hammond, Matthew D., 71–72
Hampton, Rachelle, 129
Hanciles, Jehu, 8
Hannover, Bettina, 73
Hardesty, Nancy A., 206
Heen, Sheila, 251, 258
Hentzi, Gary, 53
Herr, Ranjoo S., 20
Hibbert, Evelyn, 185, 188, 191–92, 194
Hibbert, Richard Y., 188, 191–92
Hickey, Dana, 165
Hodgson, Colleen, 159
Hofstede, Geert, 6
Homan, Patricia, 72, 74
hooks, bell, 174, 176–77, 179, 182
Hopkins, Margaret M., 230, 234
House, Robert J., 7
Howell, Susan H., 228
Hoyt, Crystal L., 189
Hyers, Lauri L., 68

Jackson
  Amy, 232
  Stevi, 197
James, Wendy, 196
Jansen, Wilhelmina, 191
Janson, Maroles, 193

Jayne, Michele E.A., 8
Jenkins, Morgan, 125–29, 136
Jewkes, Rachel, 139, 147
John Paul II, 135, 138
Johnson, Todd M., 21
Jones, Serene, 90
Jost, John T., 71, 74
Junior, Nyasha, 130–31
Juster, Susan, 192

Kaiser, Cheryl R., 67, 77, 80
Kaiser, Walter, 67
Kamalkhani, Zahra, 193
Kamp, Linda van de, 25
Kärkkäinen, Veli-Matti, 151
Katoppo, Marianne, 217–19
Kay
  Aaron C., 71
  Katty, 228
Keane, Webb, 208–9
Keener, Craig S., 129–30, 242
Kegan, Robert, 253
Kellerman, Barbara, 5
Kendall, Mikki, 177
Kiilu, Ven Scholar W., 52
Kim, Grace Ji-Sun, 93, 95, 196
Kim, Kirsteen, 206, 209, 211–12, 217, 220–21
Kim, Sebastian C.H., 206, 211–12
King, Toni C., 190
Kjesbo, Denise Muir, 3
Klein, Lilian R., 100–103, 106, 109
Knott, Stacey, 146
Kosma, Marietta, 146
Kpalam, Ebenezer T., 148
Krawec, Patty, 167
Kubichek, Amy, 222–23
Kuepers, Wendelin, 191

Lahey, Lisa Laskow, 253
Lajimodiere, Denise K., 190
Lakeland, Paul, 90
Lamarche, Veronica M., 71
Lamptey, Enoch, 140
Lapsley, Jacqueline E., 104
Lea, Bronwyn, 241, 246
Lederleitner, Mary T., 216

Lee
  Sandra S.K, 186
  Yeon-ok, 212
LenkaBula, Puleng, 57
Leung, Rebecca, 141–42
Lewis, Joini, 76
Lewis, Stephen, 76, 80, 178
Liefeld, Walter L., 207
Lienemann-Perrin, Christine, 209, 211
Longkumer, Atola, 1, 7
Lorde, Audre, 164, 167

Ma
  Julie C., 141
  Wonsuk, 141
Mack, Beverly B., 193
Mahmood, Saba, 54, 189, 191
Mallimaci, Fortunato, 26
Maltby, Lauren E., 73
Maracle, Lee, 162–63, 167–68
Maros, Susan L., 5–6, 179, 226
Martell-Otero, Loida I., 177
Masser, Barbara, 70
Matholeni, Nobuntu P., 52
Mayer, Gabriele, 209
Maynes, Elizabeth, 229
McConnell, C. Douglas, 7, 230, 233
McEwan, Bree, 141
McFarland, Sam G., 73
McMahon, Christopher, 149
McPhillips, Kathleen, 78
Mernissi, Fatima, 192–93
Meyer, Holly, 134
Miazad, Amelia, 151
Mikołajczak, Malgorzata, 73
Milkie, Melissa A., 231
Min, Anselm, 86
Mmnualefhe, Dumi O., 58
Mohanty, Chandra, 20
Mohr, Tara S., 228, 230
Moltmann, Jurgen, 9
Montañés, Pilar, 71
Moore, Carolyn, 113
Mordi, Kiki, 145
Morgan, Anna, 224–26, 231, 235
Morin, Karen M., 193
Morris, Brian, 193
Mummery, Jane, 209

Mwaura, Philomena N., 186

Nazir-Ali, Michael, 210
Ngunjiri, Faith W., 189–90
Njoroge, Nyambrua, 58
Northouse, Peter G., 5, 225

O'Donnell, Michaela, 179
Oduyoye, Mercy A., 47–48, 57–58
Okely, Judith, 193
O'Neil, James M., 75
Orsi, Robert A., 135
Osei, Phinehas N., 146, 148
Osei-Tutu, Ellen M., 140
Oswald, Debra, 71
Overall, Nickola C., 71–72
Owens, Bretlyn C., 73

Peart, Karen N., 172
Phiri, Isabel A., 48–49, 61
Pierce, Ronald W., 245
Pierce-Baker, Charlotte, 127–29, 131, 133
Pietrzak, Janina, 73
Piper, John, 245
Pizan, Christine de, 78

Quarshie, Emmanuel N., 140, 145
Quayesi-Amakye, Joseph, 145

Ramírez-Pereira, Mirliana, 197
Raudvere, Catharina, 191, 193
Raworth, Kate, 176
Ray, Stephen G., 91
Rey, Cheryl de la, 189
Robert, Dana L., 4, 7, 17, 186, 188, 207, 211, 216
Rodgers, Silvia, 187, 192
Rodino-Colocino, Michelle, 150
Rollero, Chiara, 71
Rose, Susan D., 73
Ross, Cathay, 187, 208
Rouse, Carolyn, 191
Ruffini, Giovanni, 38

Sabat, Isaac E., 76
Salazar, Marilu R., 193, 196
Sandberg, Sheryl, 229, 232
Sandoval, Chela, 177

Sauder, Laura, 83
Schmidt-Hesse, Ulrike, 209
Schmitt, David P., 229
Schreiter, Robert J., 195
Scott, Halee G., 228
Seguino, Stephanie, 73
Shaw, Karen L.H., 191
Shellnutt, Kate, 3
Shepherd, Melissa, 71
Shipman, Claire, 228
Simpson, Leanne B., 158, 168
Sinclair
    Amanda, 190–91
    Raven, 158, 191
Slater, Stanley F., 8
Smith, Christian, 6
Smith, Peter, 134
Smith, Susan E., 187, 189
Sossou, Marie-Antoinette, 140
Spencer, Grace, 98
Spivak, Gayatri C., 54
Stark, Rodney, 19
Stasson, Anneke H., 4, 188, 207–8
Steady, Filomina C., 190
Stevenson, Winona, 162
Stewart, John Robert, 253
Stone, Douglas, 240, 251
Suk, Jiyoun, 141–42
Swan, Laura, 34–36
Swim, Janet K., 68, 77

Takla, Hany N., 32
Takyi, Baffour K., 140
Tamrat, Taddesse, 32
Tannen, Deborah, 236
Teng, Fei, 70
Tenkorang, Eric Y., 139
Tietnou, Tite, 163–64
Trotter, Jonathan, 234
Trzebiatowska, Marta, 17

Tsekpoe, Christian, 141
Tucker, Ruth A., 4, 207–8

Uchem, Rose N., 25
Uhl-Bien, Mary, 5

van Vugt, Mark, 5
Veilleux, Armand, 31
Vescio, Theresa K., 71
Viki, G. Tendayi, 70
Villacorta, Wilmer G., 233
Volf, Miroslav, 191

Wallis, R.E., 33
Warren, Tish H., 226
Welsby, Derek A., 31
West, Cornel, 76–77
Whitacre, Rodney A., 242–43
Whitehouse, Harvey, 187
Wilhite, David E., 33
Wilken, Robert Louis, 123
Wilkerson, Robyn, 113
Williams, Robert, 141–42
Willimon, William H., 235
Wilson, Kory, 159
Wingard, Jason, 234
Wommack, Timothy R., 26
Woodley, Randy S., 160
Wortley, John, 34
Wright, Stephen C., 71
Wrogemann, Henning, 210

Yafeh-Deigh, Alice Y., 54, 58
Yang, Fenggang, 25
Yeh, Allen L., 210
Yogtiba, Joseph A., 140
Yong, Amos, xiv, xvi

Zenger, Jack, 176
Zurlo, Gina A., xiii, 17, 21

www.ingramcontent.com/pod-product-compliance
Lightning Source LLC
Chambersburg PA
CBHW071241230426
43668CB00011B/1541